THE SHOOTING OF

RABBIT WELLS

ALSO BY WILLIAM LOIZEAUX

Anna: A Daughter's Life

THE SHOOTING OF
RABBIT WELLS

AN AMERICAN TRAGEDY

WILLIAM LOIZEAUX

ARCADE PUBLISHING · NEW YORK

FIRST EDITION

Library of Congress Cataloging-in-Publication Data

Loizeaux, William.
    The shooting of Rabbit Wells : an American tragedy / William Loizeaux. —1st ed.
      p.   cm.
    ISBN 1-55970-380-6
    1. Basking Ridge (N.J.)—Race relations. 2. Wells, Rabbit, d. 1973—Death and burial. 3. Police shootings—New Jersey—Basking Ridge. I. Title.
F144.B24L65 1998
974.9'44—dc21   97-29707

Published in the United States by Arcade Publishing, Inc., New York
Distributed by Little, Brown and Company

10 9 8 7 6 5 4 3 2 1

Designed by API

PRINTED IN THE UNITED STATES OF AMERICA

For Beth and Emma

Acknowledgments

This book derived from interviews with many of Rabbit's friends and acquaintances, all of whom are identified in the text. I will not repeat their names here, but I would like to thank each of them for opening their homes and lives to me. They have inspired this project from beginning to end. This is as much their book as mine.

This is also, in part, William Sorgie's book, and I am very grateful for his candor in revisiting the difficult passages of his life. Like the others I've interviewed, he shares the idea behind these pages: that it is better to tell than to forget a painful, tragic story, for there may be things to learn and feel that can stop it from happening again.

A number of expert and able people assisted my research at key moments: Jean Hill and the other local history librarians at the Bernardsville Public Library; Margaret Juliano and the reference staff at the Bernards Township Library; Stephanie Bakos at the Berkeley Heights Library; Betsy Regal of the New Jersey Department of Human Services; Elaine Fishbach at the Bonnie Brae School; Willard Dolman of the Ridge High Guidance Office; Lieutenant R. Chesko at the New Jersey State Police Academy; and Victoria Kahn and Alan Pemberton, both of the legal profession, who — how can this be? — have yet to send me bills.

I am also fortunate to have steadfast friends who are fine writers and honest critics. Neil Fraistat, Rose Ann Fraistat, Joan Goldberg, Ivy Goodman, Harvey Grossinger, Ted Leinwand, and Bob Levine read my manuscript at various stages. All helped me think and write a little harder, making this a better book.

My thanks to Jennie Dunham and Joe Regal at Russell & Volkening for their efforts on my behalf, and to Tim Seldes for his sage advice and counsel. Again, I am grateful to my publishers, Jeannette Seaver and Richard Seaver. My eagle-eyed copyeditor was Jo Ann Haun. And to my editor, Tim Bent, I want to express my special thanks for his meticulous care, good cheer, and for all his acts of friendship and faith.

Finally, but foremost, there is Beth's sustaining love and wisdom. As well as a wife, mother, friend, scholar, teacher, and sometimes knitter, she is my most trusted reader. Though her thoughts no longer fill these margins, they inform every page.

BERNARDSVILLE AND
BASKING RIDGE, NEW JERSEY

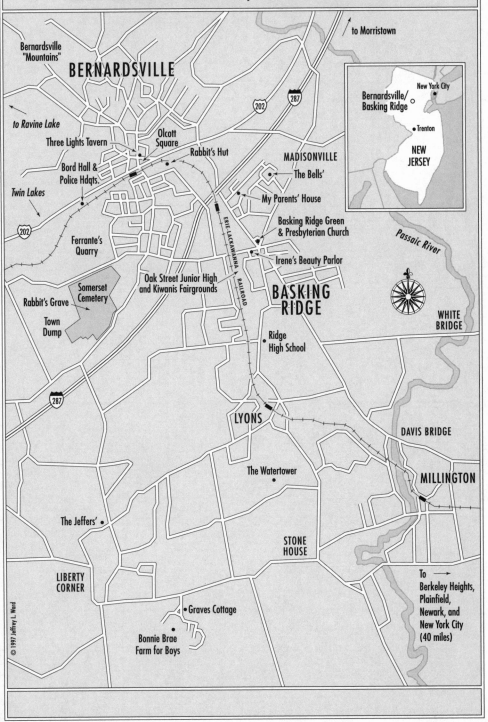

to Morristown

Bernardsville
"Mountains"

BERNARDSVILLE

New York City

Bernardsville/
Basking Ridge

Trenton

NEW
JERSEY

to Ravine Lake

Three Lights Tavern

Olcott
Square

Rabbit's Hut

MADISONVILLE

The Bells'

Bord Hall &
Police Hdqts.

Twin Lakes

My Parents' House

Basking Ridge Green
& Presbyterian Church

Passaic River

Ferrante's
Quarry

Irene's Beauty Parlor

ERIE-LACKAWANNA RAILROAD

Oak Street Junior High
and Kiwanis Fairgrounds

BASKING
RIDGE

WHITE
BRIDGE

Rabbit's Grave

Somerset
Cemetery

Town
Dump

Ridge
High School

LYONS

DAVIS BRIDGE

The Watertower

MILLINGTON

The Jeffers'

STONE
HOUSE

To
Berkeley Heights,
Plainfield,
Newark, and
New York City
(40 miles)

LIBERTY
CORNER

Graves Cottage

Bonnie Brae
Farm for Boys

© 1997 Jeffrey L. Ward

THE SHOOTING OF

RABBIT WELLS

Olcott Square

I have always liked coming into the area that I call home, which includes the small, clustered communities of Basking Ridge, Bernardsville, Liberty Corner, and Millington, New Jersey. It is the hills that most affect me. They are not dramatic, not aspiring. They are rounded like old men's shoulders, formed some two hundred million years ago and worn down ever since by wind, water, and even a glacier — all of it sculpting a gentle place of brooks, ravines, and ridges. In recorded history, the Leni-Lenape Indians, part of the Algonquin nation, first inhabited the forested hills. Then the early colonists, Scotch Presbyterians, began farming and dotting them with log and stone houses and churches, some of which still stand. Roads followed the graceful contours of the land, often along old Indian paths. In the 1840s, the great stone grist mills were built along the brooks and the Passaic River. By 1872, a single train track wound through the ravines, bringing the very rich, by 1900, to mansions and estates in the higher elevations. Then, after mid-century, came the growing migration of upper- and middle-class people leaving the crowded, troubled eastern cities for a safe, spacious suburban life in neat homes on one- and two-acre lots that spread out from the towns.

It is a pleasant, ordered, accommodating landscape with by and large decent and well-meaning people who find room in these hills to be themselves and to get along with one another. When I visit there, often harried and ill at ease in the world, I am for a time becalmed. Those hills in their old, familiar spaces. Soft and congenial, they seem to remind me that this is a place where, if I changed my life, I might still belong. The air is cleaner and drier than where I now live. Roads are less congested, lawns immaculate. At dusk the deer still emerge from the woods, and by 10 P.M., when I go out walking, the hills are dark and quiet.

In the smoothed lap of one of these hills, just a mile from Basking Ridge where my parents still live, is the center of Bernardsville, called Olcott Square. The square is actually a triangle, defined by the skewed crossing of three roads that didn't quite meet at one point. In the middle of the square stands a tall flagpole on a small green, around which cars slow and disperse, now with the aid of a traffic light. The sidewalks are clean and uncrowded. Shoppers walk briskly, yet pause to exchange greetings. Bordering the square stand neat brick storefronts, most with striped awnings shading their windows: Mansfield's Pharmacy, Autumn House Furniture, Diehl's Jewelers, and Sussman's Clothes, where my mother — incredibly, in her seventies now — still buys buttons and thread.

So this is hardly the sort of place where you'd expect to find violent death and disorder. But at 12:30 A.M. on January 13, 1973, a young man with whom I went to school was shot and killed by a Bernardsville patrolman, his blood pooling on the sidewalk across the square from Sussman's. In a lurid flash that lit up the storefronts, a human life was lost, other lives were thrown into anguish, and a community nestled among gentle hills found itself swept up in the great troubles of our time. In the aftermath, angry crowds filled the square. Riot police with loaded shotguns stood outside the storefronts. Issues of race, class, and the rippling effects of the Vietnam War broke openly upon us. The violence of "elsewhere" had happened here, in the very heart of town. Life as we knew it — or as we thought we knew it — would never be quite the same.

There is no outward sign of any of this now, unless of course you were to travel south for a mile to Somerset Hills Memorial Park, and find section 10, lot 264, grave 2: a small bronze marker, flat on the ground, about the size of a doormat, mostly covered by weeds. And if we care to look, there are other reminders in places closer to the heart. There are people today who, as they walk in Olcott Square, carry photographs of the dead young man in the worn plastic leaves of their wallets. Others keep the things he wrote, the things he made, or the gifts he gave to them in drawers and cubbyholes. And still others, many others, carry his memory, a persistent, painful, fragile thing that still brings laughter, consternation, and tears of love and rage.

His name was William Samuel Wells, though we all knew him as "Rabbit," the name in fact on his grave. He was different from most of us: a multiracial kid from the streets of Trenton, walking the halls of a suburban high school of middle-class white kids. He was tall and strong, with freckles splashed across his cheekbones, slightly hooded brown eyes, long lashes, a gap-toothed smile, and by our junior year, he had grown that afro, like some strange, dark halo.

He was handsome, a year older, cooler than most everyone else in our class. I remember him as a senior, in 1970–71, in a fringed leather jacket, boots, and jeans. He listened to Hendrix and Sly and the Family Stone. He read Eldridge Cleaver and Martin Buber, and wrote poetry on cafeteria napkins. He had a certain bravado, something a little exaggerated in the way he'd stroll into a classroom, slightly late, maybe with a pencil behind his ear, poking out through his bushy hair. Because he could never hide, he must have felt he was always on stage. He was the kind of guy that, if he were anywhere around, you always knew he was *there*.

All these years later I've come back to Rabbit because he keeps coming back to me. I didn't know him well. We were never close friends. Yet while so many other memories have faded, his recurs vividly and with a pang to which I am still unaccustomed. His name appears in my notebooks and diaries. I've talked about him to whomever would listen. His life and death haven't settled. And now that I live in a mixed neighborhood outside of Washington, D.C., where race is an issue of everyday life, he comes back with even greater insistence. When I think of my hometown and all that was good, safe, and nurturing there, his story imposes. He is as present for me as those rolling hills, or the bright awnings in Olcott Square, or the twang of bullfrogs through my old bedroom window. How could his death have happened amid such beauty and apparent benevolence, and in a place I still call "mine"?

Rabbit's life was neither celebrated nor well-documented, and yet the loss of it carries a weight and significance that do not lie quietly buried. In this book I have tried to recover his life and to understand why it came to an end. I have returned to the places he lived and walked again on the streets, through the fields, and among some of the rooms where he walked and ran. Though most records of his life have been lost or destroyed, I have found some of his poetry, artwork, and a few official documents. I have spoken at length with the policeman who shot him and with those who saw him die. But mainly this book grew from the rich memories of the kids — now adults — he went to school with, and of their parents who took him in and called him family. Had they not held fast to him in their minds, there would be little to tell.

This is a particular and local story, but in it are echoes of our national life: of our efforts at racial harmony and of the persistence of prejudice and devastation. At a time when "integration" no longer embodies a dream and "community" can mean a walled, racial enclave, his story has something to tell about the difficult necessity for engagement, tolerance, and compassion.

Bonnie Brae, 1966

I begin by thinking of how Rabbit first came to town, a fourteen-year-old, in the fall of 1966. Most of what I know or can imagine about his life then comes from my conversations with his cousin Donald Baker, and with his friends, and from a state summary of his confidential foster care records.

I see him in the back seat of a shiny white car with the state seal of New Jersey on its doors. He is a big, gangly kid, yet just now he seems small in the wide seat. On his lap sits a canvas duffel bag, about two feet long, whose leather handles he holds tightly in his palms. His hair is nappy and short. His skin has the hue and smoothness of coffee with cream. As he looks out his side window without altering his gaze, his freckled face is open, apparently impassive, and there is the sense that even as he takes in the streaming landscape, he is lost inside himself. If someone spoke or touched his arm, he might not even notice.

Probably the driver is an official from the Mercer County Youth House, a juvenile correctional facility outside of Trenton, where Rabbit had been confined for a month. And per normal procedure, a social worker, with a pen and a crisp folder in her lap, is sitting in the front passenger seat. This is not the only time that Rabbit has been driven in such a car by people he barely knows, but this is the first time that any of these trips has taken quite so long. They are passing through hills where there aren't many buildings. They have been on the road for an hour.

His very first trip was in a car like this. It took place on June 7, 1955, when he was three years old and the New Jersey Bureau of Children's Services was driving him to his first foster family. He must have been terribly afraid and confused, and when he turned to look out the back window he may not have had the sensation that he was moving, but that his mother in the doorway with her crumpled face was oddly receding, getting smaller, without her arms or legs doing anything, or a hand rising to wave. In that doorway of the row house on Perry Street, Trenton, she was small and round, her lips sealed inside her mouth, a look all sad and worn.

Now, as again Rabbit is being driven somewhere, I imagine he remembers his mother standing in that doorway not so much with that old sting in his throat, as with a grudging acceptance, like a giving in, that doesn't feel very good either. Outside his window, the hills, like waves, rise and fall, and telephone wires bounce. In the fields, there are fences and grazing horses, and he thinks he smells burning leaves. They've told him of course; they've shown him on a map. But what he keeps thinking is, *Where are they taking me?*

"Pretty nice country, eh, William?" asks the thick-shouldered man who is driving.

In the back seat, Rabbit doesn't know what to say. The clothes they have given him don't quite fit. They itch him under his arms.

"You know, you're pretty lucky to be coming here, all things considered."

Rabbit wishes the man wouldn't call him "William" — he was "Billy" then, or "Bill." And he wishes the man hadn't said "all things considered," because it makes him think of all the things that had gotten him into this fix in the first place.

"Guilty as charged," Judge J. Willison Noden had said. "Incorrigible and runaway." I doubt that Rabbit knew what "incorrigible" meant, but he knew a good bit about "runaway." Twice, at ten and twelve years old, he had run away from his first foster parents. According to the state — and this is as specific as the record gets — they "became quite upset" and Rabbit was moved to another foster family. Then, three times, all within a couple of months, he ran away from that family as well. They were all too strict, he had told his case worker. They just didn't understand. The last time his foster father had tried to ground him, Rabbit was out the upstairs bathroom window and back on the street in seconds. For eight days they couldn't catch him, and when they did he wasn't running anymore. He was sleeping in a shed. From there he had landed in Juvenile Court and then the Mercer County Youth House, which was actually a jail.

Now he is on probation. His social worker had been unable to place him in another foster home. "So this is it," she'd have told him when they had gotten into the car. "Bill, this is your last chance. Understand?"

It hadn't always been this way for Rabbit. For so long things seemed to have gone pretty well. For nine years, from age three to twelve, he had lived near Trenton with his first foster family, a black family, whose identity, because of their privacy interest, has been withheld from me. The state says that at eight years old, he was "very happy" and "his foster family was very fond of him." His "standing and deportment" in elementary school were consistently "good" or "excellent." He regularly attended Witherspoon Methodist Church and collected merit badges as a Boy Scout. As late as January 1965, he was on the honor roll at Trenton Junior School #5.

As he sits silently now in the moving car, all that must seem like another life. Outside, the fields give way to big houses with winding driveways and mailboxes, some with pictures of pheasants and hunting dogs. He sees a neat park with a pond, benches, and a wooden bandstand. There's an old stone train station and a bank with a clock. A policeman directs cars around a grassy circle with a tall flagpole in the middle. Awnings shade the storefront windows. Women clutch children and wicker purses. From station wagons, teenagers spill out, chattering, shoving, some with freckles as big as Rabbit's, none with his hair or skin.

Just a mile away, they drive through another town center, with a green, a big church with a gold-domed steeple and white columns, and more quaint shops. This is Basking Ridge, a colonial town named for the deer seen basking in the sun on the ridge. They pass clapboard houses, wide lawns, and then they are heading again toward open, rolling fields. They go over the Passaic River. They weave down a road beside a stone wall and pass a water tower. At last they turn into a long, straight lane. Tall trees spaced at regular intervals line either side. It feels like entering a tunnel, though light shivers through yellow leaves.

BONNIE BRAE FARM FOR BOYS, the sign reads. EST. 1916.

"Bonnie Brae," the social worker explains, "means beautiful hillside."

At the end of the lane, they approach some buildings that the man who is driving refers to as "cottages." But they are huge, three-story, brick-and-stucco Tudor dormitories, like no houses Rabbit has ever seen. One is where Rabbit will live, with fifteen other boys and two "cottage parents." This, as long as he doesn't screw up, will be his home for the next four years.

They park at the Turrell Administration Building and get out in the bright sun. All around are fields, some dotted with bales of hay. It is such a sudden, glaring openness that for an instant Rabbit feels an urge to take cover; he'd like to nestle somewhere.

"You all right?" the social worker asks. Her hand touches his shoulder.

Rabbit nods and follows them inside, big and uneasy, his eyes on the carpet ahead of him. He meets Robert West, the assistant director, who welcomes him and gives him the usual spiel for all the new boys. Rabbit is entering another environment, "another family," as the Bonnie Brae brochures explain. Here he will live "a more wholesome life" and no longer need the "ways of the street." Here he will be provided for: food, clothing, medical care, and counseling. Bonnie Brae is a working farm, and like all the other hundred or so boys, Rabbit will do daily farm chores, and thereby "develop character." He will also take classes, participate in sports and recreational programs, and if he does well and proves responsible, he might enter the local public school and eventually "fit into the community at large."

Rabbit says yes, he understands, but keeps his eyes on the carpet. While the social worker and the man from the Youth House remain in the office to take care of paperwork, Bob Saracino, the recreation director, leads Rabbit on a short walking tour. I have spoken with Bob. He is retired now, living in Oregon, though he still thinks a lot about Bonnie Brae, he says, and remembers Rabbit well. "He was a big frightened kid when he arrived, more frightened than most. He was reluctant to open up or bond with anyone, yet when he did, when he took that plunge, it was usually for keeps."

With Bob, Rabbit visits the barn, chicken coop, and cow pastures — things he has never seen, or smelled, close-up before. Down a hill from the barn are acres of tan corn and hay, a pond with rowboats, and an orchard where stepladders stand beneath splayed apple trees. He visits classrooms, the new Buttenheim Gym and recreation hall. Outside again, he watches guys his age playing soccer on a football field. They wear matching yellow sweatshirts and shorts. A few kids, he notices, look like him, some a little lighter, some darker; all are shouting and wildly sprinting. *I can do that,* he thinks.

Back at the parking lot, he shakes hands with the man from the Youth House and with the social worker, who says she will see him next week. From the back seat, he gets his duffel bag with all his things inside: a change of clothes, sneakers, toothbrush, a bar of soap in a plastic bag, a pack of cigarettes hidden in a sock; in the matching sock are a flattened nickel that once he had put on a train track and a rumpled, wallet-size photo of himself when he was ten years old. I am guessing at most of the contents of his bag, except for the photograph, which I've seen. *That* I'm sure he had.

Now they all say good-bye, good luck. The car with the state seal moves away, and as it does, Rabbit again feels that slight pull of air, like a breath, while he stands with a bag in his hand.

Later that afternoon, he yanks out his shirttails and lets

them hang low. Though the air is crisp, he rolls his sleeves up to his biceps and walks hard and slinky. He is going to meet his suite-mates in Graves Cottage. He climbs three flights of stairs and comes to the doorway of a room with battered desks and bureaus. Three guys are talking inside. One black, two white. The black kid has spindly legs that seem to extend up to his armpits; the first white kid is small, stumpy, and scrappy-looking, with curly orange hair; the second has dark, greased-back hair, and leans against a bureau.

Rabbit stands in the doorway, bag in hand. The three guys stop talking and look at him.

"You must be the new guy," the stumpy one says.

"Wells!" says the kid with greased hair, standing upright. "Jesus, I don't believe it!"

Then Rabbit recognizes him: Fred Simko, a toughass kid with whom Rabbit had collided once at a Trenton roller rink, before he knew anything about skating. Now Fred tells the story of how Rabbit had plowed into him, how they had exchanged insults, then duked it out in the parking lot; then how they had met again at the rink, called a truce; and how, for weeks afterward, Fred had taught Rabbit how to skate, how to push on one foot and glide on the other, how to turn and go backward without falling.

Now the black kid speaks. His name is Cy Hardy, from Camden. "Well, I guess you could say you guys have already run into each other."

Rabbit smiles — dimples, freckles, the gap in his teeth. So much for his hard, slinky look.

"Hey, that dude looks like a rabbit," Cy says.

"Rabbit?" Fred asks.

"Rabbit," Cy says. "Yeah. Rabbit. Look, that's him. It's perfect."

The stumpy kid nods. He is Doug Robb, from Newark. Like everyone else, he is here because his family has blown apart and there is no other place to go.

Fred is still thinking about the name, and Rabbit is saying it to himself, *Rabbit. Rabbit. Cool. I like it.*

Then Fred says, "Hey Rabbit, come on in. You and me are sharing this room. You got the bottom bunk."

So within hours after Rabbit arrived, already in somebody else's clothes, he was renamed. Seldom would he hear William or Bill again, except from adults. Cy, Fred, and Doug remember that day. I've spoken with all of them recently. They are middle-aged now and married, with jobs, kids, and homes in the area. They've made it to the middle class. Like me, they have changed since our days at school. All of us have let out our belts a few notches and are wearing down at our sharper edges. When they talk about Rabbit, they smile, laugh, though sometimes they nod and don't say anything. Together with him, they spent four years as suite-mates at Bonnie Brae Farm. They did everything together. They cleaned out cow stalls. They threw bales of hay on flatbed trucks. They copied homework and wore one another's clothes. "We were all like this," Fred tells me, entwining his thick fingers. "But Rabbit was also a little different. Most of us had people come visit each Sunday, on Family Visiting Day. Rabbit, I don't think, had anyone ever come. He was alone a lot."

Again I think of that day he arrived. It is well after dinner and after the usual horseplay of fourteen-year-old boys who are supposedly getting ready for bed. Blobs of toothpaste lie in sinks. Grass-stained clothes are strewn on floors. It's ten-thirty. Lights out. From downstairs their cottage parents call, "Pipe down!" and one by one the boys, exhausted, fall into sleep, leaving the sounds of the night. From his bottom bunk, Rabbit hears a dripping faucet and something electrical humming. Through the dormer windows comes a pale, bluish light and the flutter of leaves, like sheets on a laundry line.

Now, with a start, he remembers something that he would

never forget and would describe to his friends years later. He remembers another group of windows, steel-barred, way up on a cinder block wall, and then a fine, delicate snow slanting through the bars. It was at the County Youth House, soon after he was sent there. Dressed in a light cotton prison suit, he was with a group of guys in a holding room, waiting for some kind of "processing." The group had gotten rowdy. There were shouts, complaints, some punches thrown, but he wasn't involved. The guards warned them to settle down, or else. When they didn't, the guards opened all the windows wide and let the snow come in. The fighting stopped. Nobody moved. Everyone looked up, without a word, as snow sifted down on their hair and shoulders — he can still hear its feathery sound. It was a beautiful thing, a stunning, miraculous, magical thing! Yet it froze him to the bone.

In his sleep, Fred shifts his weight in the bunk above, making everything shake.

"Hey, Fred?" Rabbit whispers, and there's no reply, just that slow, rhythmic breathing. Wearing only his underwear, Rabbit gets up softly and goes to his duffel bag in the corner, crouching beneath the sloping ceiling. In the light from the windows, he has an odd, shivering, translucent look, as though he's not wholly there. It's his own bag, yet he feels like a thief; the air is cool, but he's sweating. He pulls back the zipper, tooth by tooth, as quietly as he can. Inside he feels for the sock that contains the coin and the photograph, then slides them out, and though his eyes can only see their shapes, he knows them with his hands. The coin is flat and cool, almost like liquid, all its imprints gone. He turns it in his fingers and thinks of train wheels going over and over it, something so terribly hard and heavy pressing out something so smooth.

The photograph is rumpled and frayed at the edges. Though invisible in the dark, he sees it clearly in his mind: he wears a tan printed necktie with a white shirt, and he likes the crisp, sharp look of the collar against his brown skin. For a ten-year-old, he holds himself proud and erect, his eyes serene, un-afraid of the flashbulb. His lips are closed, but on the verge of a smile, holding in some small enjoyment. His freckles are as big as ladybugs. His hair is even shorter here, a "butch," and his ears stick out like pontoons, as if to give him balance.

It would be embarrassing if any of the guys ever saw this photo, with the ears and the Sunday school face. Still he holds it, because while it's not exactly comforting, it reminds him of a time before the running away, before all the trouble and dread. Yet it also reminds him how the bottom falls out, and how fast he fell with no sense of stopping. In so short a time, he had gone from honor student, from "doing well," from that smart, serene kid in the photo, to a scared, angry runaway in a shed, to an in-carcerated "incorrigible offender," shuddering in the snow. *One moment you're standing proud and the next you're whirling down.* It was a sense he carried with him for the rest of his life, even through his most triumphant moments. And it must have been among the last things he felt in the seconds before he died.

He has the coin in one hand and the photo in the other. Be-sides his memories, these are his history, all he holds of his past. He has no photo albums or scrapbooks. On shelves in the New Jersey Bureau of Children's Services lie folders labeled with his name, but he knows nothing of these. All he knows is that if sud-denly he were to disappear, there would be only this coin and this photograph to say he had ever been.

Now he walks to the pale dormer windows, as if following the sound of those fluttering leaves outside. I, too, have stood at those windows upstairs in Graves Cottage. In the last decade, Rabbit's old room has been remodeled and now is part of the Bonnie Brae Development Office, humming with computers and printers. But I can stand there and see what he must have seen and try to imagine what it was like: in the distance, the hills, like beached whales, and on one the shape of a water tower, an onion turned upside down. On its top shines a small, pert, blinking red light, so pitiful in all that sky. On another ridge stand a few houses, TVs flickering in upstairs windows. There's the smell of the fields. From somewhere a train whistles thin and wild. *Someone is going someplace.*

He could run of course. No one is stopping him, no guards or locked doors here. And maybe it's because no one is stopping him that he doesn't feel like running away. Nor does he feel like staying put. All these fields, this sky, these layers of hills. All these strange people in wide yards, walking on clean sidewalks. No one out there looks anything like him. How in the world would he ever "fit in," and why would he even want to?

In a place this wide, you can fly apart, spin into tiny pieces.

He goes back to his bed and lifts the corner of his mattress, which lies on a sheet of plywood. He slides the coin and the photo under the mattress, and lets it gently down. Then he curls up beneath his blankets.

318 Perry Street, Trenton

About an hour from my hometown is Trenton, the capital of New Jersey. To get there you travel south along those same roads on which Rabbit was driven north in 1966: Route 206 through Princeton, then Route 1 past the sprawling junk yards of North Trenton to the exit marked Perry Street. Follow the ramp to the top of the hill. Then, straight through the windshield, is the three hundred block of Perry Street.

Forty-five years ago, you would have seen a broken line of three-story row houses and storefronts: Mack's Dinette, a laundry, a barber shop, and on the corner, the T 'n' N Bar. It was a racially mixed, lower- and working-class neighborhood. Most of the row houses were divided into apartments or offered rooms to let. Families and people came and went, many of them rail-road workers, for a block north was the railroad terminus and the beginning of the Delaware and Raritan Canal.

Three eighteen Perry Street was in the middle of the block. On the second floor was a small, stark apartment: a kitchen, liv-ing room, and a bedroom that looked out on an alley and a drooping web of clotheslines. It was here, in early January 1952, that thirty-eight-year-old Hannah Baker Wells brought her new-born son, whom she named William, the name of her own fa-ther. She was a mildly retarded woman who had only completed the third grade. She was physically stunted and suffered from di-abetes and a heart condition. In a photograph of her that Rab-bit's cousin has given me, her small face is kind and crumpled. Her dark hair appears greasy, parted in the middle and combed back to her earlobes. Her mouth is shut, the sort of sad, sunken mouth of people who have lost their teeth, or don't have much to say anymore. Yet her eyes hold an impish gleam, and there on her bunched cheeks and across her creased brow are the freckles she passed on to her son.

On Rabbit's birth certificate she is listed as "white," though, according to Rabbit's cousin, she was also part Chero-kee. Years before, she had had five other children, all of whom went into foster care after Hannah was arraigned and found guilty of neglect in 1943. Their father was her frequently absent husband Charles Wells, a white man, a laborer, who is also listed as the father on Rabbit's birth certificate. But this child didn't look like the others, and according to summarized state records, Hannah said Rabbit was conceived at a party, his father an African-American whose name she never knew. For three years she cared for Rabbit. She wanted to keep him, says Rabbit's cousin, but it all became too much for her. When, in the words of the state, she "realized the social implications in raising an in-terracial child, she requested" — and I suspect the state also ad-vised — "that he be placed into foster care."

Today, in the three hundred block of Perry Street, you will

not find that apartment or row house, nor any of the other row houses or storefronts. Some ten years ago the block was razed to make room for a government building that has yet to materialize. The home where Rabbit lived for his first three years is now a vacant lot: some skittering rubbish, a single tree, a tangle of tire tracks in the mud.

On the end of the two hundred block the old stone firehouse remains, as does Speckle Reds Soul Food. Outside of these buildings, firemen and neighbors sit on folding chairs in the morning sun, chatting, playing cards, or waiting for the next alarm. All of them remember the three hundred block before the wrecking balls and bulldozers came. Had anyone ever heard of a Hannah Wells? Or a Hannah Catherine Baker? Had anyone ever heard of a Charles Henry Wells? Or a freckle-faced kid named William, Bill, or Billy Wells? He would have been a toddler, probably funny and rambunctious.

But no, no luck. No one remembers. "That was a long time ago."

I have read stories of ancient bodies found preserved in bogs or glaciers, their clothing more or less intact, a tool in a clenched hand, an expression still on a face. It's as if they have been rescued from oblivion, and we are reassured by a remote possibility that something of ourselves might likewise be rescued, somewhere far ahead. There are bits of Rabbit's life that I might recover through memory, luck, and hard searching. But if I am to be truthful, I must also acknowledge the weight of what I do not recover; that my searches can end less in dazzling discovery than in vacancy, confusion, or exhaustion.

Three eighteen Perry Street is gone. And Hannah Wells, like her son, is dead — she died in 1983. As for Rabbit's father, I've found even less. Evidently he disappeared before Rabbit was born, a man whom Rabbit would never know, and we may never

know either. I don't know his name. I don't know where he
went or what he did. I don't even know if he is dead or alive, or
if by some strange chain of events, he might be reading these
pages.

Plainfield, 1967

In 1954, a year after I was born, my parents built our house and
moved about twenty miles from their hometown of Plainfield to
Basking Ridge. They were near the beginning of that migration
of upper- and middle-class people, almost exclusively white, who
left the towns and cities of eastern New Jersey for a landscape of
pastures and weathered barns in the hill country to the west.
Some of my father's family remained in Plainfield, however, and
so on Sunday afternoons when I was a boy, after my mother had
taken my sisters and me to church and we were still in our
starched clothes, my father, in his white shirt and clip-on bow tie,
would drive us all to Plainfield to visit my grandmother. She lived
in the same house that my grandparents had built when they
were married in 1910, and where, five years later, my father, the
second of five children, was born. It is still there at 915 Grant Avenue, among towering oaks and thick rhododendrons: a stately,
white, three-story home, with dormers, two columns, forest
green shutters, and a glassed-in porch on each end.

Beginning around the turn of the century and continuing
through the 1940s, Plainfield, the "Queen City," was perhaps
the most fashionable commuter stop on the Jersey Central line.
Along tree-lined Grant, Central, and Plainfield Avenues, huge
Greek Revival and Victorian homes were built with columns,
wide porches, turrets, and gingerbread moldings. Just a quick
train and ferry ride to lower Manhattan, Plainfield was perfect

for prosperous businessmen and their burgeoning families. Cheap domestic help was always available. In my grandparents' house while my father grew up, Mrs. Kane, an Irish immigrant, did laundry each day, while a succession of German, Scottish, or African-American "girls" cleaned, cooked, and served meals. In their crisp uniforms and white aprons, they were summoned by a secret button beneath the rug at the dining room table. They roomed on the third floor and used the toilet stall for the help in the basement.

By the time I was a boy, most of my grandmother's domestic help had been let go. Her children had married and moved on; my grandfather had died in 1955, and my proud grandmother now lived alone in the big house — except, of course, for Frank.

Frank, my grandmother's "yardman," was a soft-spoken black man with a paunch, loose pants, a kind smile, and a smudgy cap that covered the bald spot on his head. He had no last name that I knew of. He came from the West End of Plainfield, the poor "colored section" down around Second and West Front Streets, where the Jersey Central came through. According to my father, Frank had unspecified family troubles, and so after my grandfather died and the kitchen help was unnecessary, my grandmother offered Frank a room on the third floor of the house. There they lived for many years, during all of my childhood visits to Plainfield: that quiet, retiring man with the baggy pants, a rake in hand; and my aging grandmother. She was a stout Christian Brethren, who, as we were leaving, would prepare herself for evening meeting — her Bible clenched under her arm, her hawthorn cane tapping the stairs, and on her head a black feathered hat, like a crow that had fallen there.

To get to her house we drove through the West End of Plainfield, near the housing projects and the recently abandoned businesses on Grove and Second Streets. Despite its proud and prosperous heritage, Plainfield, as we were told, was on its way down by the midsixties. Crime was on the rise. Whites moving out, blacks moving in. "They" were now thirty percent of the population: a black middle-class community in the East Side "gilded ghetto," and the poor in the crowded West End, only ten blocks from my grandmother's house.

On Friday and Saturday, July 14 and 15, 1967, my grandmother, in her nightly phone conversations with my father, spoke of hearing a number of sirens off in the distance. By Sunday morning though, after a heavy rain, things seemed to have settled down. Saturday's *Courier News* reported some minor disturbances, what Plainfield's mayor called "youthful lawlessness" now under control — and all of it overshadowed by what was happening in Newark: three horrific days and nights of arson, looting, and sniping, leaving blocks in ruin and twenty-four people dead.

About midday on Sunday, July 16, my family, all dressed up and in our mint green Ford Ranchwagon, visited my grandmother. As always, she poured tea for my parents while my sisters and I looked through her leather-bound photo albums of gray-haired relatives and listened to her stories of the old days. Then, as usual, we left in the afternoon and returned home in time for my mother to prepare supper, for my father to water his garden, and for me to hear the last innings of a doubleheader on my transistor radio.

Because nothing extraordinary had happened, I have no precise recollection of that visit to my grandmother's, and it hasn't been until recently, after studying the old accounts, that I've realized how close we were, how we just missed it: when all hell broke loose in Plainfield that day.

At about 3:30 P.M. a group of two hundred people from the housing projects were dispersed from a park where they had been meeting to draw up a petition of grievances, complaining of police brutality and inadequate housing and recreational facilities. In an angry caravan, they turned up West End Avenue, probably minutes behind our green Ranchwagon. Some were drunk. Some threw stones at pedestrians and cars. Within an hour all was mayhem. Stores were looted and firebombed, cars were overturned and torched, snipers shot at fire trucks. A sixty-three-year-old white man was pulled from his vehicle and beaten up; another was snatched from a motorcycle. Later, snipers riddled passing cars on West Fourth Street, wounding a young woman from Somerville. Gunmen pinned down firemen in the Central Avenue firehouse. About 8 P.M. Patrolman John Gleason, who had left his post to chase, confront, and wound a suspected looter, was trapped by approximately forty youths, then stoned and beaten to death.

How frightening it must have been for everyone in Plainfield, and I wonder how my grandmother spent that night. Surely she opened her Bible and prayed. Surely she locked her windows and doors and talked on the phone with my father. I doubt that she slept through all the sirens, helicopters, and not-so-distant gunfire. I imagine her in her kitchen, at her avocado-colored table, sitting up all night with Frank. What did they think was happening around them? To the town where she was born, married, and raised her children? And to the town where he had come to settle his family, who were somewhere among those sirens and fires?

I imagine they talked, then just sat listening for long periods. They might even have touched hands across that table, beside the sugar bowl. Yet of course, with the first light in the calico curtains, they would have stood abruptly, as from a dream. My grandmother would have turned, grasping her cane, and climbed the stairs to her second-floor bedroom. And then Frank, after visiting his stall in the basement, would have gone up to his room on the third.

By dawn on Monday, Plainfield was strangely quiet. A few trains ran, but the platforms were vacant. The only cars on Central, Grant, and Second Streets were charred and upside down. On West Front Street, trash ruffled in the breeze and shards of glass glittered. Six blocks from my grandmother's stately home, stores smoldered in the early sun, and from her old butcher's shop on West Fourth Street came the stench of burning meat.

I do not remember all of this — much is secondhand — and yet I do remember my father's face on that Monday afternoon, as he unfurled the *Courier News* and read it all, over and over, in his corner of the living room couch. In a headline as large as when Kennedy was shot, he read,

INSURRECTION RAKES CITY
Mob Stomps Wounded Policeman to Death

In grisly detail he read just how the policeman had died. He read of "hundreds of Negroes on a wild rampage," of "all-out war on the streets" of his hometown, of fires burning at Grant and West Fourth Street, at the address where his parents were married. He saw photographs of the policeman and the wounded young woman from Somerville, her blonde hair fanned on the pavement. He saw ravaged streets and stores he barely recognized. He saw a photo of the Plainfield Avenue railroad bridge, under which we passed to visit my grandmother, and from which snipers had fired.

The look on my father's face was not one of anger or even resentment. It was more like a child's blank bewilderment, as though right there in our own house, among our familiar hills, he wasn't sure of where he was. I remember he didn't say anything at all, but wandered outside and watered his garden. I remember he came in, locked the doors (in the middle of the day!), and went into his bedroom. He drew the curtains and drew back the bedspread. Then lying down on crisp sheets, he laced his fingers over his eyes.

*   *   *

The Plainfield riot was important to us, and is important to this story, because it happened not far from my hometown. We were scared in a way we had never been scared before. Things were coming unhinged. For my own family, a part of our history, our way of life, seemed under siege. We were scared for our relatives and friends in Plainfield, and we were even scared for ourselves. The *Courier News* didn't discuss in detail the grievances of those who had gathered in the park; most attention was paid to the ensuing violence that seemed to be spreading west. The police in neighboring Passaic Township bought tear gas and riot gear. I remember rumors (completely false) of roving gangs heading in our direction. Though it was still at a distance, we felt a looming menace, and the menace came with a face, or faces — the faces of young, dark men, bold and wild with anger.

Most of the people in my town, including my family and certainly myself, believed in the ideals of equal justice and equal opportunity, civil rights and desegregation. We had been stirred by the words of Martin Luther King, and when we thought of those virtues, we thought of him, so dignified, principled, and restrained in his dark suit and tie. Yet we seldom thought about what those ideals might have implied for our lives or our relations with others. We didn't live among people of color, and if and when they touched our lives, it was as cleaning ladies, garbagemen, and yardmen, with the same worn shoulders and quiet smiles as Frank. That was comfortable — for us. But then came the Plainfield riot, and with it our heightened fear of those dark young men and our uncertainty about our relation to those people of color whom for years we thought we had known. Was there something behind Frank's diffidence? What was he thinking? What was he feeling? When we offered lunch to the cleaning lady, were we being generous, condescending, or both? Did she resent us? *Should* she resent us? Just who were these people who, like swallows, flew into and out of our lives, leaving our floors immaculate, our garbage cans empty, and returning to

places like Plainfield? Was this an acceptable state of race relations? And what, if anything, should be done about it?

It took a riot for many of us to even begin asking such unsettling questions. Some responded with compassion and even
activism. In others, the old perceptions hardened, and perhaps
in more of us than would care to admit, *both* attitudes wrestled
for dominance, leaving us swaying and confused, deeply am-
bivalent, by turns open-minded, idealistic, "committed to
equality and civil rights," and then fearful of what real social
change might bring.

This was the atmosphere, or part of the atmosphere, about
the time that Rabbit came into our lives. All the old records
from Bonnie Brae Farm are gone, destroyed by a flood in the
1980s. So I can't say for sure, though I can surmise that Rabbit
did pretty well at the Bonnie Brae school, for by the spring of
1967 he had joined our eighth-grade class at Oak Street Junior
High. He was a "Bonnie Brae kid," a "colored kid," and a weird
color at that. He wasn't immediately friendly or unfriendly. He
didn't invite your sympathy or enmity — that didn't seem to
matter to him. Suddenly, implacably, he was just there, among
us, inside his skin. While some held nothing at all against him,
many regarded him warily.

Joanne

I wish I could remember meeting Rabbit, but I can't — probably
because, if I remember myself correctly, I steered away from him
then. I was a wiseass on occasion, but usually the straitlaced, studious son of a Christian Brethren businessman and a Presbyterian schoolteacher. I didn't get involved with the boys from
Bonnie Brae. They were known as hoods, they were fiercely loyal

to one another, they came from "who knows where." And as I've said, there was Rabbit's color. Looking back, I wince at that part of my fear of him, and I wish I had had the vision or experience then that might have stood up against it.

So rather than meeting him, I became cautiously aware of him as some odd but avoidable part of my surroundings. What I have from that junior high year is but a single memory of him that feels more like a composite of memories. I see him after classes near the corner of Henry Street and Brownlee Place, just beyond the edge of school property. He is smoking a cigarette there, where the teachers can't touch him, with a group of other guys from Bonnie Brae and some townies, as they were called — kids from the older, now poorer, families who lived in the old frame houses. Standing there, Rabbit draws in smoke, holds it like a slow sensual pleasure, and blows it out through his nostrils. As if they are all the cares in the world, he flicks ashes off on the sidewalk, then squashes the butt with his boot. He has a high-pitched laugh, almost a giggle. He wears tight, dark pants, a turtleneck, and those two thin smudges above the corners of his mouth mean he's trying to grow a mustache.

They are hanging out together, these tough kids in a quiet town, shooting the breeze, shooting the shit, and they will not be hurried or hassled. They are cool, but not menacing, unless you dare challenge them. Perhaps they are talking about some teacher they have it in for, or how bored they are, or how boss the Rolling Stones are. But I can't really hear just what they are saying, because, walking home with my friend Dave Wallace, with our books and baseball gloves, I am crossing to the other side of the street.

It was only through playing ball that I had my limited contact with the less privileged kids in town. I was small, thin, I couldn't hit much, but I could scoop up ground balls and peg them to first, so I got into some of those Saturday afternoon pickup games on the field at Oak Street School. There I became friends with Johnny Cross, a shortstop and a pitcher who at fourteen years old could actually throw a sharp curve. He lived with his parents in a small, semidetached house on Brownlee Place, a narrow street between the junior high and the backs of the shops in Basking Ridge. His father was a construction worker, and his mother, in a housedress, would bring us lemonade as we sat on their front porch steps after games, overlooking the school and the weedy ball field, discussing our futures in the majors. This was heady stuff for me. For we all knew Johnny was big league timber, and I believed that somehow by being his friend, I might tag along.

So for hours on Saturdays, we discussed these weighty matters. Which team would we play for? Where would we hit in the batting order? Would we have to waste time in the minors?

I hadn't thought of any of this for a long time, until some months ago when I spoke with Joanne Mingus, whom we knew as Joanne Calantoni back in school. Though it wasn't exactly her home, she lived in the other half of the semidetached house where Johnny Cross lived. She lived there with the family of her married older sister, because her mother had died when she was two, her father had recently committed suicide, and her eight brothers had been dispersed to distant family elsewhere.

I didn't know this during all our years at school. And if you look at the photos of her in our yearbooks — her smile, her long, black, Joan Baez hair — you can hardly see a trace of tragedy. Except perhaps in the softness of her eyes, in their reserve and slight aversion — as perhaps it was in Rabbit's eyes, in their stare-you-down hardness.

They became special friends, Joanne and Rabbit. He was big, exotic, and he could dance. "He had long lashes that girls would kill for," she says. But there was more going on than that. On those same porch steps where Johnny Cross and I talked about baseball on weekends, Joanne and Rabbit "talked about everything" on those late afternoons after school. I can see them now, she sitting with her knees together on the top step and he leaning back on the railing. Their cigarettes glow as evening approaches. Rabbit should be back at the Farm. The six o'clock whistle has blown at the firehouse. Already he's missed the late bus, his demerits are mounting, and next weekend he's sure to be grounded. Still, for the life of him, he doesn't stub his cigarette. He doesn't rouse himself and go down those stairs.

And it's not just because her hair, like water, flows over her shoulders. And it's not just because of her tight sweater or her plaid skirt that shows her thighs — though of course that helps, a lot. It's mainly because of the way she sits there, not scared or nervous, not looking at him funny or turning away as if she's got a better place to be. And it's because when she speaks, he doesn't feel strange, and when he tells her some things, he doesn't feel strange, and even when they are quiet, he doesn't feel strange, like he does so much of the time.

They talk about a stupid quiz in math, that bitch of a librarian, and that stuff they served at lunch. As he keeps the beat with his hand on the railing, they hum the riff from "Satisfaction."

She straightens her skirt on her knees. Then in her easy voice, she says through the dusk, "My dad — he hung himself in his bedroom."

Rabbit looks at the wooden stair between his feet, the way the paint has worn with walking. "Why?" he asks.

She shrugs her shoulders, an answer he understands. "I guess it was better than in the kitchen," she says, making a laugh. And this too he understands.

Now that image of his own mother passes before him: her sealed lips and crumpled face. *She couldn't even wave.* Then, although Joanne hasn't said another word or asked, he says, "My father? Well, I've never met him. I don't even know his name." Rabbit lights his "last" cigarette, using hers as a starter, and draws her glow into his. Beyond the field and the school, the train rattles over the Oak Street bridge, moving toward the Basking Ridge station. There are squares of light in each of the cars, and shadows in each of the squares. Little houses, they seem, flying by on wheels. And then they are gone through the trees.

Some day, they swear, they'll go to California where everything's got to be better. Sun. Sand. Flowers in your hair. Some day it'll be all right.

Years later, after high school, and while the rest of us were off at college, Joanne and Rabbit would in fact go to California, though at different times, independently. Over the holidays they both returned to Basking Ridge, their closest thing to home. For Rabbit, California would be his last trip — he died two weeks after returning. For Joanne there would be marriage, children, a life afterward, though there would be more tragedy as well. She was in a terrible car accident. She is a quadriplegic now. And as she speaks to me from a small town in Wisconsin, I wonder how often, in all her suffering, she might have thought about Rabbit, about talking with him on those evenings on Brownlee Place, with their cigarettes glowing in the dusk.

"My brother," is how she still describes him. And it's more than a figure of speech.

"To my little Sis," he wrote in her yearbook. "I'll always love you, Rab."

Things Corporeal

I was taught about sex Presbyterian-style. I believe it was in confirmation class at our church, when I was twelve or thirteen years old. Reverend Felmeth led all the boys into Westminster Hall, where we sat on metal folding chairs. In the middle of the wide, well-lit stage, like a small suitcase flat on the floor, lay a black record player — and nothing else — its electrical cord snaking off toward the wings. All during my childhood, I had come to this hall for special church-related events and performances: potluck dinners, "youth stewardship" meetings, Christmas plays, et cetera. It was here that I mangled "Joy to the World" in Mrs. Kraus's piano recital, and it was here that I saw Christ, in the person of Craig Kampmier, ascend to heaven on a stepladder. He wore a white sheet and a rope belt. His blue flip-flops were the last thing I saw as he climbed into a cloud.

Now there was just that record player on stage, and a hush, like prayer, filled the hall. In his khakis and a plaid shirt, Reverend Felmeth walked up on stage with the same slow solemnity with which he moved to the pulpit each Sunday morning in his black robe. He didn't say anything that I remember. Perhaps he just said, "I'm going to play you a record." Then he pulled the vinyl disk from a plain blue album jacket. It didn't look like *Meet the Beatles,* or *Surfin' USA,* and it couldn't have been the Rolling Stones. The record was warped, and when he leaned over, put it on the turntable, and got it going, it undulated like dark ocean waves. From his pocket he took a quarter, then balanced it carefully on the end of the tonearm, right above the needle. He set the needle into its groove on the outer edge of the record. It rode the waves like a buoy. We heard scratches and clicks, and before we heard anything else, Reverend Felmeth had left the stage, a faint fluttering in the wings.

From a warpy record, with ten other fidgeting, pubescent boys: that was how I learned, or partially learned, the awesome facts of life. Through the scratches and clicks, came a man's voice, even deeper than Reverend Felmeth's. He could have been God speaking, except for a slight impediment as he strained over the waves.

He began, I recall, vaguely enough, with something about love, the Christian family, our responsibilities as young men. But as he veered toward certain things corporeal, parts of the

anatomy, their functions, male and female, as he actually described things *inside* the body — and with the record whirling
and the needle bounding toward its awful center — my legs began to shake, the sweat poured down, my vision narrowed,
blurred, blackened. . . . And then I was out, stone cold on the
linoleum, crucified in my Hush Puppies.

This was followed, in the weeks thereafter, by a number of
books and pamphlets from the church library that appeared in
my room with perky instructions from my mother to look them
over and ask her if I had any questions. I didn't have any questions, of course; I barely glanced at the books. So one day, as my
father hammered at his workbench in the basement, she sat me
down in the living room chair beside the bookshelf where, to
this day, there stand a porcelain goldfinch, Compton's Encyclopedia, the Bible, *The Gardener's Handbook,* and her thumbed
copy of *Noblesse Oblige.* There she spoke of certain urges that I
might have, that they should not cause me fear or embarrass-
ment, but when I felt them — *if* I felt them — it would probably be best for me to focus my mind on baseball.

Thus my interest in our national pastime. Which seems to
have developed, hand in hand, with my interest in the thick
Playboys that Dave Wallace would slide from beneath his lumpy
mattress, like stacks of money.

How did Rabbit learn about sex? I doubt it was Presbyterian-
style. While I was in confirmation class, he was on the streets and
roller rinks of Trenton, or even in the Mercer County Youth
House. Perhaps his foster parents or his social worker discussed
it with him, though I suspect he mainly got the word from older
guys who at least claimed to have already "done it."

When he first arrived in our lives, most of us assumed that
Rabbit was more experienced in the sexual arts. After all, he was
a year older, cooler, and — this was the clincher — he was

darker. Moreover, he seemed to do little that dispelled our assumptions. He hung around with some of the faster girls, the ones that someday, I was warned, might get themselves in trouble. He flirted. He was smooth. He was often the first out on a dance floor. "Hey man, get your ass out here. Help me with some of these chicks!"

With time, as we all grew our hair and wore bell-bottom jeans, as Hendrix careened from subdivision windows ("Are you Experienced?"), Rabbit's friendships widened. He was *in*. Exotic. A measure of our tolerance, liberality, perhaps even our conscience. He was charismatic, together, and friendly "when you got to know him." His girlfriends extended into my own development. And there seemed to be lots of them.

"The guy must be an incredible stud," we'd say with that mixture of envy and aversion. "How does he do it?"

Well, it seems that he didn't "do it" with all the frequency and virtuosity that many of us had imagined. He didn't flat-out faint at the prospect of sex, but nor was he unusually slick at the moves, the slow grind in the back seat of a car, the slide of the hand, the girl melting — I was told — like taffy.

There was a gulf between what, with his help, we imagined, and what, in all likelihood, transpired. According to some of his old high school girlfriends, he was more reticent than most other guys, often more reticent than *they* were. In the hallways, on the dance floor, he was Mr. Cool, all strut and swagger. But get him alone in some quiet place — the place you're supposed to be getting to — out of the lights, away from the noise, away from the other guys he's trying to impress. You're in the field beyond the gym, behind the bleachers in the shaggy grass. There's the paper bag with the bottle of Thunderbird that he left by a tree. Your cigarettes glow, the crickets ring; you smell the dewy grass. Now lean back and see the planes circling for Newark airport, so high you can't even hear them. Say that they look like shooting stars; that you're glad you're out here, together with him, away from those jerks in the gym. Then toss back your hair and lean into his arm. Let his hand fall on your breast. You wouldn't mind if he moved it there, if he moved it in slow whorls. And you wouldn't even mind if he undid your blouse and touched you skin to skin. So you wait and wait with the planes, the dew, the reek of Thunderbird, and his hand all wide and resting. He breathes slowly, as though gaining strength. His chest is like a hillside. You can't see them now, but his lashes *are* long, the palms of his hands are white. From somewhere comes a tremor that feels like a sign, the place where things go faster. But what he does is remove his hand, and turn his face away. It is not in anger, at least not at you. It seems to be in spite of you. In another guy, you might think he was losing his nerve, or coming apart at the seams. Whatever it is, it curls him inward — you'd like to take him into your lap. But is it in him, or in you, or in you both, this thing that now stills *your* hand? After all the jive, bump, grind, and wincing slow dances, even out here in the night — you are almost invisible! — there is this thing about darkness and light.

In all our years with Rabbit, there were *no* African-American girls in our school, which put him in a terrible bind. For him to be a red-blooded male, he had to cross the color line. But in so doing, he triggered fears of miscegenation and our deep myths about black sexuality. This getting-together of young males and females is awkward enough without crossing such lines. For Rabbit it was at least equally awkward, equally exciting, equally imperative, but more forbidden, more fearful, fraught with a kind of danger that I have never known.

On the Border

On an early morning in the summer of 1967, around the time of the Plainfield riot, after Rabbit had been at Bonnie Brae for most of a year, while Sgt. Pepper ruled the charts and U.S. troop strength in Vietnam approached 450,000, a yellow school bus pulled away from Graves Cottage, turned out of the lane, and eventually headed north on I-287. On board were two harried cottage parents, the driver John Hendershot, and fifteen rollicking boys, including Cy, Doug, Fred, and Rabbit. They were going to Montreal, to Expo 67. Few of them had ever left New Jersey, and none had been out of the country. As they bounced in their seats they sang "Everyday People" at the tops of their lungs, strumming their air guitars. They drummed on suitcases and whistled out windows. The boys of Bonnie Brae were on vacation.

They went over the George Washington Bridge and saw from a distance the big city. They went up the Hudson. They stayed for a day at a farm in Vermont where they didn't have to do any chores. They ran around in the fields. On hands and knees, they drank from a stream, their mouths right in the water. "Amazing," Cy says, remembering it now — they all remember this trip. In the evening, before bed, they had maple syrup on crushed ice, "syrup from the trees right there!"

Then back in the bus the next morning, they followed Route 7 through towns of white houses with green shutters, the sun rising over the mountains to the east, Lake Champlain to the west. Middlebury, Vergennes, Ferrisburg, the covered bridge at the Shelburne museum. I remember this road myself. For each summer, and during *that* summer when I was a kid, my family traveled the same route toward a cottage on Lake Memphremagog in Canada, a hundred miles from Montreal. So I know the feel of those winding roads, with the barns, the corn, the distant mountains, and with every mile, the approach of the border, like a girl you've heard of but never seen, a strange new land. Québec. St. Jérôme. St.-Jean-sur-Richelieu. They've got weird little marks all around their letters. How do you say that? What does it mean?

It means you're a long distance from Bonnie Brae, from Basking Ridge, Camden, Trenton. You're a long distance from anywhere you know. And it feels better than running away.

Near the border itself there's a small, white house with a dirt pull-off and a sign on the clapboard: *Arrêt*. In the window of the house sits a man in a uniform, reading a newspaper at a table.

"Let's run it!" the boys yell, but Hendershot pulls up the brake. The man comes out of the house, straightening his hat, a clipboard in his other hand. He asks Hendershot for his name, license, and registration. He has an accent they've never heard before.

"Do you have anything you plan to take into Canada and leave or sell here?"

Hendershot, exhausted, nods back toward his passengers. "These kids." He laughs, and the officer laughs with him.

"Yeah! All right!" the boys yell together.

Then the officer again speaks to Hendershot: "So where are you going?"

"Montreal. Expo."

"Any perishables on board? Fruits? Vegetables?"

"Nope."

"And how long do you plan to be staying?"

"Forever!" the boys cheer. "Or 'til they kick us out!"

"Quiet!" says one of the cottage parents.

"Any valuable items you plan to take back?"

Hendershot hasn't an instant to answer. "Girls!" Rabbit says from his seat in the back.

"French curves!" Fred yells. And they all buckle over — the boys, Hendershot, even the cottage parents. They are all crossing the border.

The bus parks a little way up the road, and the boys, cooped up, tumble out. They want to see the boundary itself. On the maps they've been shown, it's a thick line between the two countries, but except for a small pylon, there is no sense of a border here, no line, no fence, no wall, nothing. The grass on one side is like the grass on the other. So this is it? What's the big deal? At first this is disappointing, then oddly exhilarating. What's in a boundary to stop them? Spreading his legs, Rabbit stands with one foot in the U.S. and one in Canada. He has a vague sense that he might split in half, then a little thrill when nothing happens. The other guys try it. Nothing happens. Then, whooping, they all race back and forth from country to country. Rabbit runs with a wild, whirring, ungraceful exuberance, all knees, elbows, and knotted calves. They are outlaws, smugglers with Mounties in hot pursuit. These are the times of their lives.

I must remember these times, these boys, like colts, leaping over the border — when things like "forever" seemed remotely possible, when "perishable" didn't snag in the mind, and boundaries might be illusory. How easily they run and jump over that line, and run right back again. Rabbit had many of these times in his life. I must not let his death erase them.

Community Relations

One evening in the following winter of 1968, when Rabbit had just turned sixteen, Bonnie Brae hosted the annual basketball game between their team and the Volunteer Fire and Rescue Squad from Liberty Corner, a neighboring town. It was usually a hard-played, good-natured affair, covered by the *Bernardsville News:* the strapping local firemen and the disadvantaged boys, a celebration of "community relations."

Rabbit was never on the Bonnie Brae basketball team. He liked the game, he looked the part, but was not particularly well coordinated. I remember in gym classes that he was best — and he was *very* fast — when sprinting flat-out, alone in his body, with all that propelled him directed in a straight line toward a single goal.

So on that evening, Rabbit sat in the stands with Fred Simko, watching their team, which included Doug and Cy. Cy was a lanky forward; Doug a small, scrappy guard, quick on the dribble, quick with his hands — I know, because I remember him stealing the ball from me in high school pick-up games. Anyway, some of the firemen didn't like the way he played. "City ball," they called it. So they jawed at Doug, which spurred him on. He stole the ball again, and perhaps he hacked someone hard across the arm. Then "the next thing you know," as Doug tells it now, "they jumped me. They were all over my back."

What followed — and was not reported in the local paper — was an old-fashioned rumble. The teams got into it, cursing, punching, wrestling on the floor. Almost immediately so did some fans. According to Fred, "Rabbit was sitting right beside me. And then he wasn't." Enraged at what was happening to Doug, he was among the first to leap from the stands. "He wasn't a very good fighter," in Fred's estimation, "he didn't know how to use his fists. But he was big and strong enough to throw guys out of the way. That's what he did to those firemen."

Much of this feels exaggerated to me, almost the stuff of legend: Rabbit leaping into the fray, coming to the aid of his friend, tossing aside firemen like sacks of flour. A few years later I had a summer job with the township road department and got to know some of those firemen. Big, jovial, ham-handed guys. Few of them could have been thrown around, even by the likes of Rabbit. But maybe the precise truth matters less here than the legend, less than these stories, like distillations, that his friends still carry with them. When the brawl had petered out and everyone was cooling down, Rabbit went up to the firemen, some still lying on the floor. To each of them he offered his hand — Fred and Doug swear this is true. "Hey, you all right?" he asked.

Five winters later, at 12:30 A.M. on January 13, 1973, the Liberty Corner Fire and Rescue Squad, along with other neighboring police and rescue units, responded to a ten-ten police emergency from Olcott Square. Some of the men on that call had scuffled with Rabbit in that rumble at Bonnie Brae. When they arrived in the square, the Bernardsville rescue squad was already at work on the scene. Still, those men from Liberty Corner stood by and saw Rabbit sprawled outside the doorway of the Three Lights Tavern, much as some of them had been sprawled, those years before, on the floor of the Buttenheim Gym. They watched as the other rescuers pumped his chest, bagged him with oxygen, felt for a pulse, and finally left him lying on the pavement.

"Hey, you all right?" Maybe some of them remembered, remembered that big kid, remembered taking his hand — all brown on top and white in the palm — and how he had helped them up off the floor.

Newspaper Title Winner

Although it isn't a farm anymore and is now a very different kind of "facility" for "troubled youths," Bonnie Brae remains a going concern. You still enter down the long, tree-lined lane, past the playing fields, toward Graves Cottage, the Turrell Administration Building, and the Buttenheim Gym. But when you visit, you will not find much evidence that for four years Rabbit lived here. As I've said, his old room is now part of the Development Office, and the records from his time were destroyed by a flood. In the foyer of the small theater (which used to be the cafeteria) hang framed photographs dating back to "the farm years," yet in none of them does Rabbit appear.

Where he appears, mostly, from this time of his life, is in the memories of his friends. Cy, Fred, and Doug are filled with stories. They see him skinny-dipping at midnight in the Bonnie Brae pool, his long arms in the moonlight, then diving deep beneath the water's surface, coming up where you'd never expect him. They see him climbing, on a dare, to the peak of the barn, way up by the lightning rods. He seems bigger than life in many of these memories, bold and brash, "a smooth talker," but "there was always something else about him," Cy says, "like something you couldn't touch or talk about. Maybe he felt it even more than the rest of us: he didn't seem to have *any* family." Sometimes, when everyone was playing out on the fields, he would come back to his room, and half-shutting the door, lie down on his bed and read for hours. They all remember these moments of Rabbit's withdrawal, which in retrospect seem inevitable and healthy, though at the time they were a little perplexing, so at odds with "his usual self."

When I last visited Bonnie Brae, the director of development took me on a short tour. She pointed out all the new buildings and improvements, while I was more interested in what was old. Toward the back of the property I spotted the barn still standing, though its silo has been dismantled. Inside were the old wooden stalls for the cows. It even smelled faintly of manure and silage. There were things around that didn't belong in a barn: battered sofas, rickety booths from fund-raising events, some artificial palm trees from a play of some sort. Upstairs in the loft lay old hay bales, all pillaged and scattered by birds. Along one side, where the slanting rafters met the floorboards, some dishes were neatly stacked. I counted over a hundred plates, a hundred cups, saucers, and bowls — old white china with a teal floral pattern that my mother could probably identify.

These, said the director, were the cafeteria dishes used through the 1960s, before they changed over to plastic. So these were the dishes from which Rabbit and all the boys ate their canned corn, steamed broccoli, sloppy joes, and viscous fruit cup. I can almost taste it now. I can hear the scrape and clatter of trays and silverware, the boys' jiving and riotous jokes. They are back from school and from playing in the fields. Rabbit is flush and full of himself, holding forth while scarfing his food, reliving some feat of power and speed, bits of grass in the sweat on his arms.

Returning then to the Development Office, the director pointed me toward a hall closet where she said I'd find some "old stuff," though no official records. Inside stood a tilting stack of tattered scrapbooks, crammed with newspaper clippings, old brochures, and copies of letters to various philanthropists, in no particular order.

In all the brochures and clippings, though, there were no photos or mention of Rabbit, and no real sense of the boys' lives. But in one of the scrapbooks, between the last page and back cover, lay copies of two issues, perhaps the only issues, of the Bonnie Brae student newspaper. One was six pages long, the other eight. They were filled with riddles, puzzles, a sports page, a poetry corner, and bits of avuncular advice on avoiding poison ivy or washing hands — "Surely before meals!"

Then this caught my eye, on the front page of the May 5, 1968, issue:

Newspaper Title Winner

It's all over. The titles have been judged. The winner, the owner of FIVE DOLLARS, is *Bill Wells.* His entry of the *Campus Communications,* judged the best of twelve entries, is now heading our pages. We thank Bill for his excellent suggestion, and we hope that he does not spend it all in one place.

It is such a small item, yet it feels important to me. For here is a thing that I can hold in my hands, as Rabbit held it in his. It says where he was, and what for a short time he was doing. On or about May 5, 1968, nearly two years after he arrived, he won a contest at Bonnie Brae Farm. He gave a newspaper its name, he won five dollars, and saw his own name in print. I bet he felt proud, though he might have been too cool to admit it. Five bucks back then wouldn't buy you the ranch, but it could get you a pizza at Pistilli's with all the works, or a pair of jeans, or a fringed leather vest, or a couple of paperbacks, with a carton of Camels thrown in.

Perhaps he didn't spend it at all, but, along with a folded copy of this newspaper item, took it back to his room and put it into a drawer, or added it to his things under his mattress. As a kid, I used to hide little things in the backs of drawers. Maybe this is what Rabbit hid in his: a five-dollar bill and his name in italics — another thing he could touch to know it was there, another thing to remind him, when things got bad, just how good, how proud, he could feel.

Billy Sorgie

The person who shot and killed Rabbit on that night years ago
in Olcott Square was William Sorgie (pronounced "Sorg*ee*"),
twenty-four years old, a Bernardsville patrolman. He and Rabbit
had never met nor heard of one another before. Their lives
touched but for a matter of seconds, at most a minute, a trifling
space of time. Yet the story of Sorgie's part in that moment had
begun many years before.

Five stops, or about twelve minutes, east of Basking Ridge on
the train toward New York is the small town of Berkeley
Heights. The train slows as it crosses the trestle above the Passaic River. Then it whistles beneath the bridge at Route 512, the
same road that, a few miles back, passes in front of Bonnie Brae.
To the left, as you stop, you will see the old wooden "stick style"
station, recently painted green, with the initial-carved benches
on the platform. Few people sit on the benches here. Few get on
or off the train. This is but another bedroom community on
your way to work, with a Shop Rite and a Rexall Drug Store,
where the houses, though neat with their groomed shrubbery,
are more pinched together than they were in those grassy hills to
the west. Through your window to the right is a parking lot,
and, as the train pulls away, you can see, beyond the glinting
hoods and windshields, the brick front of the Municipal Building that houses the Berkeley Heights Police Department.

Had you taken the Erie Lackawanna in the late fifties and
early sixties, and had you lowered your newspaper and looked
through the window as the train pulled out of the station, you
might have seen on those stone steps to the Police Department
a kid in jeans with a ball, a glove, and a blue Yankees cap. That
was Billy Sorgie. Anyone would have recognized him, anyone

who knew anything about Berkeley Heights. He was Frances and Charlie Sorgie's boy, a clean-cut, "yes sir, no sir" kind of kid, with black, crew-cut hair and two consuming passions: to play centerfield for the Yankees, and to be a policeman.

All spring and summer he played in the C.Y.O. and Police Athletic League, running down fly balls like Mickey Mantle. He was good. He was strong for his age, and had a rifle arm. He could hit fast pitching, and he could hit hard — he seemed to be unafraid of the ball. Evidently the local policemen took a special liking to him, and he was thrilled by their attention. When he wasn't at home, at school, or on the base paths at Memorial Field, he was across the street, hanging around the police station. He'd chew the fat with the desk sergeant. He'd listen in on the radio. On the steps he'd greet the cops as they came in from their shifts, or he'd watch them hurrying off on an emergency, in their crisp uniforms and shining shoes, with their guns snapped tight in their holsters.

His mother was Scotch-Irish, and his paternal forebears came over from Sicily as marble masons. His grandfather was an American infantryman in the First World War, his father an infantryman in the Second, fighting at Guam and Okinawa, some of the bloodiest battles in the Pacific. After the war, his parents married, settled in Passaic, and his father got a job with the Pullman Car Company, repairing brakes on trains in Hoboken. There were two children: a daughter Caroline, and born in 1949, a son they called Billy.

By the time Billy was eight years old, his father had become an assistant superintendent for Pullman at the astounding wage of $350 per week. They had bought a 1954 Cadillac. Then in 1957 they moved west along the path of the Erie Lackawanna to Berkeley Heights, where they bought a brand-new development house, a shag-shingled colonial with a two-car garage, not too different from the house my parents, just two years earlier, had built in Basking Ridge.

These were heady times for the Sorgies. The Pullman

money rolled in. They got free tickets to travel the rails — to Buffalo, Chicago — on vacations. In '59 they replaced the old Cadillac with the brand-new, longer tail-finned model, which Billy's father drove to the station. At home his mother cooked big Italian dinners, or they splurged at the Pine Tree Inn. After school, on weekends, and all summer long, Billy rode his Schwinn a mile into town, where he played ball and hung out on the police department steps. It was great, just then, to be a kid: to shoot your pellet gun at muskrats along the Passaic, to jaw with the cops, to smell the grass that stains your sneakers, the linseed oil, like a holy ointment, slick in the pocket of your glove. Each evening you'd meet your old man at the train and race him home on your bike. The Plainfield *Courier News* or the *Newark Star Ledger* would lie curled on the driveway. The smell of dinner, all ready, would drift through the screens; fireflies would hover and blink. But best of all, when you slide into bed, your transistor radio lies under your pillow. The Yanks are playing. The dial is set, and nobody else in the whole world knows it. On the card in your mind, you pencil-in the lineup: Kubek, Richardson, Maris, Mantle; Whitey Ford on the hill. It feels so good, it must be a sin. Christ, they were unstoppable then.

Of course, it is my own youth that I am imagining. Billy Sorgie may not have had a transistor radio, and his bike may not have been a Schwinn. Yet all boyhoods overlap in some way, especially the boyhoods of Yankees fans who grew up near the Passaic. We all know the feel of those late-August nights, with the plaintive train whistle, the sweat and mosquitoes, with the smell of the river, forbidden, fecund, and Red Barber closing out the ninth, soft as a benediction.

I never knew Billy Sorgie. He was four years older than I was. He lived ten miles away in another county, another school system, and I had never even heard of him until that night more than twenty years ago, when I was away at college and my mother was on the phone, telling me what had happened to Rabbit.

"He was shot and killed by a policeman," she said. "By a William Sorgie," she added.

Now I think a lot about Billy Sorgie, just as I think a lot about Rabbit. We were all named William, called Billy or Bill. For all our differences, we were all once boys. We threw stones. We admired men in uniforms. We had our heroes, some of whom we shared. All of us thought we were good at sports, then good at girls, and all of us would be disillusioned. It may not be true, but it *feels* true: that some part of me resides in each of these boys, and some part of them in me.

The Yankees went on to have a few more great years, though for the Sorgies it all fell apart in '62. Bobby Kennedy, then attorney general, broke up the Pullman Car Company, and Charlie Sorgie lost his job. The family sold the Cadillac, then the house, and rented a tiny, second-floor apartment near the station and the "Little Italy" part of town. Frances Sorgie found work as a crossing guard. Charlie got another job in Hoboken repairing brakes, this time for the Erie Lackawanna, but for just the minimum wage. He had to walk each day to the train.

As for Billy, he still played ball most afternoons; he washed dishes at local restaurants some evenings, and long before dawn on winter mornings, he tossed newspapers from the back of a truck. At Livingston Regional High School, he got average grades. He took industrial arts classes all four years. He was smart enough, but by then it was clear: college just wasn't in the cards.

By chance, while prowling around his old high school library, I ran into someone who knew Billy Sorgie back then: Dan Gomula, his old industrial arts teacher, now in his sixties.

Did he remember him?

"Hell, of course. A good kid. A solid kid." He even remembered a project of Billy's that they worked on after school.

On the lathe, they repaired an old shotgun for duck hunting —
something wrong with the barrel or bore.

In the same library, in the *Claymore Yearbook* of 1966 —
the year Rabbit was sent to Bonnie Brae — there, in the group
photo of Homeroom 101, stands "B. Sorgie" in his junior year:
tall and broad-shouldered in his coat and narrow tie. He must
have turned girls' heads. He seems good-natured, courteous,
yet wickedly handsome, the sort of looks the rest of us would
have died for: his clean-shaven square jaw, hinting of Aqua-Velva
and manhood; his small ears that don't stick out; his piercing
eyes; dark brows; black hair combed back in a tidal wave, stiff
and shining with Brylcreem.

He played outfield every year in school, and in that same
yearbook, some pages later, is a team picture with him standing,
his thick arms crossed in front of him, his sleeves pushed up to
his biceps. There is an L on his cap, a big LR on his jersey, and
through black-rimmed glasses with flipped-up shades, he stares,
dead serious, at the camera.

This, I recognize, is his "game face," the one with which he
steeled himself, the one that he — and all ballplayers — shows
to opposing pitchers. It is not especially mean or angry, but is
unflinching, unimpressed, almost a dare. It means business. I'm
not backing down, it seems to say. So go ahead, throw it, give
me your best stuff. I'll blast it the hell out of here.

With a jolt, it strikes me that this could be the face that he
showed to Rabbit as they stood face to face, ten feet apart, on
that night twenty-five years ago. It was a human face that in
other circumstances had smiled and laughed, had softened in
sympathy and love. But here it was stern, steel-jawed, and un-
forgiving. A stranger's face, a slugger's face, a policeman's face,
a hard and handsome white man's face. The last face Rabbit ever
saw.

*   *   *

The last high school photo that I've seen of Billy Sorgie is his graduation picture of 1967. Here he is "William F. Sorgie." The same dark, chiseled eyebrows and wave of shining hair, the same coat and narrow tie. His thin lips are closed, determined, with a small, knowing smile. His eyes gaze off toward a point in the distance, as if he can see his brave future. Despite the turn in his family's fortunes, he is dashing, confident, invincible here. Above his photo is this inscription: "Happy the man who . . . makes all his pleasure dependent on his liberty of action."

Probably before this photo was taken, in February 1967, Sorgie had already signed his letter of intention to enlist in the Army. A war was on in a faraway place and, unlike many of his college-bound classmates, he wanted to serve his country. Like his grandfather and father, he would join the infantry. He expected no more or less of himself. In July '67 he began ten weeks of basic training at Fort Dix, New Jersey, followed by infantry training in Missouri, and duty as a wire man in Germany. Then six months after he had graduated and got his yearbook, while Rabbit and I were freshmen in high school, this kid — this other William who had grown up along the Passaic — arrived in Vietnam.

High School

It is hard to imagine many places in America that seemed more distant from the war in Vietnam than Basking Ridge and Bernardsville. It just didn't touch very many of us directly. Of course it was in the news, on television, but so were *Laugh-In, Gidget, Lawrence Welk,* and we were all on our way to the moon. As late as 1971, student deferments were given by our local draft board, and more than ninety percent of our high school graduates enrolled in college. No one I knew closely had served in Vietnam. Sure, I had heard of some guys who went, and when I had that summer job with the township road department, I worked with a few who had recently returned: Paul Knoll and Dave Gorsky — both of them townies, sons of plumbers or janitors, who, like the guys from Bonnie Brae, didn't have the means to be anywhere else when Uncle Sam came knocking.

Had Rabbit been an outstanding student, he might, by his senior year, have hoped for a college scholarship as a way of avoiding the war. But his school records show that his performance was terrible, particularly during his ninth- and tenth-grade years. Except for his consistent Bs in Art, he got almost straight Ds. English, Algebra, Social Studies, General Science, Earth Science, History, Math: D, D, D, D, D, D, E — he barely scraped by. In our freshman class of 268, his rank was 256. A year later he was 237 of 249, still right at the bottom of the barrel.

At first this surprises me, for he was clearly intelligent. His standardized tests bore this out. His I.Q. was measured at 109. His quantitative aptitude was around the fiftieth percentile, his verbal aptitude in the ninetieth. Except for his writing skills, which were judged average, his measured knowledge of math, science, and social studies all exceeded the seventieth percentile.

In short, Rabbit was probably smarter than most of us. Yet at school, he often seemed bored, distracted, and at times supercilious. There's an early high school story, told by some guys from Bonnie Brae, about Rabbit and a certain math teacher, whom I will call Mr. Bennett. Bennett — God forgive me — was a smallish, wormy man who could get under your skin. As the story goes, Rabbit had again come to class without having done his homework. I can see him tilted back in the last row, his arms crossed, his long legs stretched out, that bored, sleepy look on his face.

"Tell me something about prime numbers, Mr. Wells."
Bennett called you "mister" if he thought you were unprepared.

"I dunno," Rabbit said, whether he knew or not.

"Well, take a guess, Mr. Wells. Take a flying leap. You've
read pages forty-eight to fifty. You did your assignment last
night."

"Prime numbers?" Rabbit asked, and Bennett nodded.
Rabbit thought for a moment, making Bennett wait. "Prime
numbers. Well, I suppose they're *good* numbers," he said mildly.
"You know: Prime. Good. Like meat that's juicy. Not the chewy
part."

The rest of the class cracked up at this, and Rabbit enjoyed
their laughter.

But Bennett, so the story goes, was unamused. He walked
down the aisle and stood in front of Rabbit. "Get up, Mr.
Wells," he said, and slowly Rabbit did. "So you think you're
smart. Is that it?" And then, before Rabbit's classmates, Bennett
laid it on thick: how Rabbit was irresponsible, lazy, or just plain
stupid, how he was holding back the entire class, how he should
be embarrassed for himself.

Some of this Rabbit might have deserved, and some of it,
judging by his response, struck a deeper wound. A moment earlier the class had been laughing — he seemed part of them; they
were with him. Now they were silent, watchful, something receding in their eyes. And this cool kid was suddenly trembling,
humiliated, alone in his glaring darkness.

Rabbit's own eyes were all awake and strangely squinting,
sweat on his face like tears. He tried to say something, his hands
fluttering, but words didn't come. Then his fist flew out and, depending on who is telling the story, it struck Bennett in the
chest or square on the jaw, knocking him back down the aisle.
"Decked him!" is how the tale, with a flourish, generally ends.

The tale doesn't tell the whole story, though, of how Rabbit might have felt about this — the sharp, searing exhilaration

as Bennett staggered backward. *Son of a bitch. White son of a bitch. Don't you ever mess with me again.* But what was it like to sit back in his chair in that suddenly quiet classroom? Or to walk down the hall as a few kids patted his back and others, whispering, hustled out of his way? ("See? I told you he was like that," meaning: they're *all* like that.) Or then later that night to lie in his bunk, with his knuckles throbbing, his sheets cold, and that blinking red light on the water tower?

By his friends he was loved for his sympathy, and by his teachers (who knows, maybe even Bennett) he got high marks on his "personality record" for his "concern for others." So, if in fact this did happen, he might have felt that searing exhilaration, though that wasn't all he felt. *He was daring me to do it, to be what he thinks I am. So what am I supposed to do? Stand there? Take it? Do nothing? . . . But when you do it, that's no good either. Why do I do these things?*

It wasn't the last time that Rabbit would lash out at someone, even someone he loved, and then be appalled by himself.

Things would get better for Rabbit in school. You can see it in his class photos: a pride and dignity, held hard against his uncertainties. His eyes stare right at the camera, as if to make a point. In our junior year, his Ds turned into Bs and Cs. His class rank improved to 157. But already it was clear that, without a miracle or money, he wasn't on his way to a college deferment. On his eighteenth birthday, in our junior year, he registered for the draft, and by all accounts he feared what might be coming. Then there was another looming problem: Where in the world would he live? By the end of that summer of 1970, his eighteenth year, he was required by state law to leave Bonnie Brae Farm. He must have felt how on his own he was. Everyone else was planning for college. What was to become of him?

At Irene's

On Saturday mornings, about every month or six weeks, my mother drove into town to get her hair done. She went to a place she called Irene's, though the sign on the window, beside the photo of a woman who looked like Doris Day, always read "Ridge Beauty Salon." It was on West Oak Street, near the corner of Brownlee Place, about fifty yards from the town green and the Presbyterian Church. Though I walked by there every school day, I hardly noticed it then: an old two-story stucco frame house, with the beauty shop on the first floor. I have a memory of a faint astringent smell wafting out through the screened front door. Inside were a whirring row of domed hair driers, engulfing the heads of women seated with magazines on their laps.

My mother never returned from the beauty salon looking like Doris Day, but always a little more like herself: her neat brown hair slightly shorter, shining, wavy and soft to the casual eye, yet stiff as Brillo pads. All this was courtesy of Irene Wilkerson, who owned the shop and lived with her daughter Sharon in the apartment upstairs. Sharon was in my oldest sister's class, a year behind mine. She was a great friend of Joanne Calantoni, who lived around the corner, and a friend of some of the boys from Bonnie Brae. She would eventually marry Doug Robb.

Irene also took an interest in the boys, and began inviting them to the house for dinner. "It felt good," she tells me over the phone, "to have more people around." Years before, she and her husband had divorced, and Sharon was her only child. So on Friday or Saturday evenings, after she had swept the floor downstairs, she pulled up the leaves of her kitchen table and cooked. Rabbit, Doug, Cy, Fred — they came week in, week out. They came for her heaping plates of spaghetti and meatballs; they came for her slabs of Carvel ice cream; they came to get away from Bonnie Brae for a while. But mostly, she says, they came because "it felt like family": those clomping boys crowding into her kitchen, where they were made to wipe their feet, to wash their hands, to not lean back like that in their chairs, and to mind their language.

Irene remembers them laughing a lot, jostling and teasing one another. For all his size and bravado, though, Rabbit was "the most sensitive." "He was really just a big lummox," she says, laughing, and then stops laughing: "I guess he had it the worst." On holidays, while other guys at Bonnie Brae visited relatives, Rabbit always hung around town and usually ate at Irene's. As the boys approached their eighteenth birthdays and would soon have to leave Bonnie Brae, they talked for hours around her table about "what in the world they would do." Doug and Fred would go to community college, and Cy to the Police Academy. Rabbit had another year of high school. By now he was writing what he called poetry. He was getting more interested in politics, in the peace and civil rights movements. He seemed to have bigger and better plans, or maybe no plans at all. Where would he live? What would he do? "Something will turn up," he always said, and they dug into their food.

"I really liked those boys," says Irene, "I guess, for a while, I was there for them."

After writing the above, based on conversations I had with her some months ago, I've learned that Irene Wilkerson has died and has been buried in Holy Cross Cemetery, adjacent to Somerset Hills Memorial Park, on the same hillside where Rabbit lies. At her funeral were some old friends, the remains of her extended family, and Doug, Cy, and Fred. Years before, she had moved to Liberty Corner, after retiring and selling the old shop. Now it has a fresh coat of tan paint and is some sort of "unisex hair cuttery." Her daughter Sharon has been divorced from Doug, has remarried, and today is the township animal warden, what we used to call the dogcatcher. She has an office in the Health Department, which is next door to our old high school. She drives a white van — with the town insignia, an oak leaf, on the door — wears work boots and jeans, and has a thick waist, strong arms, and hair like a black mane. When we speak of Rabbit, she smiles and laughs. She remembers his tie-dyed shirts. She remembers, too, that he wrote her a poem. "He was the only one who would *ever* do that!"

After her lunch break, she goes out to her van with a clipboard, a leash, and a pair of heavy leather gloves. She has just received a call. She has to go, she tells me. Her job is to take in strays and try to find them homes.

Marian

Something did turn up for Rabbit — and just in time — before he had to leave Bonnie Brae. What turned up was love, or whatever it is that burns through us when we are seventeen or eighteen years old. The girl was Marian Jeffers, whose very name still causes guys who remember her to wince in exquisite pain. She was that beautiful. And that unattainable, except, of course, for Rabbit. She had long, extraordinarily straight blonde hair that might have spent hours each night on an ironing board, or coiled around oversize juice cans. It was parted in the middle and fell like a cape around her narrow face, over her shoulders, and all the way down near the small of her back, where it swayed as she walked to her locker. Her sort of beauty was altogether different than other girls' beaming wholesomeness. Marian's was more reserved and somber. In our yearbooks, you will not find her front and center in any group photos. She appears more on the edge of things, to emerge, when she did, from the shadows. She was small, slender, and shy, I had thought. So when

you first saw them together, Marian and Rabbit, you couldn't
help but stare. All his height, depth, swagger, and darkness. And
all her quiet delicacy.

She lived with her family in a modest, split-level, 1960s development house that was painted olive green at the time. It
stood behind a row of evergreens on Lyons Road, a mile or two
from Bonnie Brae Farm. Across the street were fields and stables
where the Jeffers boarded a couple of horses that Marian rode
every day.

How did they meet? Even Marian doesn't recall. She and
Rabbit probably took the same bus to school, and they were in
some of the same classes. After school, or on the weekends, they
might have run into each other at Somerset Farms, a small grocery store in Liberty Corner, where Rabbit sometimes hung out
on the front porch and where Marian's older brother Bobby was
a stock boy.

I like to think that they met near her home. Maybe Rabbit
was hitching into town. It could be cloudy, drizzling, or almost
dark, but he'd still have had on his shades — a cool dude ready
for action, though nobody's picking him up. In fact, the cars
seem to speed up around him. His mouth is dust and exhaust.
From someplace, a strange blur touches his eye, and he turns his
head to catch up with it. Beyond a white fence, a girl rides a
horse, her hair streaming behind her. It's like in the movies, he
thinks, or maybe this is religion. He can feel her flying across
that field; he can feel himself flying with her. Wind. Speed. The
curve of her ass in the saddle. Maybe this is what it means: *trans-
ported*.

However they met, they began going out in March 1970,
and according to friends, they were crazy about each other. In
the girls' room between classes, Marian checked her face and
brushed her hair; Rabbit actually ironed his bell-bottoms. They
double-dated with Walt Schneider and Donna Gabory. They sat
in the back of the Bernardsville Cinema, went to parties, the
usual things. When people stared, they tried to ignore them, or

sometimes Rabbit stared right back. They listened to Sly, Hendrix, Jefferson Airplane, Smokey Robinson, Simon and Garfunkel, Tammi Terrell and Marvin Gaye. The counterculture came but slowly to our town, so Rabbit was smoking just cigarettes. He wore a jacket with an American flag on the back, and he had recently gotten an electric guitar, but he couldn't play a riff. I imagine he and Marian found places to be alone: a musty sofa in a basement rec room, or that pull-over out by Ravine Lake, where kids still take the old man's car, with a six-pack or a bottle of sloe gin, and, like most of us at one time or another, discover the wonders of "parking."

In the end, it was surprisingly easy, the resolution of what had gnawed at Rabbit for months. Marian told her parents that soon he would be without a home, and they invited him to live with their family. They set another place at the dining room table, and put another bed in their son Bobby's room — he was almost exactly Rabbit's age.

The Woodchopping Story

I will not say that the Jeffers then had a normal family life, for it was hardly a normal practice where I come from to share your home with your seventeen-year-old daughter's mixed-race boyfriend from Bonnie Brae Farm. Ruth Jeffers, Marian's mother, is a small unprepossessing woman of about seventy, with a soft round face, no make-up, and worn eyes rimmed with red, as though she suffers from allergies. She carries a scuffed, square, navy blue purse. She was born in New Zealand where, as a nurse during the Second World War, she met and married Robert Jeffers, a wounded American serviceman who brought her to the States to settle in Liberty Corner. There they raised their three children, and when they found out about Rabbit's situation, "Well, it was only natural to ask him in," Ruth tells me matter-of-factly with her New Zealand accent. "I was taught that children of all colors belong to everyone." For her, it was that simple.

Aside from this, the Jeffers lived pretty much as the rest of us did. In the mornings Bobby, Rabbit, and Marian (an older daughter, Christine, was at college) went off to high school. Robert Sr. drove to work, while Ruth Jeffers did errands, kept the house, and prepared supper. In the evenings they reassembled at the dining room table, ate, then dispersed to read the paper, do homework, or skip it and watch TV. They did chores with appropriate reluctance: washed cars, cut grass, and vacuumed beneath the beds. Ruth tells a story about asking Rabbit to chop wood, soon after he had moved in.

It was the fall of 1970 and they were still getting to know one another. The Jeffers had recently had a tree taken down and the wood cut into lengths. So one Saturday morning Ruth asked Rabbit if he would mind taking a turn chopping and stacking some of it. She was taken aback when, flat out, he told her no, he had better things to do.

"All right," she said. "If that's how you want it. The wood will get chopped without you."

They parted ways for the rest of the day and at dinner they made no mention of their previous discussion. Rabbit and Marian went out late that night, and Ruth went to bed before they returned, leaving the front door unlocked and the light on in the kitchen. It took her a while to fall asleep, after talking with Robert Sr. about it. Had they done the right thing? Suddenly Rabbit seemed so intractable. Who was this new person under their roof and now out with their daughter after midnight?

Even then Ruth knew pretty much what it meant — that firm "no" in Rabbit's voice and that hard look in his face. He was drawing a line. He was holding to what he felt was his. After all, he was eighteen years old, a young man, and despite the fact that they sheltered, fed, and clothed him now, he was certainly not their son.

Finally Ruth went to sleep. She never heard Rabbit and Marian return. Instead, what she heard, and what awoke her before dawn, was a slow, rhythmic thunking sound, accompanied by sharp chuffs of breath, building in intensity. The sounds stopped for a while and started again. She made herself get up to see. On her way to her door, she pushed open her curtains, and in the pale light, she could make out a figure, standing alone in the yard. It was Rabbit, swinging the big, wedge-headed maul, splitting the wood, his breath coming out in plumes.

I imagine him now in his jeans, gloves, and gray sweatshirt. He is still feeling a little hung over, and a little pissed off that he's actually dragged himself out here at this ridiculous time of day. Yet the air and exercise brace him. There's frost on the ground; he smells withered leaves. He stands a log on the stump, holds his feet apart, and lifts the maul over his head. In a glinting arc, he powers it downward and through the log, which teeters and falls in two. It gives him an old, warm, wild pleasure, to see something cleave by his hands. Now and then he takes the maul a few steps away and leans it against a tree. He collects the split wood, stacks it, and this gives him yet another pleasure: piece by piece the pile grows; he can measure what he's done.

Now he picks up the maul again and hefts it over his shoulder, both hands on the handle, before carrying it back toward the stump. Look at him now. Remember him now. For this is how he stood when he was shot. Tall and proud in the dim light. His feet apart, his breath hard, a heavy weight on his shoulder.

Eroded Bones

What impresses me about his time with the Jeffers is the apparent fullness of Rabbit's life. Something always seemed to be happening. It was during this period that he read *Soul on Ice* and the *Autobiography of Malcolm X,* stories of injustice, hatred, near self-destruction, imprisonment, self-assertion, discipline, redemption. I think of Malcolm X, then Malcolm Little, a light-toned black kid in Michigan, the only nonwhite kid in *his* class. He loses his home (burned down by the KKK), his father (beneath the wheels of a streetcar), and his mother (to an insane asylum). At the age of thirteen, he is farmed off to foster homes and reform school. At twenty, he goes to prison. Then I think of how all that must have rung in Rabbit's head. He must have read that book until dawn.

Of course, when he finished it, he didn't run off and join the Nation of Islam — Rabbit was hardly a separatist. Yet he did, for a time, take an African name, though no one, even his closest friends, can remember it precisely now. It is possible that Rabbit didn't take it that seriously. But it is more possible, I think, that he did take it seriously, and that very few others recognized it.

What his friends tend to remember are the more conventional forms of his nonconformity. The beads and peace symbols. Even the Hendrix look. He called everyone "brother" or "sister." Like any number of us, he took a stab at Eastern religion. Buddhism, Zen Buddhism, transcendental meditation. In the summer, he exchanged his boots for those Indian buffalo-hide sandals everyone was wearing. I have a hard time imagining him meditating, eyes closed in divine communion, cross-legged on a shag carpet. Still, I can almost smell the incense, and hear Ravi Shankar's sitar twanging in the speakers.

In school, he was most engaged in art classes, and at least

one teacher thought him talented. He took courses in print-making, ceramics, drawing, sculpture, and photography, which became a lasting passion. He bought, or the Jeffers bought him, a camera, and he took it on long walks in the woods with Marian, snapping photos of their meandering footprints in the snow, or a glaze of ice encasing a twig, or the rippled shadows of leaves on water. We were all into Nature then.

I have found none of his photos or other artifacts, except for two small ceramic sculptures Ruth Jeffers has shown me. We were sitting in the Bernardsville Library, around the corner from Olcott Square, when she took them out of her purse. One is terra-cotta, the other painted a dull white; each fits into your palm. At first they remind me of something like coral: organic forms with rounded protuberances and hollows, all the surfaces smooth, even soft. One has holes that go clear through, inviting your fingers to follow — to follow, in fact, where Rabbit's own fingers went. Here a socket-like cave, perhaps the size of his thumb; here a tunnel the length of his pinkie; here a curve as gentle as the back of a thigh; here a bump like a knuckle.

Like eroded bones, now, these sculptures seem to me, worn smooth by use and time. And as with bones, it's the space around and through them that occupies all your groping. What pulsing thing ran through this hole? What curled in this dark hollow? You turn these things over and over in your hand, and the clay itself gives no wonder. Its life resides in its holes and hollows, in its absences, in the shapes we can only imagine.

Rabbit's own bones were big, blunt, and wide. In photos of him, I focus on his wrists and hands; you might even call him heavy-handed. Yet there is a delicacy in the way that he holds a cigarette between his index and middle fingers. His hand hangs languidly over a chair arm; I would even call the posture feminine. So where did all the delicacy come from, to hold a cigarette like Marlene Dietrich, to form with his bluntness those small, smooth sculptures?

It came from the holes and hollows, from what, though absent, has left its impression, a shape we can only imagine.

Why has Ruth kept them? And why, like so many other remains, have they not disappeared?

Perhaps because what we hold of the loved and dead can be a measure of our living. Those sculptures — Ruth hasn't sealed them in plastic, or put them away on some shelf. They are grimy with ground-in dirt and oil, with years of turning in her palm.

Lieutenant Sorgie

On January 8, 1968, Specialist Fourth Class Bill Sorgie had completed his basic and advanced training and landed in Chu Lai, joining 485,000 other Americans in South Vietnam. After ten days at the Americal Combat Center, he joined Company C, Third Battalion, Twenty-first Infantry, 196th Light Infantry Brigade, Americal Division, in Quang Tin province. He was eighteen years old, a long way from home, a light weapons infantryman.

Today he is Lieutenant Sorgie, getting on toward fifty, the second in command at the same Bernardsville Police Department where he worked when, in January 1973, he shot and killed Rabbit. At first this astonishes me, that he is still there. And then it doesn't astonish me at all. For these are towns where policemen settle into their jobs for a long time, where townspeople expect to know policemen personally, and to believe in their integrity and judgment almost as firmly as they believe in their own.

Sorgie has his own office in the old stone headquarters, just beyond the park and duck pond on Route 202, before the base-

ball field and Ferrante's Quarry, a half mile west of Olcott
Square. When I first met him, he stood behind his desk in his
crisp blue uniform. He asked me to come in, and we shook
hands stiffly. He is shorter than I had expected, less than six feet
tall, and like all of us, he looks different from his high school
photographs. Gone is that shining Brylcreemed tidal wave that
swept back from his forehead. His hair now is short, his hairline
ebbing, his eyebrows less emphatic. His eyes themselves seem to
have receded. They appear smaller, as though condensed
through the years, behind his wire-rimmed glasses. His jaw has
softened, his shoulders thickened. He's grown a thin mustache.
Gone is his angular outfielder's body, though his strength, I can
tell, remains. Some decorations cascade down the front of his
left shoulder and end at his bright badge. A tiny gold rifle adorns
his tie clip, and on his belt, with just the handle exposed, he
wears his gun strapped in its holster.

I tell him I'd like to talk about the Wells shooting, about his
time in the service, about how and why what happened happened. The things that he remembers.

"Well, that's all in the past," he says straightaway, though
without anger or impatience. I notice that his head seems small
for his body, and his voice, while deep, is gentle.

On a shelf in his open locker lie his rubber-cleated shoes
and Rawlings glove wrapped around a softball. Photographs of
his kids stand on a file cabinet. And as we sit down, I see on the
wall directly behind him that familiar hook-like shape, like a
comma: a map of South Vietnam. Along its right-hand border,
as he would explain, are insignias of his old division, brigade,
and infantry unit. On the map itself, some red dots cluster in an
area south of Da Nang, the places where he saw action.

"That's all in the past," he says again. But there's that map.
There are those dots. And then we talk of the past for over an
hour — and we've talked for many hours since. Whenever I visit
my parents in Basking Ridge, I call him, I drop by his office, and
he always makes time. He closes his door, we sit with the map

behind him, and he folds his big hands on his desk. Often we talk about baseball, the Yankees' glory years when we were kids. Yet we always come back to the shooting and his time in Vietnam, those things of the past that he remembers like yesterday.

He says he can draw a clear dividing line between what he did in the military and what he's done in civilian life, that the two are "unrelated." But I don't think even he entirely believes this: that the habits and reactions of soldiering stop at the edge of a battlefield, or at the coast of a faraway country, or can't ever resurface in moments of extremity, in places like Bernardsville, New Jersey.

When we talk, he always asks how my research is going. Then I tell him, and I ask him questions that he answers without hesitation. He seems to *need* to answer such questions, as much as I need to ask them. What was it like in Vietnam? What did you do? What happened? Or on that night in Olcott Square, where were you standing? Where was he standing? What did you see? What did you hear? What were you thinking? What were you feeling? Why did you do this? Why didn't you do that? What might you do differently now?

Bill Sorgie has been very helpful to me. He seems to have nothing to hide. He has authorized the release of his military and police training records, but mostly he has talked and talked about these difficult things in his life, as though he hasn't talked about them for a while.

I don't know if I like him or if he likes me. Maybe that doesn't matter. He knows that Rabbit and I were classmates, and he knows that I see some things differently than he does. Still, he is interested in what I find, what I think, and in knowing about the person he killed.

For that I respect him. And it makes me uneasy. It would be oddly comforting if he were monstrous, overtly racist, if he gloated over Rabbit's death. That would make it simple for me; that could be the whole explanation. But he is a straightforward, hard-working, family man — this man who shot Rabbit through the heart. He is reserved, cool, yet not unfriendly, a man like many I think I've known, a man, in some measure, like myself.

Walking Point

"What I've mostly wanted to do is serve," he says, thinking back on his working life, "to do a job the best I can, and of course to get paid and recognized for it. That's why I went into the military. That's why I'm a cop. I still think of myself as a servant."

Early in his military service, Bill Sorgie got a buzz cut, a new wardrobe, innumerable inoculations, and said "Yes, sir!" maybe a million times. Around calisthenics, he took classes in military courtesy, and then classes in the somewhat less courteous activities of bayonet thrusting, rifle firing, and live-grenade throwing. In his Advanced Individual Training in Missouri, he encountered mock Vietcong hamlets, complete with thatched huts, tunnels, booby traps, punji-stakes, "enemy" soldiers, and even flocks of chickens. The mess hall featured inspiring signs such as:

AGGRESSIVENESS and FIRE POWER will WIN

BONG the CONG

Much of this has a surreal, distant, even humorous flavor to me, seen across so many years. Then I read a passage in the Time/Life series *The Vietnam Experience* that stops me cold, when I think of what happened in Olcott Square.

Since much shooting contact with the enemy [in Vietnam] occurred unexpectedly at close range, and ended abruptly, frequently without sight of the foe, soldiers were trained in the techniques of "instant reaction" and "quick kill." Ordered to shoot at sound and movement without consciously aiming, men on mock patrols fired automatically at pop-up targets.

"In the infantry I was taught to react and stay alive," Sorgie tells me now. "It was my most important training." It honed what he calls his survival instincts. "I was not going to get myself killed."

Indeed, he was not killed in Vietnam mainly because of his quick responses, and a good dose of luck. In war, the infantry does the dirty work, and this war was no exception. On his map on the wall, he shows me where his battalion was stationed at LZ (landing zone) Center, a Fire Support Base in the largely Vietcong-controlled mountains northwest of Chu Lai. From there, along with thirty-two others in his platoon from Company C, he would go on search-and-destroy patrols out in the field, often through triple canopy jungle. He was a "grunt," he says, like most everyone else. Days of exhaustion, boredom, starting, stopping, "humping" your stuff, slogging in muck and sweat, keeping the leeches out of your crotch, the mosquitoes out of your ears. Weeks and even months went by like this. Waiting, searching. Patrol, guard duty, patrol, stand down, guard duty, patrol, patrol. Suddenly in the middle of nowhere, a sound. A broken twig? A cricket? A clicking cartridge? Or was it a smell? Or nothing? And then, as if all your days poured into this, you are ripping loose with a fear like ecstasy, spraying the bush with all that is in you, killing to stay alive.

Bill Sorgie killed two enemy soldiers in Vietnam, and probably a few more. He tells me this without apparent pride, more with sad resignation. "It was something I had to do," he says. This is what happens in war.

On one of the patrols, he was walking point, the first in the line of his squad, often the first to hit a booby trap or an ambush, the first to "make contact." He saw a shape through the foliage before the shape saw him. It was only twenty feet away on a low ridge, wearing a pith helmet, carrying a gun. Sorgie wheeled, fired an entire clip, eighteen rounds, and the shape fell from view. Immediately the rest of the platoon fanned out, found cover, then cautiously searched the area. But if there were others along with the shape, they had already melted into the jungle. Now Sorgie and his squad approached the low ridge. There was no sound or movement. On the far side, he found the shape face down, its slender arms outstretched, as though swimming. Its black shirt was shiny, wet, and ripped with bullet holes. One rubber sandal was on a foot, the other was someplace else. The rifle lay a few feet away, and the pith helmet, strapped but twisted cock-eyed, covered the side of the head.

"What did you feel?" I ask Sorgie now.

He thinks and says, "Afraid."

"Of what?" I ask. And I expect him to say that he was afraid that the shape was still alive, still dangerous, or that others were lurking in the bush, planning a revenge attack.

Instead, he says, "I was scared that the body might be a female. That's what really got me." Then he explains that he had seen it happen before. After a firefight, a buddy of his had shot at a shape carrying a gun, sprinting across a field. But the gun, it turned out, was a long, wooden farm tool, and the shape, moaning then in the mud, with its hair pulled back in a small, soft bun, was that of a teenage girl.

So what Sorgie most remembers about this "incident" was sliding the muzzle of his M16 beneath the brim of the pith helmet. He tilted it back. He saw a neck, an ear. On the side of the head, he saw neat, black, short-cropped hair, not much longer than his. Then, feeling relieved, nauseous, his gun trembling, he let the pith helmet down.

January 7, 1969, LZ Center

In the war they were called "sapper attacks." After the costly Tet Offensive, when Sorgie was just arriving "in country," the Vietcong and North Vietnamese Army broke up many of their larger, depleted fighting units into smaller, more elite commando-style sapper units that harassed, sabotaged, or, often under cover of darkness, conducted meticulously planned raids against U.S. and South Vietnamese bases. There were thousands of these attacks; some were mere nuisances, some downright assaults. Hot, tired men were jolted from sleep by exploding mortars, screams, automatic fire. . . . From who knows where? From inside the perimeter? Inside your head? A dream? What? Where? People rushing. Hootches burning. The ammo dump. The latrine.

LZ Center was in the mountains west of Chu Lai, Sorgie's home away from home when he wasn't out in the field: an artillery emplacement, a warren of trenches, foxholes, sandbag bunkers, ripe latrines, with the smoke and thunk of outgoing shells, then hours of silence, tedium, then incoming dead, the living and wounded, borne on whomping helicopters. For weeks the base had been probed by quick bursts of fire from outside the perimeter. One night Sorgie was on guard duty in a trench near his squad bunker, peering down the mountainside, across the mine field, and into the darkness beyond the barbed wire. There was activity out there, scurrying around. The radioman asked headquarters for illumination, then got permission for them to throw grenades. With his outfielder's arm, Sorgie could easily reach the wire and whatever else was out there — it was like hitting the cut-off man. He put down his gun and threw a grenade, ducking back into the trench and listening for the popping sound. He threw another, and another. He was reaching to get one more when he heard the faint whistling, and then all was a bright flash that he couldn't hear, and he was oddly airborne, drifting, draining, then in the dirt — he wasn't sure where — a moist pain in his buttocks and the backs of his upper legs.

The Vietcong mortar round had struck his gun, just a few feet away. His helmet had protected his head; his flack jacket had covered his back and kidneys. But his pants were torn up; there was all this blood. He was out of the trench. His teeth hurt. He felt suddenly cold, suddenly scared. He seemed to hear through yards of concrete. Where the hell were his glasses?

"You're not gonna die!" he remembers the medic yelling over and over. "You're all fucked up, but you're not gonna die! You hear me? Man, you hear me?"

The medic bandaged his wounds, and, with others, carried him to the MASH unit at the center of the base. There they stopped the bleeding. Then he was helicoptered to Da Nang, where, at a hospital, most of the shrapnel was removed with long probes. For a couple of weeks he lay in bed, and then stood, using crutches that were too small and that kept falling apart. Apparently the army didn't encourage a long convalescence. In just over two months, after his recuperation in Chu Lai, he was back in the field.

Today there is still shrapnel in Bill Sorgie's buttocks and upper right leg. "Fragments" they are called, parts of some exploded whole, things of that war that he carries, literally, inside him. They don't seem to bother him. He sits and walks with ease. He says he doesn't think about them, and I suppose that like many things you've lived with for a while, they become indistinguishable from you. The wounds heal. Tissue enfolds the foreign objects. The mind can do this too.

But in the act of enfolding, the body must change, as does the mind. Things are lodged inside that shouldn't be there, and they just don't go away. Fragments of some exploded whole.

They were there on that night in Olcott Square. They are there as we speak, Sorgie and I, these days in his white-walled office. They will even be there — why do I keep thinking of this? — long after his body unfolds them.

John Peterson

In Sorgie's squad of eight men was a guy named John Peterson, their RTO, or radio/telephone operator, who usually walked near the back of the squad when they were on patrol, an antenna wagging behind his head. He was their link with headquarters or other units in the area. Sorgie remembers liking him, a tall rangy kid, "a human antenna," though what he most remembers was the way that Peterson could draw. "Whenever we were back at base, he'd have his pencil out. He could draw anything, every detail, every blade of grass, clear as a photograph. Once he drew each of our names, for souvenirs, on sheets of paper. The letters were so straight, so exact, it was like printing you'd see in a book."

On March 10, 1969, some days before Sorgie was to return to combat duty, John Peterson was killed in an ambush while on patrol. His remains were taken to Graves Registration, an army morgue in Chu Lai. Because he was a squad-mate, and perhaps because he was already in Chu Lai, Bill Sorgie was detailed to identify Peterson's body.

None of this was very remarkable, it seems. That year, 11,527 Americans were killed in Vietnam, and all of them had to be identified. What is remarkable is that for the four years before joining the Army, before he was to walk patrol with Bill Sorgie and die halfway around the world, John Peterson lived at Bonnie Brae Farm and went to Ridge High School.

Rabbit may not have known him. Peterson was four years

older, and probably left the Farm in the fall of 1966, around the time that Rabbit arrived. But perhaps they met in the gym, in the barn, or out on the playing fields. It's impossible to know. Still I imagine: two tall kids, one thin and white, one darker and broad shouldered; two kids who would never see their twenty-second birthdays, who would die on opposite sides of the globe, each of their bodies resting for a time within a few feet of the same man, Bill Sorgie.

As it happened, Sorgie didn't identify Peterson's remains. He went into the morgue and saw the big drawer, like a drawer in a filing cabinet, where Peterson's body lay. But they wouldn't open it for him; his orders had been canceled, and he still doesn't know why. "Maybe Peterson was too messed up," Sorgie says today. "Or maybe they didn't think it a good idea, seeing as I was heading back to the field."

I don't know where Peterson's remains are now. According to the army, his hometown was Dover, New Jersey, but I wouldn't bet on their being there. What I do know is that his name is on the Vietnam Memorial in Washington, D.C., on panel 29W in that long wedge of black granite, on the second line from the top, about ten feet above the pavement. Unless you're a basketball player, you'll have to reach it with one of those stepladders that the Park Service keeps on hand. In the polished stone that reflects your own image, it reads, JOHN B. PETERSON Jr. in perfect block letters, perfectly spaced, perfectly aligned. Like printing you'd read in a book.

May 12, 1969, LZ Baldy

Sorgie's tour of duty in Vietnam was scheduled to end in early June, 1969, and as was common practice, the army removed him from combat activity about a month in advance and reassigned him to supposedly safer work at the rear. He became the liaison between the Third Battalion/Twenty-first Infantry and the 196th Light Infantry Brigade. Much of this job was paperwork and daily helicopter rides between LZ Center and LZ Baldy, a larger base, brigade headquarters, twenty-three miles south of Da Nang in the Que Son Valley. "They treated me nice," he says, and he thought that the worst was surely over, that this, at last, was the gravy train, the soft winding down that might help him forget some of the other things. "I thought my killing days were done," he remembers. And it wasn't the last time he would think it.

About 2:00 A.M. on the morning of May 12, while Sorgie slept in his hootch, the Vietcong launched a coordinated large-scale sapper attack against LZ Baldy. Mortar rounds and rocket-propelled grenades exploded all over. The supply depot was hit. Buildings, tents, vehicles were set ablaze, and enemy soldiers with satchel bombs came through the wire and into the camp itself.

Slammed from sleep, Sorgie ran out his tent door, M16 in hand. The first thing he saw in the flashing darkness was another shape, a Vietcong soldier, just fifteen feet away. Again Sorgie was the first to fire, or at least to fire accurately. This was the second man — yes, a man — that he killed.

Now he ran to the communications bunker, some hundred yards away. There he learned that Aaron Lowe, a buddy, was dead, shot through the neck, and that Lt. Bigzo, the commanding officer, had been wounded while in his tent. In the chaos, Sorgie radioed for help, then noticed that no one was returning fire from the parapet out near the perimeter. So with a guy he only remembers as "Ski" — "not even an infantryman, but a cook or something" — he got an M60 machine gun, and together, under fire themselves, they ran out to the parapet, set up the gun, and began shooting at anything that moved, or seemed to move, in the darkness out by the wire. Ski held the ammo belt, feeding it in, while Sorgie just kept firing. For perhaps a half hour he blasted away, until a helicopter swooped in and, pouring down tracers "like red piss," strafed the whole perimeter.

Eventually it got quiet. Eventually the fires came under control. Eventually, I imagine, Sorgie heard crickets. And eventually, from across the South China Sea, came the first hint of morning, not even light, but a strange softness in the dark. The air moved with something moist and sweet, like the smell, he'd swear, of mown grass. There, now, is the dull line of hills and there the pale sky. In another, distant place, the Yanks are on, people are reading the *Courier News* and finishing the dinner dishes. They are yesterday's dishes. Yesterday's paper. On the other side of the world, today hasn't happened. None of *this* has happened.

Now out on the perimeter a saffron mist curls up, and the stillness is almost unbearable. Sorgie's lips are cold, white, his eyes hollow, all his youth sucked out of them. Rising out of the parapet and into the day, he realizes he's wearing just his skivvies. They are muddy, piss wet. He hasn't had this accident since he was a boy; it makes him laugh, then cry. Looking out at the perimeter where the mist has lifted, he sees mangled bodies, or parts of bodies, and there: Christ, an entire rib cage, hanging like laundry on the wire.

In the Field

The word "autopsy" means "to see with one's own eyes," and for months I have been searching for a copy of Rabbit's autopsy report — I've wanted to see it with my own eyes. I've found the name of the medical examiner, but he's now deceased; and as for the New Jersey Medical Examiner's Office itself, it has no record of that report. "That was twenty years ago." Ancient history.

"Ten years ago, that file would have been destroyed. We have space limitations, you know."

And so, apparently, does the Somerset County Prosecutor's Office, which conducted a grand jury investigation shortly after the shooting. No bill, or indictment, was made against William Sorgie, so that file, I was told, "is vacant." All of the physical evidence presented, all the reports, all the testimony taken, were "secreted" for some years, then destroyed, as if they never existed. That is "standard procedure."

My last chance then to find Rabbit's autopsy report was to call Somerville Hospital (now Somerset Medical Center), where the autopsy was reportedly performed. Amazingly, the hospital kept records as deep into history as 1973. I was stunned with gratitude.

"Could you find that report?" Then I told the woman Rabbit's name and exact date of death.

After some moments she returned to the phone. "I'm afraid we have nothing under that name. Are you sure the autopsy was conducted here?"

"Pretty sure," I said.

She thought for a moment. "Well, where did this William Wells actually die?"

"In Olcott Square. In the middle of Bernardsville."

She sighed as though I were wasting her time. I could imagine her shaking her head, drumming her fingernails. "We only keep autopsies of those who die here under hospital care. This person died in the field."

I don't want to make too much of this, but how can I possibly ignore it: "In the field" was where the enemy lurked, where war was waged, where Bill Sorgie earned a Purple Heart and the Bronze Star, the nation's third highest award for valor.

In the field was also where Rabbit died.

The Reverend

The spring of 1970 was the spring of Kent State and the "incursion" into Cambodia, an apparent widening of the "winding down" war. Though I was still eligible for a college deferment from our local draft board, as an extra precaution I had obtained a 4-F military disqualification for a congenital hip abnormality. Rabbit, however, was in perfect health and, of course, he would not get a college deferment, so he had to be lucky or resourceful to avoid the draft. His opposition to the war was more visceral and virulent than that of anyone else I knew. On his own, he hitchhiked to demonstrations in Washington, leaving the Jeffers in fearful admiration. By now he had heard of John Peterson's death. He knew of the disproportionate number of black men killed in the fighting. He knew that Martin Luther King, Jr., had turned against the war. He read Cleaver and others on "The Black Man's Stake in Vietnam." He knew what was going on.

At about this time, our Presbyterian church, like many institutions then, began reaching out to young people. The church did this by opening the Oaken Bucket, named after the giant oak tree, now some 500 years old, that still arches over the graveyard. It was a decidedly secular meeting place in the basement of the new church office building, where kids could hang out, play foozeball, smoke, blow off steam — and all of it under the casual oversight of a responsible adult. I was down in The Bucket only a couple of times, and what I remember is sketchy: cinder block walls, a fireplace, sofas, stools, a stereo, pool table, and somewhere in the background, being unobtrusive, one of the church deacons, or a parent, or Reverend Felmeth — without his collar, in khakis and penny loafers. It was a weird sort of Presbyterian bar. No beer, booze, or blood of the Lord. Just soft drinks, chips, pretzels, and Cheeze-its. The amazing thing was it worked.

Kids came in off the street, guys you'd never expect to see inside a church building. Jimmy Streeter. Rich Glasser. Doug "Whoogie" O'Fee. They walked across the green from the Village Fountain, and they brought their girlfriends, too. Sarah Talpy, Joanne Calantoni. Now and then Rabbit also dropped in. It was here that he met Reverend Felmeth, and they began an unlikely friendship that would help keep Rabbit from the war.

Felmeth was the head of the oldest, wealthiest, and most prestigious church in town, if not in the entire county. It was founded around 1700, and according to local history, George Washington, while leading the revolutionary army, encamped beneath the oak tree. The present brick structure, with its four stately front pillars, was built after a fire in the 1840s. It stands at the absolute center of Basking Ridge, on the north end of the small green. You can't miss the shining gold-leaf dome, and the bells you can hear for miles.

The reverend lived with his family in the large white house with black shutters across from the church. He had studied at the Princeton Theological Seminary and served in the artillery in the Second World War. Evidently he had some sense of the glory and horror of battle, and a sense of when war was worth the horror, and when it was all a waste.

At any rate, he and Rabbit got to know one another. They had long talks over Cokes at the Bucket, and it must have been strange and enlivening for them both: the studious, dignified, slightly balding clergyman, and the kid with the afro, sandals, and insistent, vital questions. Would Jesus have fought in this war? Would *you*? Why would I want to kill a bunch of Vietnamese? Why shouldn't I be afraid to die?

Now and then, Rabbit dropped by Felmeth's office, and they continued their discussions. I can imagine them beside the window overlooking the ancient tree and graveyard, citing lines from those well-worn texts of the time: Thoreau's "Civil Disobedience," King's "Letter from the Birmingham Jail," or even that part of the Twenty-Second Psalm. I hear it in Felmeth's deep voice.

> But thou, O Lord, be not far off.
> Oh thou my help, hasten to my aid.
> Deliver my soul from the sword,
> my life from the power of the dog.
> Save me from the mouth of the lion,
> my afflicted soul from the horns of the wild oxen.

With the reverend's help, Rabbit apparently applied for Conscientious Objector's status. And while it took some time getting through the bureaucracy — by then our part in the war was nearly over — the military finally granted it to him, according to Rabbit's friends. I have been unable to find proof of this in the disorganized records of the Selective Service. Still, those friends swear it's true: that Rabbit got the good news just months before he died.

Today Reverend Felmeth is in a nursing home, dying from a degenerative illness that has affected his mind. It is hard to believe, but this man of softness and grace has terrible, uncontrollable flights of rage and violence. I haven't seen him in thirty years, not since those tumultuous early days in high school when I stopped going to church with my mother. But recently I've wanted to talk with him, to thank him for what he did for Rabbit, and for what he did, by example, for me. "I'm afraid, though, that he won't recognize you," Kay, his wife, has told me. "I'm afraid you won't recognize him either. He hasn't taken visitors for many months. I think it's best to remember him as he was."

So now I am looking at an old news photo that includes him, dated January 19, 1973, the day of Rabbit's funeral. In its background are the familiar pillars of the church, the steps, and the tall mahogany doors through which I used to walk with my sisters and mother. In the foreground stands a hearse with its rear door flung open. And there — I recognize them — are Tom King, Greg Easton, Jim Stout, Andy Cutting, Rusty Cook, and Walt Schneider, the pall bearers, their faces pinched and, except for Walt, their hair as long and stringy as John Lennon's. They are stepping off the curb and wrestling with Rabbit's weight in the coffin. Beside them, and seen from behind and slightly to the side, stands Reverend Felmeth. In his fanned-out cassock, he looks like a large dark bird. There are his glasses over his ear, and there is the small bald spot on his head. At the instant of the photo, he is leaning toward the coffin, reaching out, as if to help with the carrying.

In the service just ended, he had recalled his discussions with Rabbit about the war, violence, and draft exemption. "He was a warm and likable person," Felmeth had said. "He was curious, interested in people, and concerned about their welfare. He was sensitive in spirit, seeking where he was going. He was, incredibly, without bitterness."

I don't think that this is altogether true — that Rabbit was in fact "without bitterness." Why else might he have lashed out at Mr. Bennett, the math teacher? Why else did he respond to Cleaver and Malcolm X, as well as to King and Thoreau? Perhaps, like most of us, Felmeth never saw his bitterness, or chose not to see it, because of what it might have said about us, about what we didn't or couldn't do for Rabbit. Many of us wanted, desperately at times, for Rabbit to have been happy and unembittered. Even now I feel it. I wish he had been more happy. And yes, that would have made us all feel better; that would have been validating, something like soothing the conscience.

But is it *all* just selfish, condescending paternalism, these feelings, words, and deeds that Rabbit inspired in his life and death? There was a time when I might have believed this, but I don't anymore. While complicated, the good and helpful acts of some should not be so cynically dismissed. Here was a man who listened to Rabbit, who befriended him, who counseled him in avoiding his death and the killing of others in a distant, dangerous place. He may have helped Rabbit get out of that war. But then Rabbit was killed a mile away, in a peaceful place, a safe distance, it seemed, from the madness.

Maybe that is why, in his last days, the pious man rages at the walls.

COMMING HOME

I have recently received from Ruth Jeffers a photocopy of a poem of Rabbit's that she found in some old files. I copy it here, exactly as it appears. The poem is untitled, contains numerous misspellings and typos, and is typed all in capital letters.

> HIS FINALLY COMMING HOME.
> HOME TO THE THINGS HE MISSED SO MUCH.
> THE THING HE LEFT BEHIND BECAUSE HIS
> COUNTRY ASKED.
> HE LEFT FOR THE JUNGLES OF SOME FAR OFF
> LAND.
> IT IS REALLY STRANGE FOR HE LEFT ONE
> JUNGLE FOR ANOTHER.
> IN BOTH CASES HE HAD TO FIGHT.
> ONLY THIS TIME IT WAS DIFFERENT FOR HIS
> FIGHT NOW WAS FOR HIS LIFE.
> YES FOR HIS LIFE.
> AFTER HIS NINETEEN YEARS OF FIGHTING
> FOR THE THINGS HE THOUGHT TONEFUL OF
> HIMSELF.

NOW HE FOUGHT FOR HIS LIFE IN AN AREA ALIEN
TO HIMSELF IN A BATTLE IN A WAR ALIEN TO
HIMSELF.
WHY DID HE DO THIS THING SO WRONG TO
HIS CONSCIENCE.
BECAUSE HIE COUNTRY ASKED?
NO BECAUSE HE KNEW NO BETTER.
FOR HE WAS BROUGHT UP WITH THE KNOWL-
EDGE THAT TO ASLED IS TO BE COWARDIST.
AND HE COULD BE NO COWARD FOR HIS FAM-
ILY, SOCIETY AND COUNTRY TOLD HIM HOW TO
BE A HERO.
A HERO IN THEIR EYES NOT HIS OWN.
BUT THEN HIS WAS NOT TO REASON WHY, HIS
WAS BUT TO DO AND DIE.
THAT WAS HIS ANSWER TO HIS QUESTION HE
NEVER ASKED.
THE QUESTION OF WHAT IS A HERO.
AND HIS ANSWER DID NOT SHOCK HIM FOR HE
WAS NEVER WANTED ANY WAY.
FOR IF HE WAS WANTED THERE NEVER
WOULD HAVE BEEN A WAR.
BUT HE WENT NOT BECAUSE OF HIS WANT OR BE-
LIFE, BUT BECAUSE OF HIS BRAIN WASHING.
AND THE BRAIN WASHING DID ITS JOB FOR
NOW HE IS DEAD
AND HE WAS KILLED BY THE PEOPLE THAT
SUPPOSITLY LOVED HIM.
YES HE IS COMMING HOME ONLY HE IS NOT
COMMING IN ON HIS OWN POWER, HIS COMMING
IN AS A DEAD WEIGHT,
A WEIGHT THAT HE WILL NEVER CARRY
AGAIN FOR HE IS DEAD.
YES HE IS COMMING HOME.
COMMING IN DEAD AND THAT IS JUST THE
OPPOSITE OF HIS
LEAVING.

AND HE WAS KILLED NOT BY THE SO CALLED EN-
EMY, BUT BY THE PEOPLE HE LOVED AN TRUSTED
TO LED HIM.
    SO LET US STOP LEDING OUR FRIENDS AND
RELATIVES TO THESE FAR OFF PLACES AGAINST
THEIR WILLS.
NO LET US STOP THESE WARS PERIOD.
    NO LET US STOP THESE UNCALLED FOR
PROPHOSIES ABOUT RIGHT AND WRONG AND
THEN STOP THE WARS.
                                    — Rabbit 1970

A common assignment in English class in junior high
school was to copy a famous poem. The idea was, if you wrote
out the words in your own ink, you'd know the poem better. I
doubt kids have to do this anymore. Probably it smacks of rote
learning and authoritarianism. Yet I can still recite "Stopping By
Woods on a Snowy Evening" because I've written those words
in my own hand.

Copying Rabbit's poem here also helps me know it better,
and I hope helps me know him, helps me hear his voice —
clichés, originality, tortured syntax, and all. It's not his cool, jiving, "Hey man, what's happenin'?" voice; nor is this his high-
pitched, toothy laugh careening down the hall. This is a voice
that I don't remember, though his close friends speak of it often,
a voice at once wistful, angry, awkward, earnest, and afraid —
perhaps the voice he heard most often inside his own head.

While it isn't written in the first person, the poem is about
Rabbit himself, about his concerns for his own survival and integrity — for being "toneful of himself." He is making his own
case against the war and foreseeing his death and sad return if in
fact he were to go. In the light of Rabbit's life and death, there
is an eerie and powerful sadness here: a character who suspects
"he was never wanted anyway," who is sent away and comes

home, "killed by the people that suppos100ly loved him," "by the
people he loved an trusted."

Almost directly, Rabbit is describing the fears at the center
of his being. That he is not wanted. That his life doesn't matter.
That love is not trustworthy. That he might be ignored, or be-
trayed, and die. That he might not, ever, make it "home."

Seizures

Through much of his life, and especially during his high school
years, Rabbit took a special liking to certain older men, and they
took a liking to him. Reverend Felmeth was one. Another was
Marian's father and Ruth's husband, Robert Jeffers, Sr. Like Felmeth, he was a World War II veteran, and perhaps because he
had seen the worst, he became an ardent pacifist. He had fought
on Okinawa and Guam, in some of the same horrific battles as
Bill Sorgie's father. He received two Purple Hearts and a Silver
Star. He was wounded and almost died. A bullet grazed, but
didn't break, the delicate sac around his heart.

I've never met Robert Jeffers — he's been dead now for ten
years — but I think I know, from the bits that his children and
wife have told me, why Rabbit liked him. He was not unlike
many of our fathers, with a button-down shirt, an open collar, a
little pudgy in middle age. In a photograph that Marian has
shown me, he has a round, affable face, thinning hair, and what
looks like a whimsical mustache. He was a chemist who drove to
work a half-hour away and came home for dinner. On Saturdays
he flipped pancakes with great fanfare, then, forgetting the
dishes, strode out to the yard or down to his Peg-Boarded basement. Next came the roar of the mower, or the whir of power
tools. A man in his home. A man in his element. With important
things to do.

Combined with all this, though, was an unusual social conscience. He not only believed in equality and justice, he believed
that they actually ought to happen, even, if possible, in Basking
Ridge and Bernardsville, New Jersey. What explains this? Ruth
points to the war and the wound that almost killed him. War and
suffering harden some; others they wear out and deaden. In still
others they tap wells of compassion — that, she says, happened
to him.

So, like Ruth, he didn't think twice when Marian asked if
Rabbit could live with their family. I'm sure there were
quarrels — how could there not be? — but what everyone remembers is how Robert Sr. and Rabbit hit it off: their long talks
in the circle of light at the kitchen table, lasting through who
knows how many beers, and well past anyone else's endurance.
Vietnam, Cambodia, Kent State, Civil Rights, the Berrigans,
Agnew, the Panthers, *M*A*S*H*, My Lai, *The Greening of
America*, Consciousness III . . . and by the way, someone's got
to take out that trash — Jesus Christ, it's almost morning.

There were also the conversations about what, after high
school, Rabbit might do with his life, and how the Jeffers might
help. Possibly because Ruth had been a nurse and Robert was a
chemist, Rabbit seized on the notion of being a physician's assistant or maybe a medical photographer.

I had few of these discussions with my own father. We were
on different wavelengths then. In the last years, though, a vein
has opened because of course we are getting older, and because,
though we don't mention it, we can sense an end. Four months
ago, my father had a stroke, and most of his faculties have
slowed. He thinks a little differently, he speaks a little differently.
A physical therapist helps him bathe, and, with his legs like
crooked sticks in his corduroys, he moves around his room with
a walker.

Robert Jeffers, Sr. had a seizure, probably a stroke, in 1972.
He collapsed at Auntie Mame's restaurant in Bernardsville,
some months after Rabbit had left their family and moved in

with another family across town. When Rabbit heard about it, he hitchhiked to Overlook Hospital in Summit, about twenty miles away. He went up to Intensive Care — it was visiting hours — and at a desk near the door, he asked a nurse if he could see a patient inside, Robert Jeffers.

This is how Ruth has told the story to me, after hearing it years ago from Rabbit. I assume that the Intensive Care Unit at the hospital was pretty much like any other. A welter of wires and plastic tubes, bulbous bags on hooks. Beeping machines and flashing sensors. Groans, sighs, breathing by bellows, phlegm that doesn't cough up. In the air a strange yet familiar smell, chalky and antiseptic. The patients are separated by white curtains that hang from ceiling tracks. You can see some feet at the ends of beds, bumps beneath the blankets. Sometimes an ankle or a knee is exposed — they seem to lie unattached in the sheets, like auto parts on a hillside.

Which ones are his? Why don't I recognize him? Maybe there's been some mistake.

Now the nurse to whom Rabbit has spoken looks up at him, then cocks her head quizzically, something snagged in her eyes. "Yes," she says, "we have a Robert Jeffers here," but "wait," and she goes to get the head nurse. Soon they both stand before him with their solemn, sympathetic faces. In their years, they have treated the living and dying, they have met with all contingencies. Gently the head nurse asks who he is, and Rabbit tells her, then explains that he had lived with the Jeffers for about a year, that he was part of the family, that he and Robert "knew each other well" — how do you describe such things? He says he just wants to see him again, see how he's doing, say hello.

Again that flickering, quizzical look, this time from the head nurse. "I'm afraid I don't understand. You have to be his relative to come in here. You aren't his son, are you?"

Rabbit doesn't say anything. He stares at the floor, trying to distinguish Robert's breathing from all the rest of the noise.

"We have rules and regulations," she goes on politely. "These are very sick people. We have limited space. I'm sure you understand."

The nurses turn away quietly on their rubber soles to go about their business. And at this, Rabbit feels his skin literally crawl and his hair jump in its follicles. He knows — he's sure — that if he were white, the nurses would have been flexible. Now he'd like to tear the place down. How long had he hitchhiked to get here, how many rides had it taken? He could tear out all these wires and tubes, even if they're connected *to him*.

I am imagining all of this now, but the important fact is this: Rabbit was not allowed to see Robert Jeffers, the man who had welcomed him into his house, who sat up with him late to talk about everything, a man he admired and probably loved. He was not allowed to say those words that you say to the sick and possibly dying, like those words I needed to say to my father as he lay among his own tubes and wires with something all wrong in his brain.

How those words must have boiled then in Rabbit's throat as he turned back down the hall. I see the elevator opening. I see him pushing the lighted button marked "L," see the doors closing, and then that little instant, felt in the knees, when the floor falls away. I see him walking through an echoing lobby, his fists held down at his sides. I see him out on the street in the dazzling sun, hitching his way back home.

Early on Saturday morning, January 13, 1973, about six months after he had recovered and returned home from the hospital, Robert Jeffers would answer the phone. It was his son Bobby, calling from work at Somerset Farms. Rabbit, he had just heard, had been shot and killed in Bernardsville. It didn't seem possible. How could that be? They had all just seen him on the day before. He had dropped by the house — it was Bobby's birthday. He seemed to be doing fine.

Immediately Ruth and Robert got in the car and drove to the Bernardsville police station. They wanted to find out what had happened to Rabbit. They wanted to see him, and maybe, though he would never hear them, there might be some things to say. But the station was bristling with police, some of them armed with shotguns. The Jeffers were not allowed inside. (I can hear it: "You aren't his parents, are you?") So they turned back toward their car in the brisk, clear morning. Beside the police station, the pond was frozen, except for the tiny patch of water where ducks swam near the inlet. The wind swayed the trees and snapped out the flag on the pole. It was a day when, after you got home, you'd bring in the newspaper, get logs, kindling, light a fire, and settle into the couch.

"We don't live here," Ruth remembers saying as they pulled into their driveway. "We just don't live here anymore."

Black Pearl

Before all this though — before the leavings, the seizures, and all the words unsaid — things moved right along with Marian. With a girl on his arm or in his wake, Rabbit could be irrepressible. They were the hit of parties and dances, known at all the local hangouts: she with jeans that she wore like skin, and he with his shades, turtleneck, or beads and bell-bottoms. He was Hendrix, and she his Foxy Lady. He was also Sly, Shaft, and the Maharishi, somehow rolled into one. He was disposed toward grand, romantic gestures. Once, he gave away all his money, about $50 worth of allowance, so that Doug Robb could buy an engagement ring. Then, some months later, he presented to Marian a ring that he called his "mother's black pearl."

I doubt that the ring was ever his mother's, and it might

not in fact be black pearl either, though I'm hardly an expert. I've seen the ring. Marian still has it. She keeps it on a bed of cotton in a small blue box in a bureau drawer. She slides it on her finger, where it stays put for a moment, and then, with the weight of the pearl (or whatever), it spins around, upside down.

It was too big for her slender ring finger twenty-five years ago, and today it still is. Where did he get it? She shrugs her shoulders. "Probably from a pawn shop," she says. Yet it thrilled her then, and even now, as we sit in her bright breakfast nook, as she turns the ring around her finger, she seems filled with an old pleasure. Today she is as thin and willowy as ever; her black jeans still look sprayed on her legs. Her hair is shorter, but still blonde, and is pulled back in a thick ponytail. She lives with her second husband in western Jersey, where there are still some farms and horses. She is a social worker who counsels "troubled youths." Incredibly, she is a grandmother now, and her seventeen-year-old second daughter, who is her mother's age when she went out with Rabbit, chats endlessly with a boyfriend on the phone.

Along with the ring, Marian shows me a framed six-by-eight-inch photo of Rabbit, which I recognize as his senior picture. He wears a coat and tie, and there's a notch, like a neat part, cut in the left side of his afro. He has a thin, groomed mustache and goatee, and you can tell by the way that he holds his head that this is a guy with a steady girlfriend. At the time of the photo, probably in the winter of '70–'71, he couldn't have known that within a few months, some things would come unglued. And as I look at him again here, despite all the differences, he reminds me of Bill Sorgie in his own graduation photo. Both of them are gazing beyond the camera. Both hold their chins high. Both are handsome, serious, on the cusp of a wave. Both appear indomitable.

Quiet Thoughts

The last thing that Marian shows me is a book called *Quiet Thoughts* by Paul S. McElroy. She handles it differently, a little more carefully, than the photo and even the ring. She doesn't speak as she turns a few pages. She touches her neck with her hand. There is a wincing in the skin around her eyes, the only part of her that seems to have aged.

The book is a very slender volume, hardbound, just sixty pages. About every five or ten pages, a simple woodcut appears: an outlined angel, a fountain, a huge sun over fertile hillsides, a hearth, a fruit tree, entwined hearts. The text is divided into short meditative passages with titles such as "Sorrow and Joy," "Living with Others," "On Giving," "The Courage of Convictions," "The Most Priceless Possession," "Two Loving Hearts." These are neat, homey maxims for living, for co-existing, and for absorbing our disappointments. Death, for example, is but "a merciful means of getting rid of the physical body which has housed our spirit on earth." And so calmly, re-assuringly, we are told, "When death comes prematurely we need not feel that injustice has been done and that the deceased has been unfairly deprived of that precious element known as time."

There is much here on "keeping our balance," on "master-ing ourselves" through "inner-direction," on finding "content-ment" by "set[ting] our hopes in things spiritual," on "reconciliation" and "restoring relationships" through the ad-mission of guilt and forgiveness.

It is indeed a book of quiet, if sometimes saccharine, thoughts, the kind that appealed to that part of Rabbit the rest of us seldom saw. Facing the title page, in his squat, loopy hand-writing, is this short inscription:

By the time you read this, you'll most likely hate me, but I will always love you. Forgive me, and forget me, but not my love.

Love,
Rabbit

After I've read this a couple of times ("hate me"? "forgive me"?), I ask Marian the obvious. What happened? And it's another long and winding story that ends in a searing instant.

For all their outward cool and togetherness, there were ongoing difficulties for Rabbit and Marian. Though she doesn't describe it at length, there was always the matter of culture and color. A dark guy from Trenton with a white girl from the 'burbs. "We were always getting those weird, often angry looks," she says, mostly from white people, though not exclusively. She remembers traveling somewhere with Rabbit once, and meeting some black kids who called him "Oreo" — black on the outside, white on the inside. She remembers that he was so upset he could barely speak all the way home. He wasn't white enough for some, wasn't black enough for others, and for a lot of people, it seemed, he and Marian didn't look like they belonged together.

Related to this level of public scrutiny, I assume, was Rabbit's tendency — so different from his usual bravado — to withdraw into himself. All his close friends mention this. "He always held some part of himself distant," is how Marian puts it now. He'd get quiet. He'd stay in his room. There were things he wouldn't talk about, things he wouldn't do. "I wanted more and more of him," she recalls, but he wouldn't, or couldn't, give enough. He "had to have air," she remembers him telling her once, and sometimes unannounced he'd go off on his own or with other friends and not return until late at night. Thinking back, she says she can understand it, but at the time she just wanted him home.

I imagine him then, coming in the kitchen door. He

doesn't look at the clock on the stove. The house is still. The refrigerator hums. They've left the light on at the table and there's
his dinner on a plate, wrapped in cellophane. On the cellophane
lies a note: Pie in fridge. Leave some for tomorrow!

He isn't hungry, but he is grateful for this, to come into a
place that awaits him. It makes a small, sharp lump in his throat,
and still he is oddly distrustful. *How long can this last? Why do
they do this for me?*

He puts the dinner in the fridge and locks the outside door.
He hangs his coat on the hook, flicks off the light, and walks toward the stairs. Even in the dark, even in this place that isn't his,
he knows where everything is. Here is the molding around the
living room door. Here is the smooth banister. He climbs quietly, but not stealthily; he has nothing to hide. Upstairs, it is dark
beneath Marian's door, but he knows she's awake, listening. He
could knock softly, go inside, and they would talk. She would
ask him where he'd been, and he'd tell her. He was just walking
the roads, nowhere in particular. A couple of guys had picked
him up, and then they had stopped at a party.

Why didn't he tell her he wasn't coming home? Why didn't
he even call?

There is an answer for this, surely there is, but it wouldn't
come easily in words. All he could say would be, *It's not what
you think. It's not that I don't love you anymore.*

He pauses at her door where just weeks ago he might have
crept in and found her waiting. This time, though, he can't go
in. And while he knows that she now is weeping into her pillow,
he walks down the hall to his room.

The most difficult thing, as they were breaking up, was that they
saw each other so often. In their pajamas in the morning with
her hair all a mess. Over breakfast, dinner, in the corridors at
school, their eyes touching and veering away. There were the
strange cars in the evenings that stopped by for him, and then

the phone calls for her from — how did they know? — other guys who were "just wondering what she was doing."

They decided to try to be "just friends," to go their own ways without hard feelings. Mostly, Marian says, this was Rabbit's idea. He said he needed space, but there wasn't more space in that modest split-level home.

Then one night Marian got another call from the guy who would become her first husband. Rabbit was in his room, wrestling with some assignment, perhaps an essay for American Lit. But how could he think straight when he was overhearing Marian on the phone a few rooms away? She was keeping her voice low, and he should have shut his door. He wasn't trying to listen, but how could he help it? In her words was that softness that was once for him. It must have ripped him in two.

She remembers that when she hung up the phone, she was startled to see Rabbit in the doorway. His eyes were big and brown as ever. And there was something else. . . .

Beyond that she wants to remember no more. She runs her hand along the spine of the book, her eyes on her clean kitchen floor. "That was when he hit me," she says. And that is all she will say.

Rabbit left the Jeffers' house and didn't return that night, or for some days thereafter. No one knew exactly where he went — to some other friend's home, they thought. Still, he and Marian saw each other passing in the halls at school, and I imagine they kept on walking. Evidently he stopped doing assignments. His grades and attendance fell off. It was spring, the prom, the last gushy weeks before graduation. Most all the kids were growing their hair, coasting, drinking, preparing for college. But suddenly Rabbit was falling apart, spiraling down, losing his way. In his last term, he flunked American Lit., and though his proud face is still in the yearbook, he wouldn't graduate that June with our class.

One day, not long after he had hit her, Marian came home to find *Quiet Thoughts* on her bed and his remaining stuff cleared from his room. As much as he wanted her, I suppose he couldn't face her. I suppose he could barely face himself. "By the time you read this, you'll most likely hate me, but I will always love you. . . ."

I have almost forgotten what it is to be that age — so much self-pity, self-loathing, pride, and burning, groping love. I imagine he gathered his books, camera, and clothes that Ruth had folded in his drawer. On top of the bureau he shared with Bobby lay his cigarettes, hairpick, and a beaded headband. He shoved them all into his old canvas duffel bag, and went down to the kitchen. Probably Ruth was there to say good-bye, and to say he could always return. Maybe they hugged. Usually Rabbit was big on hugging, holding, any kind of large gesture. Or maybe this time he just said thanks, then turned toward the door.

Ruth doesn't remember precisely when this happened, but I have the feeling it was then: Rabbit stopped in midmovement, put down his bag, and pulled his wallet from his jeans. For an instant, an inexplicably horrible instant, she thought he was going to offer her money. Instead, he took from his wallet a small rumpled photograph, much folded and flattened, furred at the edges, the photo that he had brought with him to Bonnie Brae, the one of himself as a ten-year-old boy, with the neat white shirt and printed necktie, with his hair short and ears like pontoons, and that serene look in his eyes.

"This is for you," he said, leaving it on the counter. Then he did go out the door.

What Holds

Now these years later, as I sit talking with Ruth in the Bernards-ville Library, she rummages in her worn purse and pulls out her own wallet. She flips through family photographs sheathed in cloudy plastic until she finds the one she wants, and slides it out on the table between us. It's the same photograph that Rabbit gave her, a little more faded I presume, but clear enough and unmistakably *him*, a ten-year-old, ears, freckles, and all.

For a while, without speaking, we look at the photo, then Ruth slides it back in her wallet. She is prim and old-fashioned without being dowdy. Sometimes she seems slightly confused. As I've mentioned, her eyes have that red and watery look, as though she has problems with allergies. "In New Zealand we didn't have guns," she says, looking off toward some book-shelves. "Not even the police."

Then, after a moment, "You know, we tried to see him the morning after, but we couldn't get into the station."

Then, after another moment and shaking her head, "He didn't have much. He didn't seem to need much. When he came to us, he didn't have a change of clothes, not even the tops to his pajamas."

Later we say our good-byes, then leave the library. And though I didn't altogether understand it then, what strikes me now is how extraordinary and vulnerable a gesture that was: for Rabbit to give that photo to Ruth. He had known her for a year at most, and the photo was probably the only thing he had of his childhood. Yet he gave it to her for safekeeping. He put his past into her hands, as if he knew it would last longer there than if he held it in his own.

So for more than twenty-five years now, Ruth has kept that photo in her wallet, just as he, for the eight years prior to that, kept it with him. And it strikes me, too, that in five, ten, or maybe another twenty years, Ruth will come to the end of her days, and this image, leaved with photos of her other children, will be among her effects.

I write "her other children," implying that Rabbit was one of them, and though this is not literally true, I believe it is emotionally true. This story of Rabbit is a terrible tragedy, a story of prejudice, misunderstanding, death, and how much is lost forever. But it is also a story of compassion, love, and what holds in the heart and hand. For this was a youth without a home, and this is a woman who took him in. This was a youth with just the shirt on his back, and this is a woman who clothed him. This was a youth bereft of his childhood, and this is a woman who holds a memento, enshrined in her wallet, so that anyone who cares might see.

Now, having dropped off *Quiet Thoughts,* gathered his stuff, and gone out the door, Rabbit stands for a moment on the Jeffers' lawn, like someone who, after a long ride, has gotten off a train at the wrong stop and doesn't have change in his pocket. He puts on his shades, lights a cigarette, and swings his bag up on his shoulder, clamping it there with one arm. He walks down the driveway and out to Lyons Road beside the fence with Marian's horses in the pasture. In his shades and boots he looks tough as hell. His cigarette dangles from his lips. He has a cocky, bowed, cowboy's stride, the bag bouncing beside his ear. He hears a car behind him. He turns to face it and walks backward, his heels clicking on the edge of the road, holding his thumb low. From a distance, he looks like the coolest of dudes. He even gives the impression that he'd be doing *you* a favor if you pulled over and picked him up.

But where is he hitchhiking *to?*

The Hut

On Route 202, across from Woolworth's, about midway between my parents' house and Olcott Square, is the Shop Rite where my mother has always bought her weekly groceries since the A&P closed in the midsixties. It is still a typical suburban supermarket, with a crammed parking lot in the front, a tangle of grocery carts near the doors; around the far left, almost hidden, are the loading docks with piles of wooden pallets, broken cartons, spoiled fruit, and brimming Dumpsters. You wouldn't notice it from the front, but the rear of the store backs right up to the train tracks, about midway between the Basking Ridge and Bernardsville stations. Beyond the tracks, and unseen from anywhere except a passing train, is a thicket of woods about a hundred yards wide.

I mention all this because of a story I was told by George Salko, now a retired Bernardsville policeman. He had joined in 1952, when there were only eleven men on the force. He was always known as a "small-town cop." He knew, by name, all the kids on the streets; his wife, Eunice, ran Bob's Drive-In next to the Dairy Queen; and in all his thirty years on duty, he says, he never drew his gun.

Now he tells me about a call that came in early one morning in the spring or early summer of '71. He remembers it because it seemed so weird: "There's someone in a hut behind the Shop Rite." So he got in his squad car and went to investigate. He pulled up near the loading docks. He went through a break in the fence behind the Dumpsters, then down into a gully, and up and over the gravel embankment and the tracks. On the other side he saw a vague path, like a trail that deer might make. He followed it a ways into the woods, around some fallen trees, some dense brush. . . .

And then he saw it.

It was a hut all right. A kid's abandoned fort, a clubhouse, or a pirate's den. As a boy, he too had made one of these. Banging together your father's scrap lumber. Plywood and pitchy two-by-fours. Bending nails and bashing your thumb. Maybe a tarp or an old door for a roof. Or maybe just branches laid across the top, so that when your parents let you and a friend sleep out, and when you closed your *Hardy Boys* and shut off your flashlights, you could lie back, look up, and, through the leaves, see stars.

This hut was also made from scraps: some wide boards, shipping cartons, and parts of wooden pallets from the loading docks. As he approached, though, Salko could see that it was a little larger than most kid's forts, about eight feet long, six feet wide, and five feet high. A leaning sheet of plywood served as a door, and when he called "hello," he was surprised when he heard something thump inside. He called again, and again that thump. Then slowly the plywood slid to the side. A brown hand came out, and then the rest. It was Rabbit, stooped, in his underwear and a blanket. His afro was cockeyed, flat on one side, his eyes squinting, his face wrinkled with sleep. He looked at Salko, as from a dream. "What the fuck are you doing here?"

And Salko said, "I was about to ask you the same question."

No one knows how long Rabbit stayed in that hut, less than a mile from my home and sixty yards from the Shop Rite meat display where my mother still buys those bright slabs of London broil whenever my wife, my daughter, and I come to visit. In the hut, Salko found Rabbit's clothing, a couple of books, a flashlight, a jug of water, and some rolls of toilet paper. Now, if you walk back there, you won't find much of interest. There are the shiny rails, and there, high above, the suspended electric wires. But there's no narrow path beyond the tracks. There's no makeshift habitation. The only pieces of wood around are the old, discarded railroad ties that lie at the muddy bottom of the embankment. This is still one of those strange, forgotten parts of our town, caught between commercial and residential zones. Trash skitters between the tracks, shards of glass glint in the gravel. The Dumpsters stink, and on the back wall of the Shop Rite, you can read in red spray-paint, "Muff Horner" and "Beastie Boys." Now and then a train flies by, pushing the air, crackling the wires, swirling the trash, and making the ground tremble. How often did Rabbit see, hear, and feel all this — a huge, lighted, moving thing, shooting even through his dreams?

Or did he lie awake those nights, with all those stars, the ruffling birds, then finally an immense stillness?

The Coat Story

This happened around the same time, or perhaps a little earlier that spring, as Rabbit and Marian were breaking up. It was at a party on Spencer Road, one of those parties where someone's parents leave for a weekend, and kids with dope and six-packs arrive in droves. Rabbit was there, and so was Mark Wetmore, the captain of the Bernardsville track team. I have always thought that Rabbit never ran track competitively — he is in none of the team photos or on any rosters. But Wetmore remembers running against him in the county track meets of 1970 and '71. So I am probably wrong, or perhaps Rabbit was running for a Bonnie Brae team, or somehow he was invited independently. At any rate, Wetmore swears by his memory, and I believe him. He was the county champion in the 440-yard run. At the time, he was cultivating the John Lennon look, his ragged dark hair flowing back as he ran; and Rabbit was looking like Hendrix. Each time they met, Wetmore beat Rabbit in the 440, a sort of controlled sprint, one lap around the track, with a hard kick at the end. Yet in the 220, a screaming, flat-out dash, Rabbit, who didn't bother to train for these things, would invariably leave Wetmore in the dust. It has always bugged Wetmore, though they became friends. Lennon and Hendrix, the flying freaks. It was a hip, good-natured rivalry.

At the party on that night in '71, Wetmore was wearing what he describes as a new "psychedelic afghan coat." It had bold, swirling colors and long fringe, part coat, part shawl, so cool, so far out that, especially if there were some good-looking girls around, he wouldn't take it off indoors. Evidently there were some "lookers" around that night, and Wetmore was trying to pick one of them up. He doesn't remember her now, though he thinks she was long, blonde, and wearing beads. With a beer in one hand and a joint in the other, he was talking smooth and low so she'd have to lean close, almost touching his coat, to hear him over the stereo. When Rabbit came in the room, saying, "Yo, Wetmore!" they slapped fives, and clasped hands like soul brothers.

"Nice coat!" Rabbit said. Then, standing back and taking it all in, "Man, I gotta have those threads."

Wetmore brushed him off, turning back to the girl, and Rabbit mingled with others. But later, when they ran into one another again, Rabbit said, "I just gotta have that coat."

"No way," said Wetmore.

"I'm not kidding."

"Forget it."

"How about if I borrow it?"

"Why?"

"I got my reasons."

Wetmore couldn't believe this. The guy wouldn't let up. "It's my fucking coat. Wear your own."

Still Rabbit persisted. "Let me have it an hour. A half hour. Why are you wearing it in here anyway?"

Eventually Wetmore relented and let Rabbit have the coat "for a while." Rabbit put it on, and Wetmore had to admit, it looked pretty sharp with those fluorescent colors spilling over

Rabbit's wide shoulders, with his afro looming and that long fringe swaying around his hips as he moved.

They split up, circulating in different parts of the party. There was a bong going in a back bedroom, beer in the fridge; bottles of Mateus on shag carpets, some with dribbling candles. A half hour later, Wetmore was getting nervous. He shouldered his way from room to room, through smoke and laughter, bodies wedged against book shelves and walls. But no Rabbit, no afghan coat. He knocked on a bathroom door: just somebody being sick, probably from the hash brownies. Then a glimpse across a crowded living room, toward the foyer and open front door. There was that round back of Rabbit's head, that splash of color on his shoulders. Wetmore took a step to follow, but sometimes you just have to leave it be, let it go like in the 220 — you watch from behind and admire. Rabbit was on his way out the door, and on his arm — in the crook of the arm of Wetmore's own coat! — was that girl, that long blonde. She was holding Rabbit there, leaning against him, her head all soft and nestled on his shoulder, her hair falling down near the fringe.

Radical

One of Rabbit's most enduring friends, from the early days in junior high, was Jackie Lentzsch. She came from a big family who lived in an old farmhouse way out on Somerville Road. I remember her because her last name also begins with L, and she was always in my homeroom class. She was one of those kids who had to work after school. Like her older brothers, she was tough, a townie. She was awkward, thick-limbed, and perhaps because she couldn't fit our usual models of female beauty, she seemed to grasp at a kind of flamboyant femininity. Her hair was long and flame-colored. She wore short skirts and shimmering black nylons that made cricketing sounds as she walked. She wore lip gloss, mascara, and perfume of stinging potency. She plucked her brows, wispy thin, turning them up at the ends. Her lashes, like cowcatchers on locomotives, hung thick and heavy. She was off-putting and yet deeply intriguing in a way that my mother would not have approved.

None of this daunted Rabbit, however. He took her right in stride. When in eighth grade she kicked him in the shins, he shrugged and said, "Girl, you're radical." From then on, he seldom called her Jackie. In the lunch room, on the bus, at the Village Fountain, her name was Radical. Radical and Rabbit. Step back. He in his short-sleeved black turtleneck, and she in those bulging nylons. Laughing in study hall, cruising the halls, cigarettes in pockets. There was nothing seriously romantic between them. They just liked that rough edge they brought out in each other. Together they shook things up.

Today Jackie has that same long, flame-colored hair, though I'm not sure that the color is natural anymore. "Don't I look just the same?" she says, batting her lashes as she lets me in her screen door. It is more a dare than a question, and of course I say, "You're just the same."

In truth, she looks a little heavier now, undeniably middle-aged in a loose emerald green dress. She wears the same heavy makeup. Her brows are plucked. She has a twenty-one-year-old daughter, is divorced, and lives alone in a rented house in Branchburg, though just now she is "wild in love" with a guy in Ireland, a "hot, long-range romance" she tells me within a minute after I've arrived.

Over coffee, she shows me a photo she's kept of Rabbit, where he stands in a turtleneck and sharp-creased pants outside our high school door. "He was a good dresser," she says. Then she gets out the old yearbooks.

In her '68 (our freshman) yearbook, in green pen, with loops and flourishes, he wrote, "To one of the sweetest girls in this hick town. Take care and be good." Then in our senior year-book of '71, when he knew that he wouldn't be graduating with us, he wrote in dashing red ink, "Keep Radical Kid. And Swing on." This is followed by a squiggly mark whose meaning Jackie can't remember now. Then, "To our old love. Love ya, Rabbit."

After she has read me these messages in her husky voice, she lights a cigarette and blows smoke toward the ceiling. Even when she is quiet, she seems wide open, brash and needy, not a calculating bone in her body. "He could light up a room," she says after a minute, and laughs. "He would talk about anything. Even girls' periods!"

Her fingers on the yearbooks are thick and blunt. There's lipstick on the end of her cigarette and lacquer on her nails. Then, from a crease between pages of our senior yearbook, she pulls out a folded piece of waxed paper about four inches long.

"He gave me this," she says. Yet she doesn't know or remember what it is. Carefully she unfolds the waxed paper and lays it open on her palm. "A flower!" she says in a different voice, something caught in her breath. After all these years, it surprises her again. Mascara runs at her eyes. "Can you tell what kind?" she asks.

And though it is shriveled, crisp and tan, without a scent, it is unmistakably a rose.

Coming Home

On July 16, 1969, Sergeant Bill Sorgie, wearing his Purple Heart and Bronze Star, left Vietnam for Fort Knox, Kentucky, where for the next ten months he served as a drill instructor, imparting some of what he had learned to those who would take his place in the field. After that, he had another year's service remaining. He wanted to travel, and knowing the state of his family's finances, the military was still his best chance. He requested that he be sent to Korea, and on May 23, 1970, that's where he arrived. Again, he was a training officer, a buck sergeant, drilling his men as he had been drilled: marching, calisthenics, basic uses of sidearms and rifles — he had a good eye and a calm hand. It was agreeable work, predictable, routine. But after all that had happened in Vietnam, much of it honed by the nearness of death, these were hardly his memorable days. In his mind now, many of them have blended into one another. He has forgotten the names of some friends. Of course he remembers his marriage there to a small, pretty Korean girl, but he is reluctant to discuss it. He was young, and probably lonely and impulsive. I have the impression that it happened too fast. Suddenly, someone gave herself over to him, and what was he to do? I imagine a fierce love that had little chance to endure. But he didn't want to *not* love her, and he didn't want to leave her behind. So they married in Korea, and Sorgie's best man, a friend whose name he doesn't forget, was Jay Mock, an African-American.

Then about June 19, 1971 — during our last week in high school, and perhaps while Rabbit was living in his hut — Bill Sorgie, having completed his four-year tour of duty, came home to Berkeley Heights. Two weeks later, his wife joined him. It was an awkward time for them. They rented a small house on Springfield Avenue, across the street from his parents' apartment. Almost immediately he got a job as a mail carrier in New Providence. On weekends he worked puttying, sanding, and spray-painting at Berkeley Auto Body, and some nights he pumped gas at Joe Benham's Amoco station. He was picking up where he had left off. Things seemed the same, but they weren't the same. Many of his friends had split town, and some of those who had stayed had changed. Their hair was longer, they grew beards and smoked dope, and he still wanted to be a policeman — he was applying at local departments. I imagine him down at the Pine Tree Inn, introducing his wife to some old buddies.

"You're a lucky dog," they'd tell him out in the hall, digging him in the ribs. "I bet she can really make you happy. A regular China doll."

But she looked so much stranger here than in Korea. And she hardly said a word. I see him jogging toward the outfield on a warm Saturday evening. There's a pickup game at Memorial Field with guys from the police and fire departments. They've got a keg, and someone's brought pizza. There's the smell of his glove and damp cut grass. There's that soft, familiar crush of steel and iron, as the train settles into the station. At this moment he has almost forgotten those fragments that twinge now and then in his ass. And he has almost forgotten how she — *my* "*wife*"? — sits alone in the bleachers, not even watching, with her pale, oval face and almond eyes, and her black hair coming down like a veil.

Southern Cross

On November 1, 1971, a guy in a white Dodge Road Runner pulled into Berkeley Auto Body with an aggrieved look on his face. He was pissed. The night before, on Halloween, some kids had spray-painted graffiti all over his car. He wanted to know what he could do to fix it, if some solvent might do the trick. The guy had just gotten out of the military, he said, and with his discharge pay had bought the car practically new. When he opened the door and walked around toward the front, he looked big, athletic, but he had a slight limp.

Bill Sorgie was working in the shop that day, and he put down his sander, pulled the mask away from his face, and went out to have a look. The car was a mess, and when the guy pointed toward the swirls of spray-paint on the hood, Sorgie noticed his watch. He recognized the insignia on its face: against a field of blue, four bright stars, as if at the extremities of a cross, the Southern Cross, the crest of the Americal Division.

The guy's name was Donnie Erwin, from Cincinnati, and not only had he served in Sorgie's division, but in the 196th Light Infantry (Third Brigade, Second Battalion, First Infantry) in the same forested mountains and valleys of Quang Tin province where Sorgie had served. Erwin was in Vietnam from July 1968 through July '69, when Sorgie was also there. He had walked point in the same jungles. He had done the same innumerable hours of guard duty in the rain. He knew all about LZ Center and LZ Baldy, for he was based at LZ Ross, just a few miles east, where in May '69 (four months after Sorgie was wounded at LZ Center), he was shot by a sniper.

Moreover, Erwin had been a baseball player, a catcher, recruited and signed out of high school by the Cincinnati Reds. He had made his way to AAA ball when the Selective Service got him, sending him on his way to the bullet that, hitting his throwing hand and knee, would end his baseball dreams. At Fort Dix, near the end of his tour of duty, he met and would soon marry Pat Stashluck, of Berkeley Heights, an old schoolmate of Bill Sorgie's. After his discharge, Erwin and Pat moved in with her parents, who ran the Pine Tree Inn. Then he got a job in Bernardsville, driving one of those big dump trucks for Ferrante's Quarry.

So they had a lot to talk about that day at Berkeley Auto, Sorgie and Erwin, two utter strangers. It was uncanny. Both of them wounded about the same time. Both of them knew the same girl and the same foxholes on the other side of the globe. Together they remembered certain passwords and radio codes from their days in the field. I see them chatting there outside the bays of the body shop, a fine, floury dust on Sorgie's thick arms and shoulders, and Erwin, handsome, dark-haired, leaning back against his car, even warming to a laugh, both of them shaking their heads at the way life tosses people together, surprised by all they share.

I suppose Erwin bought some solvent or perhaps a polishing compound that might, with elbow grease, have removed the spray-paint from his car. In the months that followed, he and Sorgie would see each other around, passing on Springfield Avenue in Berkeley Heights. And then after the new year, after Sorgie would land his police job, they'd wave to one another in Bernardsville — one in a patrol car or directing traffic, the other in that big red dump truck. A couple of times they played baseball together on the field outside Ferrante's Quarry. But as much as they played ball or waved on the roads, they were heading in different directions. Straitlaced Bill Sorgie was now a cop, and "Dyno" Donnie Erwin, though married, was a long way from settling down. He had killer looks and a hot temper. He had "Dyno" tattooed on his arm. Increasingly, he would spend his nights away from his wife, running with a barhopping crowd.

So they were passing acquaintances. They were never friends. And by now, today, they might have completely forgotten one another, had they not met again about fourteen months later in Olcott Square, in the last moments before Rabbit died.

That night Erwin had been asking about a job as a bartender. He was looking good, wearing a tie, a new camel hair sports coat, and again his watch with the Southern Cross. But when Sorgie saw him outside the Three Lights Tavern, he had blood on his mouth, neck, and hands. He had just been stabbed in the bar. He was wildly angry, wounded, beseeching. Then a few seconds later, at the fatal instant itself, in a black burst of realization, he would scream, "No!" to Sorgie, just that word, as if a word could stop what was happening.

But his voice was blotted out by the flash, blotted even from his own hearing. And by the time he would hear or see anything again, Rabbit's blood, too, was splattered over his coat, his watch, and the Southern Cross.

Around Town

For me, the summer of '71 was a summer of excitement, outward confidence, and even cockiness. I didn't have a girlfriend and I didn't have my own wheels, but I had just graduated from high school and soon would be off to college. While Bill Sorgie was coming home, and Rabbit was apparently staying put, I was getting out in the world. It didn't matter that "the world" in this case would be a small college in upstate New York. What mattered was that I had a purpose that would take me elsewhere, and that I was heading off. But in the meantime, there were the long summer nights of basketball on my friends' floodlit driveways. We were Willis Reed, "Clyde" Frazier, Dick Barnett, Bill Bradley, and Dave "The Rave" DeBuschere. In the mornings, with my headlights on, I drove my parents' Ranchwagon to my summer job on our township road department. I punched in with the others, got my assignment from Fred "Dirty Neck" Miller, and went out on one of the big yellow trucks to shovel blacktop into potholes.

During my comings and goings at work I'd occasionally see Rabbit around town. He seemed to have friends, all kinds of friends, all over the place. He'd be hanging out on the steps of the Village Fountain, at Buxton's, the Dairy Queen, or out in the lot in front of Woolworth's, where guys would idle their GTOs and 442s, Steppenwolf booming from tape decks: "Born to be WI . . . I . . . LD!" He'd be leaning against a wall outside the Oaken Bucket, thumbs hooked in front pockets. Or laughing with guys in front of the bowling alley. Or sitting alone beneath a tree near the Shop Rite, waiting for a friend.

A fleeting figure glimpsed through a truck window on our way to or from the quarry. That's how I saw him that summer. I didn't give him much thought.

But when I think of him now, say, beneath that tree, I know

he had much to ponder. He hadn't graduated. There was the draft. He had broken up with Marian; she was tight now with that new boyfriend; there was no way he could live with the Jeffers. At night, after parties, he'd crash at one friend's or another's. Or if he found himself with no place to sleep, he'd ask to be dropped off near Olcott Square.

"You all right?" they'd ask him as he got out of the car.

"Yeah. Cool." What else was he supposed to say?

He'd close the door, and they'd beep and take off, squealing around the green. He'd cross the square and follow Route 202 past the Texaco station and the Animal Hospital. He never heard them during the day, but at night he often did: those dogs wailing behind the dark windows. They'd shut up for a while, then one would yelp, and they'd all let loose again. At Santillo's Nursery, he'd cut back through the shrubs, avoiding the clicking sprinklers. He'd hop the fence, go down the embankment, and follow the gleaming tracks. There's the pale back of the liquor store and Shop Rite, heaped with crates and cartons. And there beside those busted barrels is his path that leads into the woods.

Rusty

One of those places where Rabbit often stayed during this period was the Cuttings' home on Walnut Circle, a new development off the end of my own street, Cherry Lane. As a boy, with my friends, I had explored this area, built tree forts, shot suction-cup arrows at imaginary Indians — it was all woods back then. By the summer of '71, most of the woods had been plowed under, and about thirty big houses stood around a wide, circular road with sidewalks and cobblestone curbs. I remember my father's jaw dropping when he learned of the cost of these homes. $100,000! Was there a mistake with the decimal point?

Sixteen years earlier, my parents had bought their lot and built their house for about $25,000. This was how fast things were changing. Corporate headquarters began blooming in the fields. Business executives snapped up the new homes and brought their burgeoning families.

I never knew the Cuttings, though I knew of them. They were "different," as my parents said. Theirs was a melded family, kids from previous marriages and two foster youngsters brought together in an eight-bedroom house by Penny and Barry Cutting. Evidently there were five kids, though I mostly remember two: Andy Cutting, a rock guitarist; and big, jovial, red-haired Rusty Cook, a rough-and-tumble lineman on the football team. In school he was a friend of Rabbit's, and often he invited him to the house. "Things were sort of loose then," Rusty tells me now. There were parties. They had a pool. Andy's band practiced in the garage, shaking picture frames around the neighborhood. Barry Cutting was often away at work, and somehow Penny lived with the chaos. According to Rusty, she just loved kids around, she wanted them all, even if they overwhelmed her. When she found out that Rabbit was homeless, of course she offered him a room. When you've already got five kids, what's a sixth? How could she turn him away?

So Rabbit was suddenly on Walnut Circle, with his own room in a big house, living the high life. He could sleep in late, lounge around the pool, have a few beers, lunch. Then turn up the music. "Truckin," "Layla." Go out in the evening, cruise the Dairy Queen and Buxton's with Rusty. Nothin' happenin'. So park on some road way up in the hills. Southern Comfort and pass that joint. Get out and lean against the warm hood. Look at the stars. Feel the buzz. Try to forget everything else.

They became party buddies, Rabbit and Rusty. "That summer we were roaring." They couldn't have imagined that in a year and a half Rusty and Andy would carry Rabbit in his coffin and slide him into a hearse.

Today, Andy still plays for a rock band that does the local bar circuit, and Rusty works for the Bernardsville road department. He's still happy-go-lucky. He's still big, strong, with his wide, tanned face and red bird's-nest hair. He wears glasses with tape on the bridge between the lenses. You can see him around in his orange T-shirt, driving a truck or working the backhoe. In the mornings, with his lunch box, he comes into the road department garage, right next to police headquarters. From the window of Bill Sorgie's office, you can often see Rusty, just twenty feet away, checking the oil in the trucks. They know one another, have coffee together, gas up their vehicles at the same pump, see each other every workday. They are good friends, if not the best of friends — this man who carried Rabbit's coffin, and this other man who put Rabbit into it.

This is, no doubt, a beautiful thing. Rusty and Sorgie over cups of coffee, or leaning on a fender, talking baseball, kids, families. It speaks of the reach and power of friendship, accommodation, and perhaps forgiveness. This is how men live together, this is called "society." And yet it bothers me. It makes me wonder: should *all* our wounds be healed, forgiven, or forgotten?

A good part of me says, Yes. Be reasonable. Let it slide. We must get over these things.

But something else gets my back up.

Forgiven? Possibly. Forgotten? No.

55 Walnut Circle

While infinitely more hospitable than the hut, the Cuttings' home was probably not the best situation for Rabbit. Things were too "loose" — too many temptations and distractions, too many people, good times. As Penny Cutting would later say, "I

have five children, and all of them together didn't want an edu-
cation as much as he [Rabbit] did. . . . We wanted to keep him,
but the house had just stretched beyond its limits."

By what seems to have been a mutual understanding, Rabbit, for yet another time in his life, would look for housing elsewhere. And this time he learned of an added twist. He would
have to find people who would not only take him in, but do the
paperwork to become his foster parents. Without a local legal
guardian, he would not be allowed to attend and finish high
school.

The answer was literally across the street and catty-corner
from the Cuttings, at 55 Walnut Circle. That is where the Bells
lived: another sprawling two-story house, with an attached
garage, two front picture windows, and a deck and glassed-in
porch in the back, looking out on a wooded yard. Every time I
return to visit my parents, I see this formidable home. It stands
on the hill, directly in front of an entrance to Walnut Circle.
Even at night, I can't miss it. My headlights sweep the front
lawn. I see andromeda, azaleas, rounded yews and rhododendrons, all nestled around the house. Thick beds of pachysandra
encircle the trees, lanterns border the brick path to the door. A
bank of low junipers, like a gentle wave, washes down to the
curb.

It couldn't have been exactly like this twenty-five years ago,
as Rabbit walked up that brick path. But it was still a world away
from Perry Street, Trenton, and from his hut behind the Shop
Rite. He knocked on the front door, and Martha and Harrison
Bell asked him in. From their daughters in high school, the Bells
had learned of Rabbit's precarious situation. Now they would
talk with him about his possibly moving into their home. They
all went into the kitchen.

The Bells are a gracious patrician couple. Today they live in
a stone house on a point of land on the Maine coast, an old family estate. At the time of their lives when many retire to condo-
miniums in warmer climes, they have returned to a lonely place

of austere beauty, of rocks, waves, and withering wind. In the winters, snow and sleet lash their windows; they wear sweaters all summer long. Years ago Harrison retired as editor-in-chief of Silver Burdette, a textbook publisher, where he worked when they lived on Walnut Circle. Now as we sit in their country kitchen overlooking the water, he has the lean, loose-fitting, long-eared look of certain men about seventy. I recognize his Maine accent, a mild reserve, and his dry, twinkling sense of humor. When we speak of Rabbit, he often defers to Martha, whom he calls Marty Lou. She is small, direct, and energetic, as soft-spoken as he, though as thoughts come, her words tumble out, while she pounds and kneads some sort of pastry, rolling it out on a slab of marble, slathering it with mashed fruit.

Was it anything like this on that day when Rabbit first spoke with them in their kitchen on Walnut Circle? Harrison, for the most part, sitting thoughtfully; and Martha standing, her back straight, her hands busy, saying just what's on her mind? "It was really an interview," she calls it now. "We were interviewing each other." At first, neither she, Harrison, nor Rabbit were sure they wanted to do this. "Our house, already, was quite full. We had to be very careful."

Straightaway, Martha had set out some rules that Rabbit would have to abide by, if he were to live with them. I imagine him shifting in his chair and craving a cigarette, yet he managed to see this thing through. They talked for an hour. They talked about school, his plans, about what they might expect of one another. The Bells, after all, were not his parents. They wouldn't monitor his every move; he could come and go as he pleased. But in their house, he must be responsible.

Rabbit's pride was what most impressed the Bells. He seemed to know who he was. He wasn't begging to move into their house. He asked, but he didn't pressure them. As Harrison remembers, Rabbit seemed to be saying, "I hope this can work out for us all, but I'll be OK if it doesn't."

By the time he walked back down the brick path, Rabbit

knew where he'd next be living. The Bells would apply to be his foster parents, and he would move in before the beginning of the school year. I don't imagine that he found much pleasure in this, though it must have been some relief. I suppose he also felt that old humiliation — *Why do I have to ask for a home?* — unwinding as he left their door.

When Martha said that their house already was "quite full," she wasn't kidding. Seven people lived there. Along with Martha and Harrison were two daughters: Martha (who would be a senior in high school) and Judith (a junior). Judith's boyfriend David had his own family problems and lived in the basement. "Grandma Sally" had a room and a sitting area upstairs. Then there was Charles, their five-year-old son, who suffered from Hunter's syndrome, a severe and progressive genetic disorder.

Now, in late August 1971, add Rabbit to this household. If the Cuttings' home had stretched beyond its limits, then what in the world was this? Thinking back on it, the Bells glance at one another, shaking their heads, surprised by their old selves. Were they crazy? Maybe, a little. But "it was the right thing to do," Martha says. "Besides, it worked out nicely. We'd do it all over, I'm sure we would — even if we knew what would happen." Her hands now come to rest on the counter, and she is looking out toward the gray water where some blasted pines cling to the rocks, to the places where nothing belongs. She takes in breath and wipes her hands on a dish cloth. "I wish you could have seen him with Charles."

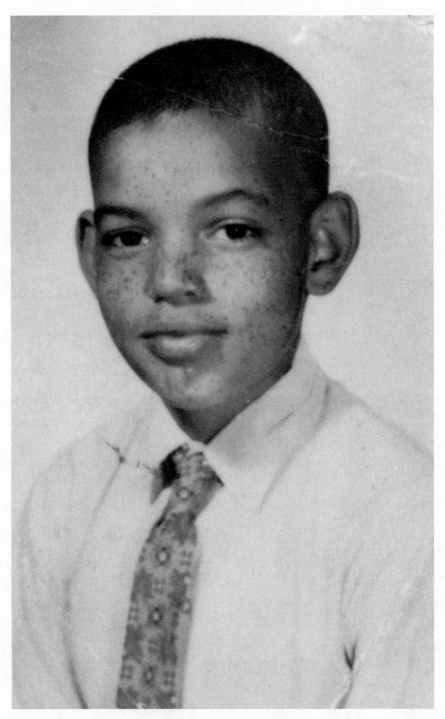

Rabbit at ten years old, 1962.

Olcott Square, Bernardsville, New Jersey, mid-1960s.
COURTESY THE SCHELLER COMPANY

Basking Ridge town green, Presbyterian Church, and ancient oak tree.
COURTESY THE SCHELLER COMPANY

ABOVE: *Entrance to Bonnie Brae Farm for Boys.*
BELOW: *Graves Cottage, Bonnie Brae Farm for Boys.*

The Bells' house,
55 Walnut Circle.

*Rabbit as high school freshman,
1967–68*
COURTESY BERNARDS TOWNSHIP
PUBLIC LIBRARY

*Standing next to the
high school door, 1968.*
COURTESY
JACKIE LENTZSCH

Rabbit's mother,
Hannah Baker Wells,
date unknown.
COURTESY DONALD BAKER

With Marian's horse in the Jeffers' yard, 1970. COURTESY JUDITH BELL

High school yearbook photo, 1971.
COURTESY BERNARDS TOWNSHIP
PUBLIC LIBRARY

MARC ANTHONY SERITELLA
"Life is far too important a thing ever
to talk seriously about."

SUSAN A. SERRETTI
"It is good to be merry and wise."

DAVID SHIVELY
"O for a life of sensations rathe
of thoughts."

Bill Sorgie, 1967 high school graduation photo with classmates.
COURTESY BERKELEY HEIGHTS
PUBLIC LIBRARY

WILLIAM F. SORGIE
"Happy the man who . . . makes all
his pleasure dependent on his liberty
of action."

JAMES M. SMITH
"I feel an earnest and humble desire to
increase the stock of harmless cheer-
fulness."

STEVE SOLOMON
"Life is a series of surprises,
would not be worth taking or ke
if it were not."

Patrolman Sorgie, 1972.
COURTESY BERNARDSVILLE NEWS

*1972 high school
yearbook photo.*
COURTESY BERNARDS TOWNSHIP
PUBLIC LIBRARY

Hey man, you got a light?

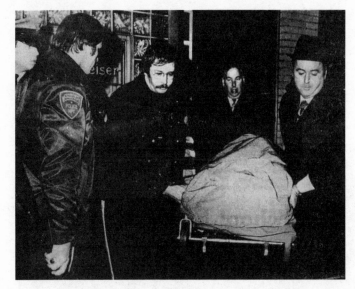

Rabbit's body being removed from the Three Lights Tavern, 1:45 A.M., January 13, 1973. COURTESY BERNARDSVILLE NEWS

Article about Rabbit's death in the Philadelphia Inquirer, *featuring picture of the Three Lights Tavern, with concrete-based No Parking sign.* COURTESY PHILADELPHIA INQUIRER

10-A Sunday, Jan. 21, 1973   Philadelphia Inquirer   11

Irresponsible Police Action?

Slaying of Black Youth Stuns Virtually All-White N.J. Community

"And it seems the only way,
if you think about it,
That man can keep his
head,
Is by taking all the living
things around him
And squeeze him 'til
they're dead."
from a song written
by William Wells

By WENDELL RAWLS JR.
Inquirer Trenton Bureau

BERNARDSVILLE, N.J. —
They came by the hundreds
Thursday and Friday to say
goodbye to William ("Rabbit")
Wells, but he did not hear.

A policeman's bullet pierced
his chest a week earlier and
his body lay in a pink satin-
lined casket.

The death of the 21-year-old
black youth had scorched the
hearts of the virtually all-
white residents of this affluent
Somerset County community.

Almost singlehandedly, Rabbit Wells had rendered Basking Ridge and its New En-
glandish atmosphere practically color-blind.

IT WAS NOT COLOR, nor
its much-heralded conflicts,
which caused his death, although authorities say they
are uncertain why first-year
Bernardsville policeman William Sorge, 31, shot Wells
outside Three Lights Tavern
shortly after midnight Jan. 13.

"If Rabbit were not here instead of in there," said one of
the more agitated young men

William Wells, slain by a policeman

on the porch of Gallaway and
Crane Funeral Home Thurs-
day evening, "he would be
saying, 'What can we do to
make sure this doesn't happen
again? What can we do to
keep things right?'"

So there have been no incidents, other than verbal, in
response to what young and
old alike here consider to be
irresponsible police action.

The Somerset County prosecutor's office says Sorge and
his shoulder as the two police-

men headed into the Three
Lights.

Prosecutor Stephen R.
Champi will confirm nothing
from that point except that
Sorge, who had been on the
force one year, fired one shot
into Wells' chest. It killed him.

THERE IS NO TESTI-
MONY from anybody to indi-
cate that Wells was involved
in the brawl. Champi dis-
missed the "No Parking" sign
was taken into the tavern by
one of the brawlers and Wells
was merely returning it to the
street as a favor to the bartender.

"In this town a policeman
doesn't even need to wear a
gun, much less shoot one," a
19-year-old youth at the funeral home said Thursday
evening.

"How can we expect young
people to respect the law and
law officials when this kind of
thing goes on?" said a man
who appeared to be in his 50s.

Basking Ridge's young people have tried to react to the
roosting the way they believe
Wells himself might have
done. More than 300 attended
a folk concert last night at
Ridge High School, with pro-
ceeds directed toward a bureau and a grave marker for
their friend.

"He was in the wrong place
at the right time
And no one will bid him
farewell

For the California beauty
he left it all behind
And his memories will
never fade away."

Three lines, written especially for the concert by Ben
Hall, son of a Basking Ridge
minister, remind all who
knew Wells of the job he was
set to begin as a California
tuna boat as he could save
$6,000 to pursue a medically
oriented college career.

"He knew he could never
get enough money to go to
medical school," said Mrs.
A. B. Cutting Jr., in whose
home Wells lived for four
months about a year and a
half ago.

"He decided he wanted to
become a medical photographer, and do something deal-
ing with sickle cell anemia or
leukemia," she added.

A 21-YEAR-OLD SELDOM
plans for death. So, the mass
of Wells who had been shifted from
foster home to foster home
since he was 3 years old had
been full of plans for life.

He graduated as one of
three blacks among the more
than 900 students at Ridge
High School, with average
grades and occasional mention on the honor roll.

It appeared he had weath-
ered the instability of his
younger days and occasional
brushes with the law for petty
violations while he was insti-
tutionalized at the Bonnie
Brae Farm for Boys in
nearby Liberty Corners.

"I found it difficult not to
steal loose money in my foster home after being at Bonnie Brae," said a youth who
had known Wells at the Farm
and since. "But Rabbit was

OTHER YOUTHS close to
Wells described him as "sensitive," "poetic," "brilliant,"
"jovial," "generous."

"He was a young man from
nowhere who wanted to be
somebody," said Mrs. Harrison Syli, who joined with her
husband to become Rabbit's
guardians. They wanted him
to have a legal residence and
he allowed to complete his
high school requirements last
year.

Those closest to him re-
member Rabbit as a person
who enjoyed reading and writing poetry, listening to
music, painting, reading
history. Involving them in
discussions.

They remember his aversion
to violence and his hatred of
drugs and the culture it repre-
sented.

PATROLMAN Sorge was
suspended from duty with pay
pending results of a special
grand jury investigation into
the incident. That will be conducted shortly after "more
than 50 pieces of evidence
from the scene" are returned
from the State Police labora-
tory, the prosecutor's office
said.

But Rabbit Wells, who
some say got his name because
of his front teeth and rather
large ears, which were shield-
ed by his Afro haircut as he
grew older, is gone.

As Ben Hall's song says:

totally honest. All the kids
there looked up to him and re-
spected him."

"To all who knew him he
was a different kind of
boy.

Sometimes being the only
one of his kind.

It could have been any-

one carrying that sign
But that's the way it
happens.

I guess you could call it
life."

Or death.

The "Three Lights" tavern where Wells died

ABOVE: *Former site of the Three Lights Tavern, today.*
RIGHT: *The Old Stone Tap Room (subsequently "Freddy's" and now a microbrewery).*

*Rabbit's grave, Somerset Hills Memorial Park,
with incorrect date of death.*

In the Basement

So in early September 1971, about the time that I went off to college, Rabbit was draping blankets over a clothesline strung across the middle of the Bells' basement, dividing his space from David's. I never knew David, and I haven't been able to track him down, or even find his photo in all our yearbooks. From his old friends, none of whom have seen him in years, I've learned that he was "troubled," "mixed up," "pretty weird," that his parents had recently split up; his father roomed in the Bernardsville Inn and his mother had gone to Texas. He was one of those kids who kept falling by the wayside, even as others tried to help him. He would disappear for days. He dropped out of school, broke up with Judith. At some point he was deep into a potpourri of drugs. Then after a car accident, he just "vanished," maybe to Texas, but no one knows. By now, says a friend, "I bet he's fried his brains. He could be anywhere." If he's anywhere at all.

Rabbit and David had never been friends. They ran in different crowds. Compared to David, Rabbit was together, focused, a model citizen. Now suddenly they were roommates, on either side of the hanging blankets, two guys in a room, without their own parents, a little like Bonnie Brae.

I see them down there, with the water heater, the furnace, the fuse box on the cinder block wall, and the silver heating ducts above. For a time, during high school, I set up my bed and desk in my parents' basement. I liked it there. It always seemed cool and secretive, a place to get away. According to the Bells, Rabbit called his place in their basement his "pad." He had a bed, bureau, lava lamp, desk, and an old record player. There might have been a ratty carpet on the concrete floor, and taped to the wall a huge peace symbol or a poster of Tommie Smith and John Carlos in the '68 Olympics, in their stocking feet, eyes lowered, and black-gloved fists upraised.

"Where you going when you leave here?" I am imagining all this: David speaking to Rabbit on the other side of the hanging blankets, and it is an odd question to ask of someone who has recently arrived.

"Cally," Rabbit says. He is lying on his bed, trying to read.

"What?"

"California."

"But what about Uncle Sam?"

Rabbit and David have different ways of approaching this problem. Rabbit has applied for a CO status, while David has been avoiding the draft by not registering and trying not to think about it. Now he is getting ready for bed. He was short, I'm told, with disheveled sandy hair, and was thin as a speed freak. His jeans stayed aloft by an act of God. Now he throws them over a chair. "So how would you get to Cally?" he asks. He says "Cally" like a girl's name.

"I'll get there," Rabbit says.

"And what you are gonna do?"

"Be a photographer or something."

With this, David goes into hysterics. "A photographer? Christ, I'll be the pope."

Now they are quiet for a while, and Rabbit turns a few pages. David shuts off his light and lays sprawled out on his mattress. In a lower voice he says, "You know Rabbit, we're fucked, you and me. Look at us down here. We're *under the ground*. Man, if you think about it, we're already gone. Cooked. Buried. Kaput."

Rabbit has heard all this before, tries to ignore it, but can't. He yawns, stretches; he is getting tired himself. Tomorrow is a school day. In the copper pipes between the beams above, he hears water running to the bathrooms upstairs, and then returning with a whoosh through that bigger pipe that elbows though the wall.

David says, "California. Man, you're crazy."

"You got a better idea?" Rabbit says. Sitting now on the edge of his bed, he peels off his shirt and pants. He is nineteen years old, getting on toward twenty, but in his skivvies he still feels like a kid — all those days and nights at the Farm. Then he turns off his light, leaving them in darkness in their room scooped out of the earth. In his nights down here he has learned to wait, to not think or feel, to try to hold everything still, to count out the seconds, a couple of minutes, until he can see those shards of light way up high on the wall. That's where that tiny window is that looks out at the bottom of a dry, shallow well. In the daylight, he has seen snakes and frogs that have fallen in there, some alive, some lacy with death. Above are the branches and leaves of shrubs, and through them at night, if he watches, waits, and holds himself calm, he can see — he swears he can almost touch — those pale slivers of sky.

Soul Food, etc.

At first their relationship was tentative and formal. Much of his free time Rabbit spent out of the house or down in the basement. He called the Bells "Mr. and Mrs. B," and they called him "Bill." In time, though, he was more and more around the house, upstairs in the kitchen, raiding the refrigerator, in the living room, or watching TV in the den. Very quickly he was "Rabbit"; the Bells were "Marty Lou" and "Hap," and teasingly, ironically, he eventually called them "Mom" and "Dad."

"Mom, can you cook up some soul food tonight?" Martha remembers Rabbit asking her this. I see him towering above her in his boots and afro. She is feverishly whisking something in a bowl. A pot is boiling, the timer buzzing. She wears a checked apron.

"Rabbit, I have eight mouths to feed in less than a half hour. I cook what I know how to cook."

"Come on. Some black-eyed peas and collard greens?"

"I don't even know what those *are*."

"Or some barbecue? It'll do you good, loosen you up. Put some glide in your stride."

She smiles and raps the whisk on the rim of the bowl. "All right, I'll buy the ingredients, and YOU cook everyone dinner."

At this, Rabbit turns and retires to the basement. Apparently they never had soul food.

As with the Jeffers, Rabbit seemed pretty well suited to the jumble and rhythms of family life at the Bells', and they made some adjustments for him. They all rushed through breakfast, went off to school, and generally ate dinners together around the big, round kitchen table. If Rabbit was to be out for a meal or gone for the evening, he was expected to — and usually did — call in. To Judith and Martha, the daughters at home, he was something between a friend and a teasing older brother. With Grandma Sally he engaged in rousing skirmishes over politics, music, everything. About this time, my own feisty grandmother moved into my family's home, so I think I've got a feel for this. Grandma Sally loved classical music and played the piano in the living room. I hear a Chopin nocturne tendriling down the basement stairs, and then Hendrix, those manic riffs and shattering feedback, "Purple Haze" pulsing up from the basement through floorboards and heating ducts.

"Turn it down!" The primal yawp of our time.

"What?" Rabbit calls.

"TURN IT DOWN!" She's come into the kitchen and is rapping her cane on the floor right above him. "You call THAT music!?"

Rabbit turns it down, but he can't listen to Hendrix low, so he turns it off altogether and leans back with a book. For some moments the house is awfully quiet for a Saturday afternoon. Again he expects to hear that soft, dull, tendriling music. But suddenly now her radio's booming, pouring down through the ducts: the opera, a guy screaming for all he's worth. It makes Rabbit laugh. You've got to hand it to her. The old bat fights fire with fire.

T-bird

Sometimes Harrison took Rabbit out in his car, a 1957 Thunderbird that he had inherited. Today he describes his relationship with Rabbit as "polite and casual," though I detect something more complex. Harrison's own son, Charles, was never easily taken out into the world, and of course Rabbit never knew his own father. So I see them in that shiny black T-bird, with those classy porthole side windows and long, narrow tail fins. Maybe they're running weekend errands. Maybe they're just driving around. If the weather is warm, they'd have taken off the top, and they'd be out there in the air and sun, the strangest sight in town. In his bucket seat, Rabbit wears his mirror shades, his afro blowing, his elbow hanging over the side. With his other hand, he casually waves to some guys at the Village Fountain. They can't believe their eyes. In the other seat, Harrison glides through the gears, a mild, middle-aged white man in a V-necked sweater, restraining a wild exuberance. He turns onto South Maple and heads out of town where, for a mile, the road is flat and straight as a string. They glance at each other and, like a current between them, they understand: not a word about this at home. Now Harrison opens her up and lets her fly, accelerating past the Somerset horse stables, past Crane's farm and produce stand, the old football field, the airplane hangar and grassy runway, all the trees, telephone poles, and bouncing wires, everything melting into the speed, until he slows and neatly weaves through the curves and over the bridge on the Passaic.

A supercharged V-8 with overhead valves. A three-speed with automatic overdrive. A Holley four-barrel carb, air scoop, power steering, power brakes, whitewalls, fender skirts, gleaming chrome, and fins as sleek as eels. . . . By lesser things are men bound together. They were both nuts about that car.

"He often asked for my opinion on one thing or another," Harrison remembers now, smiling. "And *more* often, he gave me his opinion. He usually knew where he stood." They talked about the war, the draft, and what Rabbit was doing in school. Harrison was once an English teacher, and I suppose it was no mere coincidence that Rabbit's grades improved that year. I am skipping ahead, but during the following summer of 1972, after David had split town and Martha had taken the rest of the family to vacation in Maine, Rabbit and Harrison stayed behind in the house on Walnut Circle. Harrison, of course, was working at Silver Burdette, and Rabbit had gotten a part-time job as a busboy at the Minuteman, a restaurant on Route 202. Rabbit never had a car, so in the T-bird, Harrison often took him to or brought him home from the Minuteman. I imagine it felt strange in the house, just the two of them in all that space. They had to live with one another in ways they hadn't before. Who was going to do the laundry? Who was going to take out the garbage? Who was going to make the grocery list, try to fix meals? What the hell does this mean, *sauté*?

"One time he introduced me to some friends as his father," Harrison said in an interview after Rabbit's death. "So when he went to my office I returned the compliment and introduced him to my coworkers as my son."

There is room for plenty of irony and humor here. I see the bemused smiles of Rabbit's friends. Or the quizzical, awkward glances of Harrison's coworkers. This guy with the afro? Your son? Of course, neither Rabbit nor Harrison was altogether serious. I imagine this as a sort of joke between them, a certain dancing along the racial divide to see how others might respond. What they said about their relationship was certainly not the truth. Yet from what I think I understand of Rabbit and what I see in Harrison's gray eyes, these "compliments" they paid to one another may not have been entirely false.

Months later, early on that cold January morning, after Rabbit had graduated, gone to California, and returned for the holidays to visit, Harrison was getting ready for his weekly indoor tennis outing with some colleagues — perhaps some of the same colleagues to whom he had introduced Rabbit as his son. He was in his tennis gear with a sweatsuit on top. He had finished his breakfast, and he was probably enjoying a rare moment of peace and that vague sense of virtue that comes when you are awake and your coffee is strong, in a house where everyone else still sleeps. Outside the kitchen window, the sun was barely up, the ground humped and frosted. It was cold, windy — he'd have to warm up the car, keep the choke on for a while. He was about to leave when he heard a knock on the front door. It was one of Rabbit's friends, a young woman Harrison doesn't remember now, perhaps one of those friends to whom he had been introduced as Rabbit's father. But the friend had a strange, wild look in her face. She seemed winded, her eyes red and wet.

Had the Bells heard?

No. What?

That Rabbit had been shot by a cop in Olcott Square. That he was dead.

I imagine Harrison, standing tall and lean in his baggy sweats, with his Wilson Jack Kramer in one hand and in the crook of his arm a pressurized can with three perfect yellow balls. Just yesterday evening Rabbit had knocked on this door, and, striding in, had surprised them all. He was back in town from California, making the rounds. He was looking good, riding high — he had landed a job with the tuna fleet in San Diego. They had all embraced and talked for a while. How long would he be in town? Not long. Where was he staying? With a friend. Could he come for dinner? Not tonight, but soon. Then he had taken a shower and gotten "dressed to the nines," as Harrison recalls. It was almost like he was still living there, his towel hung on the bathroom knob. He had said he was going over to Bernardsville that night with some old friends to celebrate his recent birthday.

Still standing in his sweats in the doorway that next morning, Harrison again said, "What?"

I hear Rabbit's friend slowly repeating her words, and then more slowly: "It's true. It's true."

At this, Harrison simply didn't know what to do, but soon he found himself in the T-bird. Some time before, he had dropped and broken a bottle of vermouth on the floor, and now the car smelled sweet but sickly. In his hands, he felt the smooth, cold steering wheel, with those rounded bumps on the back. He pulled out of the garage, out of the driveway, and onto Walnut Circle. He went halfway around, keeping himself between the curbs, to where Wildwood Drive leads into Cherry Lane. Where was he going? To Bernardsville? Yes. And what was he going to do? Could he pick up Rabbit and take him to the Minuteman? Could he bring him home for brunch? He went by the turnoff for Cherry Lane and continued around the circle. At his own house, he didn't stop, but passed slowly by. For some reason, he counted the windows across the front. A nice house, solid, apparently inviolable, the upstairs curtains drawn. Incredibly, astoundingly, the rest of his family was all still sleeping. No one else had awakened to *this*. He went around the circle a few more times — he doesn't remember how many. Then, with the engine all warmed up, he pulled back into his driveway.

In the kitchen, nothing at all had changed, his cereal bowl still on the counter. He walked softly in his sneakers, so as not to make noise, so as not to disturb a thing. He called his tennis friends and, whispering, said count me out, not today, and calmly explained why. Through the window he saw the T-bird in the drive, the morning light skating on the hood. In her bed upstairs, his daughter Judith suddenly sat upright from sleep. From outside her dreams, from somewhere downstairs, she had heard a low bellowing, an animal sound that went on and on, that even now she can't clear from her head.

Five days later, on the afternoon of Friday, January 19, 1973, Harrison was driving to work. During all that week he had not been able to get into the office. Life was just too hectic, too many things to do. The viewing had been the night before, and just earlier that afternoon, just hours ago: the funeral service, the burial, and all the handshakes, the soft pats on the back, the coffin fitting neatly into the earth. Now there was work at the office that he had to do, and besides, it would be good to get away for a while. At home he had changed his clothes, and now in the T-bird, he was driving what my family has always called "the back road to Morristown." It's one of the most beautiful routes you'll ever travel. It skirts the reservoir and the Great Swamp National Wildlife Refuge, then winds through rolling hills, old farms with weathered barns, and small, nestled colonial towns like New Vernon and Green Village. I suppose Harrison enjoyed this trip: the muted browns, tans, and grays of the winter fields, the curved lines of stubbled corn, the strange, sudden, warm weather, hinting impossibly of spring. He wasn't in a hurry. He doesn't remember thinking of anything in particular. He was just driving along, as though emptied out, numbed, taking in what came through the windshield.

Just past New Vernon, he noticed the flashing lights in his rear view mirror, and a policeman pulled him over.

Did he have any idea how fast he was going?

Harrison had no idea.

Thirty miles an hour *over* the limit! Are you trying to get somebody killed?

Harrison was dumbfounded. What was he doing? Sixty in a thirty-mile-an-hour zone? His hands shook on the wheel. Whatever he had done was far more menacing than anything Rabbit might have done. *He was only trying to do a good deed* — that's what everyone said.

Now here was this policeman in his crisp blue pants, with his gun buttoned up in his holster. The car still stank of sweet vermouth, but the officer didn't seem interested. "What year is this?"

"A fifty-seven," Harrison said.

The officer walked clear around the car. "She's a beauty." He wrote Harrison a ticket for just nine miles an hour over the limit: a light fine, a slap on the wrist, not even a court appearance. He said, "Here, sir, it's your lucky day."

Harrison remembers thanking the officer profusely. He felt like he had been delivered, forgiven. But why him, why was *he* off the hook? And why was Rabbit in the ground?

"Now you take it easy." The officer smiled, waving him on. "You take care of that car."

Charles

Charles Bell was five years old when Rabbit came to live with the family, and he was six when Rabbit died. He was born with the genetic disorder mucopolysaccharidosis II, or the severe form of Hunter's syndrome. From a medical dictionary in my local library, I have copied this description.

MPS II, Hunter's syndrome, originally called "Gargoylism"

Etiology   The syndrome is inherited as an X-linked recessive trait. Deficiency of the enzyme iduronate sulfatase results in an inability to metabolize mucopolysaccharides. The accumulation of large, undegraded mucopolysaccharides in the cells of the body causes physical and mental deterioration.

Epidemiology   Only males affected. The disorder occurs in 1:100,000 live births.

Signs and Symptoms   Onset of symptoms in patients with the severe form usually occurs from ages 2 to 4 years, with mental and physical progressive deterioration thereafter. Facial features become coarsened, and a short neck, widely spaced teeth, and hearing loss are also often present. Whitish nodular skin lesions may occur on the arm or back. Hydrocephalus [enlargement of the brain and skull] is commonly seen after 4 years of age. Recurrent upper respiratory infections, diarrhea, hepatomegaly [enlarged liver], joint stiffness, growth failure, and mental retardation are typical features.

Therapy   None available. Experimental evaluation of normal plasma and lymphocyte infusion.

Prognosis   In severe form, death in adolescence, usually from heart failure after progressive mental deterioration.

As I read this cool, clinical description, I am aware that none of these words can adequately describe Charles Bell. Yes, he had all the signs and symptoms: severe mental retardation, a claw hand, a flat nose with wide nostrils, thickened lips, tongue, and gums. His breathing was noisy. His nose always ran. His speech was slurred and garbled. He couldn't smell, taste, or hear very well. From the outside, he was grotesque, a dwarf, a human gargoyle. A century and a half ago, we might have called him monstrous.

And yet he was also somebody's child, a child like any

other. He hated pain and needed love. He played, ran, knocked over milk and oatmeal. He curled in his parents' arms. He laughed, hooted; "he was a character," the Bells say. He loved the light that wobbled through leaves. If you listened carefully you understood him. When he wanted ice cream, he said "from the freezer." He could make you look up at the trees.

When Rabbit first arrived, Charles was especially wary. Here was a big, strange-colored guy suddenly emerging through the basement door, sitting down at meals, diverting the family's attention. They were cool toward one another. And then it all changed. Rabbit was one of the few people who wholly engaged Charles, and Charles, for his part, "just adored" Rabbit, always wanting to sit beside him at the table, waiting for him at the door. Rabbit seemed undaunted by all the deformity, as Martha explains now. He didn't seem to see it. "And he had something for Charles that the rest of us didn't have — it had to do with them being so physical." They wrestled in the basement and rolled around in the den. Rabbit carried Charles on his shoulders. In the yard, he whirled him around, holding his forearms, legs flying out, around and around, until they both stopped and tried to walk, swaying, falling, sick with giggles and dizziness, the trees spinning above them.

Passing by in your car, they would have caught your eye. It just didn't fit into the scenery: some big colored kid with a huge-headed dwarf, staggering around on the lawn. . . .

While through the kitchen window, and through Martha's eyes, it must have seemed altogether different. Rabbit and Charles whooping it up. A proud young man with a boy still inside him. And such life in what is stunted!

Like the Bells, Rabbit knew that Charles's life would be short and this apparently affected him. Each month Martha took Charles to Johns Hopkins Hospital in Baltimore for tests, photographs, X-rays, and plasma infusions. Back home, she shared the photos and X-rays with Rabbit. These were things he wanted to see and know. How was Charles doing? What was getting better? What getting worse? For a long time Rabbit would look at these images — the lesions, the bloated liver, heart, and stunted bones — and I think I know why. Before he had arrived at the Bells', he had the idea of becoming a medical photographer. Life with Charles must have convinced him. He must have felt that by looking hard at troubling things, he might stare them down, or stare them away, or at least hold them still for a while.

Ironically, of course, Rabbit died first, and Charles lived for eleven years after. But in all those years, Charles never understood that Rabbit was really dead. The Bells tried gently to tell him. Yet he wasn't saddened, he wasn't disturbed, it never seemed to penetrate. In his own mind, he seemed to know his truth. Until he died, he continued to speak of Rabbit in the present tense, as though he had gone off again to California and might someday come back through the door.

So the Bells have buried two young men. You can see it in their eyes. Rabbit was alive, then he died in seconds. While for Charles, life seemed to merge with death over a long period of months. You cannot think of two more different people than Rabbit and Charles. And yet for the Bells, and now for me, these different lives that briefly touched are tightly bound together.

As I think of them again, I am reminded of that photo, given to me by Rabbit's cousin, of his mother, Hannah Wells. I have it here on my desk. There is her worn, crumpled face, her straight, sealed, sunken mouth, her head like a shriveled plum. She too was a grotesque, not a pretty sight, her growth and mental development stunted, yet still with that life in her eyes. I wonder if Rabbit saw something of her in Charles — and something of himself as well: his own strangeness in the town where he lived, his appearance in some eyes as peculiar as a deformity. Surely he recognized the way people stared at Charles, or glanced and looked the other way. No wonder he took the kid into his arms, and no wonder Charles adored him. I even wonder if, in all of Charles's blind adoration, Rabbit felt something like a mother's love, lost so long ago.

The Break of His Life

Early in December 1971, Bill Sorgie got what he still thinks was the break of his life. After six months of dropping off his resumé at about thirty local police departments, he received a call from Thomas Kenney, the chief at Bernardsville, inviting him to formally apply for a position as patrolman. Bernardsville was never considered a "hot" place for a policeman to work. Things didn't happen there. The town was out in the country, near the end of the train line, most of it hills, narrow roads, and huge estates where the rich — he had heard even Jackie Onassis — usually kept to themselves. Down near the center of town more regular folks lived in suburban lots and frame houses. Many of the local artisans and shopkeepers seemed to be Italian — Nardone's Bakery, Pistilli's Restaurant, Rizzo's Optical — their forebears, like Sorgie's, brought over to work on the mansions up in the hills. West along Route 202 was the Shop Rite and Woolworth's, the old high school up on the bluff, then the neat shops around Olcott Square, a couple of bars, a tiny movie theater; farther west, the train station, the bank, firehouse, a park, a pond, and down the steep driveway, before a ball field and Ferrante's Quarry: the municipal offices, including police headquarters, in an old converted grist mill.

It was a calm, quaint, prosperous town, so far as he could tell. Shoppers in down parkas and camel hair coats. Volvos, Mercedes, fake-wood-paneled Ford Country Squires, an occasional muscle car, a rusted VW bus. Here and there, a few tough-looking hoods, but mostly suburban kids, college-bound types, growing their thin sideburns and ragged hair before cutting it off a few years later to be accountants, engineers, and marketing directors.

So this job, if he got it, would mostly be patrolling in a cruiser, filing reports, directing traffic, pulling over speeders, or now and then busting punks with beer in the trunk or a film canister of grass in the glove box. On a Saturday evening there might be a few drunk and disorderlies. But this wasn't a place to make a big name for yourself. It wasn't a place for heroes.

And that was just fine by Sorgie. He was married, settling down. He had had his fill of real danger — he was still reminded of it every time he sat. In places like Plainfield and Newark, cops had been assaulted, even killed, but that wasn't likely to happen here. The starting salary was $9,100, $200 more than at any other local department! With that kind of dough he could buy his own house with a yard, and maybe some woods in the country.

Eleven candidates were given written and oral exams, and of those, five were granted face-to-face interviews. Most of the others were already policemen elsewhere, but in the end Sorgie got the nod. He had recommendations from police officers in Berkeley Heights, and evidently his military record helped do the trick. Chief Kenney had fought in the Pacific in the Second World War and Lieutenant Steinkopf had served in the Navy. In Sorgie's dossier, they saw copies of the same military records that I have obtained. They saw the awards and decorations, the Purple Hearts, battle stars, and Bronze Star. No one ever asked Sorgie what *exactly* he had been through in Vietnam, but they must have figured that it was big, that he had fought with valor, and that although this sort of valor might not be necessary for this sort of job in this sort of town . . . well, it couldn't hurt.

Some days later Sorgie received the letter from Chief Kenney — "I am pleased to inform you. . . ." — and he could barely sit still to read it through. He had done it! He would be a policeman. Within weeks they would send him to the State Police Academy for training. I can almost feel him brimming with it all, pacing around his small apartment, reading and rereading the letter to his wife, then running across the road to his parents' place, showing them, hugging; and then down the street, over the tracks, up the stairs and skidding past the dispatcher. Look! Look at this! Holy Christ, I'm in!

The next day he gave his notice to the New Providence Post Office, where he was a mail carrier. He was moving on. During the week before Christmas, even before his new job had started, he drove over to Bernardsville, passing through Basking Ridge every day, wearing a coat and tie. He met all the officers and rode around in the cruisers, learning the ropes and roads. He was measured for his uniform. They put his name on a locker. What a Christmas for him, his first at home in four years. In Bernardsville a huge lighted tree stood in the middle of Ol-cott Square, and one stood on the green in Basking Ridge as well. Crèches and carolers. Wreaths on church doors. Skaters glided on the pond beside police headquarters, *his* headquarters. How far from the places he'd been.

Silhouette

On January 1, 1972, he signed all the papers and shook the chief's hand, making it official. Two days later, he began his residency at the police academy in Sea Girt. Any number of times while I was in high school, I passed by the academy, driving with friends on our way to the boardwalk at Point Pleasant. It's a strange thing to see on the Jersey shore, so near the arcades and wafting clouds of Coppertone. From the outside it looks like a military compound, with a guard house, barracks, and drill fields, all enclosed by tall fences and barbed wire.

With Sorgie's authorization, I've gotten a copy of his training records. In the eight-week "Municipal Police Basic Course," he received 405 hours of instruction in everything from "How to Take Notes & Study" to "Criminal Law," "First Aid," "Pursuit Driving," "Human Relations," and "How to Recognize and Handle Emotionally Disturbed People." There were two forty-hour "college courses" in Sociology and Psychology, and after these, the largest investment of time was in "Firearms (including Night Fire)."

As he puts it now, Sorgie was a "regular, run-of-the-mill student." He was judged "Satisfactory" in "Self-Defense," "Notebooks" and "Speech." He got a D in Psychology, a C in Sociology, and his final average on all other police examinations was 78.5. What stands out was his marksmanship. He remembers his score to this day.

Cadets were first taught to shoot at bull's-eye targets and then, when they had gained a level of proficiency, at the standard FBI target, a human-sized silhouette — as it turns out, the silhouette of John Dillinger — but always a black silhouette against a white background. They were trained to draw their weapons when they perceived a lethal threat, and to aim not at a leg or arm, but always at the most disabling area, what is called the "center mass," a Coke bottle shape within the silhouette that includes most of the head, neck, and torso. The center, then, of the center mass is the center of the chest, the heart.

In practices and tests on the shooting range, every cadet shot sixty bullets, twelve each from sixty, fifty, twenty-five, fifteen, and seven yards away from his target. A shot through the center mass was five points. A shot through the shoulder or upper arm was four points. Other areas of the silhouette had lesser values, and a miss gave no points at all. So the highest possible test score was 300, or sixty shots, at various distances, from standing, kneeling, and prone positions, straight through the center mass.

In late February 1972, Bill Sorgie shot a 254, which is considered very good for a cadet with an old Colt .38 that had been issued by the Borough of Bernardsville. It means that the majority of his sixty bullets probably passed through the center mass, and almost all of them hit the target. He remembers his

score now, as others remember their SATs or baseball players remember their averages. It has importance for him: a measure of
proficiency and value. In the years since, he has practiced and re-
fined his skill. Today he is what is called a "three hundred shot."
When he shoots, he doesn't miss.

So I think of him then on the shooting range, practicing his
night fire. I see him standing, broad-shouldered, with his feet
apart, bent in a semisquat. His eyes are locked straight ahead, his
arms straight forward at eye level, braced and V-ed to a glinting
point that is the end of his pistol. Such a small thing for all that
focus, like the spout of a syrup pitcher. All of him seems to flow
to that point, though none of him actually moves. You can feel
his stillness, a massive calm, like a sprinter in the blocks. Then
comes the brain-splitting flash and noise. And his arms, still
braced, bounce a little upward, then settle softly, just where they
were, like a gate at a railroad crossing. Sixty flashes. Sixty bullets.
Sixty crisp round holes in the silhouette, in the black silhouette
in the darkness. Hole after hole appears as if by magic. They
cluster, little lights, at the heart.

Patrolmen Foster and Laurie

At about 10:10 on the night of January 27, 1972, on Bill
Sorgie's twenty-third birthday, while he was probably in his
bunk at the police academy in Sea Girt, twenty-two-year-old
rookie patrolman Gregory Foster, a black man, and his friend,
twenty-three-year-old rookie patrolman Rocco Laurie, a white
man of Italian ancestry, answered a call reporting an illegally
parked car outside a luncheonette at 173 Avenue B in New York
City. Foster and Laurie had served together in combat in Vietnam during the same months that Sorgie was there. Foster had

earned the Silver Star, the Bronze Star, and three Purple Hearts. Like Sorgie, he still had shrapnel in his body. He had married soon after his return to the states and, again like Sorgie, he had worked for the U.S. Postal Service. He was reunited with his friend Rocco Laurie at the New York City's police academy where they were trainees. Laurie had been an athlete in high school, a baseball player and a shot put champion. At the academy he was awarded a .38 Smith and Wesson revolver for being the most physically fit member of his class. Then, when they both joined the New York City Police Department on December 1, 1971, they requested that they work in the same precinct and walk patrol together.

Now, on the night of January 27, they talked with the manager of the luncheonette, who knew nothing about an illegally parked car. They walked out on the sidewalk. The manager turned one way and the policemen turned the other. Automatic gunfire rang out, and the policemen fell face down to the pavement. According to witnesses, three assailants approached the policemen and shot them repeatedly in their backs with automatic weapons and Laurie's own revolver. According to the same witnesses, and as was reported through the media, one of the assailants then jumped up and down, firing his gun in the air, "as if exulting over the shooting."

Gregory Foster died on the sidewalk and Rocco Laurie died later that night in the hospital. Foster was shot eight times, four times in the back. Laurie was shot six times, three times in the back. The assailants escaped, and the next day the "George Jackson Squad" of the Black Liberation Army claimed responsibility for killing the "two pigs." Four thousand police and mourners attended the funeral for the patrolmen at St. Patrick's Cathedral. The small and loosely organized Black Liberation Army was linked to other "ambush-killings" of policemen. Photographs of suspects, all young black men with moderate afros, were displayed on the front pages of newspapers on February 9. A

massive, nationwide manhunt ensued. In a gun battle with police in St. Louis on February 16, one suspect was killed and two
other members of the "army" were captured. They were in possession of Rocco Laurie's revolver.

I tell this story because of its importance to Bill Sorgie at a
particular time in his life. The story was all over the news. It riv-
eted the cadets at Sea Girt. Two rookie cops, fresh out of training. A black guy. A white guy. They survived the Vietcong to get
ambushed at home. Set up, shot down, then shot in the back.
Bullet after bullet. Hole after hole. Their bodies twitching on
the pavement.

To this day, Sorgie remembers the names of those patrolmen, and the names of the suspects, some of whom remain at
large. He remembers that the patrolmen were buddies in Vietnam and that Foster earned the Silver Star. He remembers that
both of those men had been recently married. He remembers, of
course, that they were shot in the back, "executed" is how he
puts it. He even remembers the kinds of bullets — .22, .38, and
.45 caliber — that made the holes in their flesh.

So again I imagine Sorgie practicing his night fire. He feels
the smooth gun in his hand. He holds everything still, still as
steel. He sights down the barrel at the center mass, at the dark
silhouette — no, the *black* silhouette, the black silhouette in the
darkness.

Patrolman Sorgie

Bill Sorgie graduated from the police academy on February 25,
1972, and reported for duty in Bernardsville. In an old issue of
the *Bernardsville News* I've found his academy graduation
photo. This is your amiable neighborhood cop. His face has
softened since his high school photos. He smiles broadly,

dimples and all, as though with a friendly instinct. On his chest, he wears his brand new badge, and on his head a trooper's hat. On the front of the hat, above the visor, is another badge that I recognize as the seal of New Jersey: on either side of a shield stand two classical figures in flowing togas, like no one I've ever seen in our state. One holds a staff with a droopy cap (a pileus) on top, the other a cornucopia. They depict LIBERTY and PROSPERITY, according to the banner beneath them. But where, on our seal, is the figure of Justice? That snags in my mind.

Chances are, though, that this didn't bother Bill Sorgie just then. In all of the times that we've talked together, I've never seen him as happy as in this photo. This was what he had always been getting to — what he was meant to do. He was now Patrolman Sorgie, with a good salary and a bright badge, a handsome young man in a crisp uniform, ready to step out on the street.

Paternity

About that time — the winter of 1972 — another photo of Rabbit was taken for the high school yearbook. This one is my favorite: a so-called candid shot that in all its supposed candor, its every informal detail, feels absolutely composed, composed by its subject — an image Rabbit made of himself.

He has just passed his twentieth birthday, and he is at the beginning of his last and most successful term in school. He is seated casually, one leg over the other, in a high-backed wooden armchair in what I think is our school library. As usual, he stares right at the camera. His afro, by now, is magnificent, huge, almost encircling his head. He wears polished boots with inch-high heels. His pants, not jeans, are bell-bottoms. In the fingers of his left hand, he holds an unlit cigarette; in his right he's got his wire-rimmed shades, with the plastic end of one of its sides hanging in the corner of his mouth. An open book lies on his lap, its title obscured by his left shin. His shirt has a wide suede collar, suede front panels, and long knitted sleeves. The neckline, a narrow V, plunges down his chest, and Rabbit has it open, mildly daring, masculine without being macho.

This is the hip dude, but in a smart, sensitive, even studious pose. While many kids were coming down with debilitating "senioritis," he, in his second senior year, was getting more serious. In the photo, he appears to have just glanced up from reading, absorbed in thought, that no-nonsense look in his eyes.

He had some big things to think about then. Increasingly, as graduation approached, there was the old matter of the rest of his life and how he would support himself. With part of the foster-care money that the state paid them, the Bells had set up a small savings account in his name. He had that part-time job as a busboy at the Minuteman and tried not to spend all he earned. For some years he had wanted to go to California, and he had learned that if he could land a job there for six months, he could establish residency and qualify for in-state college tuition.

That was the long-range plan. In the meantime, there were other concerns. Perhaps with the idea of moving far away came the impulse to locate what remained of his family here. According to the summary of his foster care records, in the spring of 1972 he became "interested in finding his brothers and sisters," though there is no indication that he found them. All of his stepsiblings had been committed to guardianship with the state in 1943, but their cases were all closed in the fifties, and by the time that Rabbit became interested, the state had lost track of them.

According to the Bells, Rabbit also wanted to find his father. Just as I have done some twenty-five years later, he obtained from the city of Trenton a copy of his birth certificate, which he had never seen before. There, below the big blue seal, was his own name and birthday. And there was his mother's name (Hannah Baker Wells), age (38 years), address (318 Perry Street), and her color or race, which was described as "white." Probably for the first time, he learned that she had had five other children, all much older than he. Then, in the section titled "Father of Child," he read:

Full Name: Charles Henry Wells
Age: 38 years
Birthplace: N.J.
Usual Occupation: Laborer
Kind of Business or Industry: [blank]
Color or Race: White

I see Rabbit standing then in the Bells' kitchen. He must have been thunderstruck. His father? White? If his mother was white, then how was this possible? What's going on? *Look at this hair, these hands, these arms.*

In a newspaper interview after Rabbit's death, Harrison Bell remembered this moment. "I came home one day and saw that he was disturbed. Then he showed me the birth certificate and I explained that it [his father's reported race] obviously was a mistake. He thought about it a while and said, 'Well, I guess my mother lied about it.'"

It seems such a flip, dismissive statement — "I guess my mother lied about it." But I think about what Rabbit had just surmised: that this wasn't simply a mistake, that his mother felt it necessary to lie about his darkness, to deny, as though embarrassed by, this part of his heritage, to in effect make him white.

And there was an additional, even more frightening explanation, which turned out to be the truth. It must at some point have occurred to Rabbit, though I can't imagine he voiced it: maybe this Charles Wells was in fact white, and maybe his mother was telling an even bigger lie. Maybe this Charles Wells wasn't his father at all. Then who in the world was?

Again I see Rabbit standing in the Bells' kitchen, with his birth certificate in his hand. It says he was born, that he *is*, and yet it wipes out so much of where he is from, so much of what he most wants to know: *Was my old man tall? Handsome? Was he a good guy, or a jerk? Could he turn girls' heads? Was he strong? Smart? Did he feel some things that I feel? Did shoppers veer to the far side of the street, their eyes glued to the sidewalk? Why did he go? Where did he go? Does he have these arms, these bones in his wrists? Is he alive? Does he know that I'm alive? Would he even give a shit?*

In my imagination, Rabbit goes down the basement stairs, shutting the door behind him. A few weeks before, Judith's boyfriend David had split town and, although the blankets still hang on the rope, Rabbit is alone down there. Sometimes his solitude is good, sometimes bad; most times, like this, it is both. He puts the birth certificate away in his bureau drawer and sits on the edge of his bed. It has never occurred to him, but now it does: if he was born on January 5, and if he counts back nine months, a normal pregnancy, then he would have been conceived in early April, with the leaves just budding, the ground soaked, and basements damp, about this time of the year. How did they meet? Where did it happen? *Someone should remember.* For a moment he is aroused by his own beginning. His mother was small; she wasn't smart or attractive, but she could be strong and feisty. She had a smell like wet hay in the sun. Her skin would have been smoother then, that playful glint in her eyes. It must have been in Trenton, in some upstairs bedroom, the rain spilling off gutterless roofs and sliding down grimy windows. He'd like to think that they lit some candles, played the radio low, made a little ceremony, took their own sweet time. His mother, he recalls, had a frayed blue bathrobe with a cloth belt and little loops. The door would be closed, the rain drumming down, her robe hiked on her freckled thighs. He can practically imagine it, every detail, her breath chuffing like his own when he runs. Yet on the edge of his own bed, peering into his hands, he just can't see the man beside her.

Cherokee

This is how I learned that Rabbit's mother, Hannah Baker Wells, was part Cherokee Indian, as was he — a fact that very few of his friends understood, even as it became more important to him.

The "informant" on the 1983 death certificate of Hannah Wells, which I obtained from the New Jersey Registrar of Vital Statistics, was a man named Donald Baker. His address was listed in Long Branch, New Jersey, and there, after speaking with him on the phone, I met him. He turns out to be Rabbit's cousin, who, along with his own mother, lived with Hannah and Rabbit during those years in the apartment on Perry Street, in Trenton.

Now Donald Baker is a truck driver, a big, shambling man of fifty-seven (twelve years older than Rabbit would have been) who bears no apparent resemblance to his cousin. The skin on his face is white and reddish, as if he's been out in the wind. His cheekbones are high, his straight hair the color of straw, and strangely now, I can't envision his eyes, though I remember about them a sadness, as though his life, so quickly, had slipped behind him, and it hadn't been an easy one at that. For years Donald, his second wife, and their daughter have lived in a cramped house, no larger than a mobile home, that they share with a cat, guinea pigs, and a hamster.

Over cups of coffee, Donald tells me what he remembers about Rabbit's life in Trenton. He speaks in a voice that is shockingly soft, high and fluty, a voice that seems oddly de-tached from his body, like a boy's, or even a girl's voice, from a very long time ago. Long before Rabbit was born, he says, Hannah's husband, Charles Wells, had left the household, and her five other children had "disappeared" into foster care. Rabbit (or "Bill," as Donald calls him) never knew any of them, so "as a kid, the closest thing he had to a blood brother . . . well, that would have been me."

When Rabbit was born, Donald and his mother, Alice Baker, Hannah's sister-in-law, came to live with Hannah on Perry Street. They were poor but scraped by on Hannah's disability benefits and what Alice earned selling tickets at the Garden Theater. For three years, Hannah raised Rabbit. Then, in Donald's words, "the state took him away."

As he describes this, Donald's face is filled with that wearied sadness that long ago has spent its anger. Now he just shakes his head. What he wants to make clear is that in Hannah there was never a lack of love for Rabbit. She wanted to care for and keep him, but she simply couldn't do it.

A cat jumps on Donald's lap, curls there, and slowly his face brightens as we discuss the nine or ten years after, when Rabbit, though living with other families, would often return to visit. "He was around a lot then," and there grew between Rabbit and Donald that bond that sometimes happens between younger and older boys. They "hacked around a lot together": Rabbit, the admiring six-year-old with the butch haircut and stick-out ears, and Donald, the cocky teenager with blonde hair gleaming with Wildroot, and a black comb in his hip pocket. They hit Woolworth's luncheonette for banana splits, or Stewart's for root beer floats; they wrestled; they threw rocks at pigeons and freight cars; they saw movies at the Garden Theater, where Donald's mother would always let them sneak in.

We talk for a while longer, until Donald gets up, lays the cat back down on his chair, then gets from a desk drawer the photograph of Hannah that I now have on my own desk. "She was a gentle person," he says, and holds it out for me to take. He says, "keep it," and I protest — he is being too generous. But he insists, so I thank him and put it into my wallet.

Then we are awkwardly standing there, on the point of saying good-bye, when this cousin of Rabbit's does another simple and extraordinary thing. He takes my right hand and instead of shaking it, he lifts it to his cheek and slides my fingers along his skin. I don't resist, but neither am I comfortable. I'd rather he wasn't doing this.

"What do you feel?" he asks in that strange, soft voice of his. His skin is as smooth as an eggplant.

"Nothing," I say.

"Do you know why?"

"No."

He lets go of my hand. "That's because I've never shaved. I've never had to. It's in my blood. My father was half Cherokee and so was Hannah. I am a quarter Cherokee and so was Bill."

I remember that in high school Rabbit used to claim he was part American Indian. Of course we didn't believe him. "Oh sure, Rabbit. Dream on!" This was at the time when, even in Bernards Township, it was hip for kids to wear beads and Indian belts and bracelets. But it was all make-believe, ridiculous: pimply boys from split-level houses in moccasins and fringed leather jackets. Along the banks of the Passaic River, the Leni-Lenape Indians were long since extinct, and kids like me were what replaced them. Rabbit, we thought, was no more Indian than we were. We saw him as black and white, and mostly, because he didn't look white, we thought of him as black.

Yet if there is truth in the smoothness of Donald's face, then Rabbit *was* what he claimed to be: part black, part white, part Native American — so much of our history in his skin — and all of it mixed into something indivisible that defies our pure and simple categories, our need to have things stark and tidy, to so clearly differentiate.

I remember that Rabbit would sometimes ask, "Why do I have to be one thing or another?"

I still have no answer for that.

That photograph of Hannah Wells. My hand on Donald's face. Why would he insist that I keep that photo? And why would he take my hand through the space between us and make me feel his skin?

Perhaps he knew how little I know. And perhaps he knew how I might know more. Perhaps he thought that you can't know a thing — you can't come close to knowing a thing — until you've touched it.

Commencement

On June 22, four months after Bill Sorgie graduated from the police academy, Rabbit graduated from Ridge High. The ceremony began at 7 P.M. in the big grassy courtyard behind the school library. My parents were there, and though I don't distinctly remember it — it may be mixed up with memories of my own graduation — I was also on hand. I had just finished my freshman year in college, had returned for the summer to work again for the road department, and this was my sister's big day.

In those days it was cool to skip graduation, a clear sign of one's nonconformity, and you might have expected that of Rabbit. Yet, surprisingly, according to the Bells, he was a willing participant. He was amused by the hokey pomp and ritual, but also struck by his own achievement, the momentum his life seemed to be gaining. Just a year earlier, he had flunked and was living in that hut behind the Shop Rite. Now it looked like he'd get out of the draft, or the draft would just dry up. He had made the honor roll, and was thinking of college. That would have been hard to imagine back then.

Still, I can't believe he took it all *too* seriously. Below his forest green gown, he might have worn his black Converse hightops. In the solemn procession, he stood a head taller than most, his mortarboard perched on his afro. Next came the National Anthem, during which he would have remained seated. Then an endless invocation, then the endless salutatory address, then the band wheezing through more music, then the endless valedictory, additional music, and finally, as mosquitoes swirled, reclaiming an ancient habitat, the presentation of the class for graduation: our august principal, William "Moon" Keeler, squat and sweating, bald as a cue ball, standing beside the rolled diplomas stacked like firewood.

Rabbit was back near the end of the line, along with the others whose last names began with W, those poor souls who had waited for so long. But right there on the program between Jeffery Dalton Welch and Bonnie Beth Welsh, there was his name, though slightly misspelled: William Samule Wells. And now at last on the diploma itself, his name again — amazingly! — with all the letters right.

> Upon a windswept hillside stands a school so proud,
> And to her reputation we lift our voices loud:
> A shining light that shall not fail as the years go by,
> Forever in our memories, Ridge High will never die!

With these stirring words, sung in near darkness, the ceremony drew to a merciful close. "He wouldn't admit it," says Martha Bell, "but he was awfully proud of himself." Perhaps as proud as Bill Sorgie was in his trooper's hat and bright new badge — two young men who had lived through a lot, again at the beginning of things.

Back at the Bells' that evening, there were more congratulations, as Rabbit probably shrugged, "It's no big deal." He said he was heading out to a party. Some friends were beeping their horns in the drive. But first I imagine him going down to the basement, saying he wants to change his clothes. In the moist quiet of his own space, he unrolls the diploma, then rerolls it in the opposite direction. He flattens it out on top of his bureau, placing a book on each of its corners. Then he leaves it there, smooth as a place mat, where he'd see it, his name, those big, bold letters, when he'd put on his jeans in the morning.

Paternity, cont.

In my own life, the summer of '72 was the summer of my '63 Volkswagen bug. I bought it for thirty-five dollars, and I swore it was a great deal. The odometer read 103,000 miles. It moved under its own power and was in custody of all its wheels, fenders, even its wobbly running boards. It lacked only a rear bumper, which gave it an offbeat, sleek, unencumbered look, a look that I, with questionable effect, was trying to make for myself.

I had never owned a car before, and I knew nothing about machines. But by the end of that summer, I could tell you anything you ever wanted to know about pistons, rings, cylinders, solenoids, cam- and crankshafts, heads, wrist pins, steering knuckles and rocker arms, free play, end play, torque, toe-in, male and female electrical connections, bushings, bearings, valves, lobes, fuel pumps and feeler gauges, rods and gleaming gland nuts.

I was nineteen years old, brimming, restless, living at home and working again for the local road department. Another summer without a girlfriend. But at least there was this car.

Two weeks after I bought it, though, I spun a main bearing

and blew the engine. I had it towed from some place north on 287, then I pushed it (yes, you can!) into the garage adjoining my grandmother's apartment on the end of my parents' house. That is where I lived for a good part of that summer, perhaps for most of it. I bought a ratchet, socket set, wrenches, visegrips, and quarts of Liquid Wrench. With friends who knew little more than I did, and with a smudgy book called *How to Keep Your Volkswagen Alive: A Manual for the Compleat Idiot,* I removed and dismantled the engine piece by piece, down to its innermost chamber. I split the case, pulled out the crankshaft, and found the remains of my mangled bearing. Two months later, the car was all more or less back together, in time for my return to college.

In history books, there is mention of other things that happened that summer, but I have no independent memory of them. What I mostly remember is the feel of those evenings, sitting on cinder blocks in my parents' garage, with grime and oil up to my elbows, the guts of my car laid out on the floor, the radio going — loud when the Allman Brothers came on, and then a little softer, but only a little, when my grandmother rapped on the wall.

Sometimes my father would come out in his silent, crepe-soled shoes, and sit on another cinder block. He was (and still is) a strange, retiring, affectionate man. Working in his office in a corner of our basement, he seldom engaged with the world — today we might call him agoraphobic. Things, he said, were changing too fast, and for long periods, he wouldn't leave our home, even to go shopping. So when things went wrong, he'd often let them be, or make do with what he found around the house. He replaced lawn mower mufflers with tin orange juice cans dimpled with little holes. A toothache never called for a dentist; he'd always "chew on the other side." Too often we drove each other up the wall. I had been away at college for a year, and I suppose I thought I knew everything. Like many sons, from a father's view, I had been getting "some oddball ideas." Stop the war. Impeach Nixon. I was "too impulsive," "too impatient." And he had more patience, passivity (or was it some odd forbearance?) than I could ever understand.

Yet I remember once, when I had almost finished rebuilding that engine, I dropped a 10 mm nut down the narrow distributor hole and into the heart of the crankcase. I threw up my hands. I'd have to take everything apart, start all over — I might as well junk the heap. But from a pencil, paper clip, Scotch tape, and a magnet, my father fashioned a weird, bendable gadget. For hours he sat on that cinder block, leaning over the little hole in the engine, a flashlight in one hand, manipulating the gadget with the other, until he fished out the nut, still without a word, and dropped it into my palm.

Rabbit never owned a car. He never even had a driver's license, an almost unthinkable thing in our town. Friends picked him up and dropped him off, he hitchhiked, or the Bells took him where he needed to go. Whenever he was heading into Bernardsville, he would have walked or been driven down Cherry Lane, the fastest route, and passed in front of my parents' house, not thirty yards away from where I worked in the garage. Probably because I was so obsessed with my car, my back turned, my hands in the engine, I never noticed Rabbit go by. Now I wonder if he recognized me, a scrawny guy he used to see in the halls. Maybe he did. Maybe he didn't. But if my father was out there with me on the cinder blocks, I bet there's one thing Rabbit would have recognized, and that with an old pang: *Those two in that garage, bent over that engine, they've got to be father and son. Look at the way their backs arch. Look at their bony shoulders and arms. Look at how one stands, squats, fidgets, and frets, while the other sits so calmly. Between them, of course, there's a world of difference. Yet they bend toward the same purpose.*

(W)Retch

One day, probably in late June of that summer, a friend dropped Rabbit off at the Bells, but Rabbit didn't get out of the car alone. He opened the back door, and a large, gangly dog bounded out and whipped around the yard, trailing its leash behind it. That was Wretch, or Retch. The Bells still aren't sure of the spelling.

Wretch (I am only guessing which was its name) was part setter, part wolfhound, part who-knows-what, a female, a huge, exuberant, tongue-lolling thing; and now, it seemed, she was Rabbit's dog — and the Bells'. Never mind that the Bells already had their own dog. And never mind that Rabbit was hoping to leave for California sometime in the next few months. He was in love with this dog; he had to have her. Some friend of his had said he would have to give her away or put her to sleep. So what was Rabbit supposed to do?

I can imagine Martha and Harrison glancing at one another, shaking their heads and shrugging their shoulders. This would be more humorous if it were happening to someone else. Now what are they supposed to do?

Wretch slept in the Bells' basement with Rabbit and for much of the day was tied by a rope to a tree in the back yard, some distance from another tree where the Bells' dog also was tied. I suppose there was a chorus of barking out there, and within a worn circle around each tree, you might have had to watch your step. I wonder what the neighbors had to say. Or maybe, because most had their own dogs and hazardous circles around trees, they frowned and bit their tongues.

I remember a lot of dogs in our development then. We had our own lugubrious basset hound, Daphne. The Andersons had Dutch, a dachshund. The Hammels, Dunhams, and Rehms had hunting dogs: perky beagles and spaniels. Then of course there were the manic, regal Irish setters, imperious poodles, and daffy, blonde golden retrievers, biting and shaking their leashes. You'd see them early in the mornings, usually on weekends; and for some reason I remember only women out walking these dogs, all brisk with purpose, in pleated skirts, as brisk as husbands on weekday mornings, striding toward the station.

It gives me pleasure to think of Wretch and Rabbit out among these industrious walkers. According to the Bells, Rabbit walked Wretch around Walnut Circle. I can see him from behind, with his cool-dude slinky gait, swishing bell-bottoms, and on the other end of the thrashing leash, this big, gallumphing Dr. Seuss of a dog, sniffing at every juniper and mailbox.

A couple of mixed breeds out for a stroll in the land of pedigrees. I see Rabbit stopping as Wretch studies a particular expanse of yard, immaculate as a putting green. She finds her place, wriggles into a squat. There's the hiss of urine. A pause. Relief. The hips unbend with satisfaction. It's small, but it's a mark.

Edlynne & Friends

In September 1969, our junior year, Edlynne Sillman, a twenty-six-year-old Brooklyn Jew, a feminist who spoke her mind, a gifted ceramicist and graphic artist, came to teach in our high school. Need I say that she didn't easily fit in? She had frequent scrapes with the administration. She was prohibited from wearing pants. She was "too pushy," her classes were "too experimental," her art room too messy; she was said to get "too close" to her students. Some she invited to her apartment near New Brunswick. With a few, she drank beer and smoked pot.

This, at the time, was extraordinary stuff for our school.

Treacherous or liberating, depending on your point of view. Certain members of the faculty despised her, and she despised them right back. Often without having taken her classes, many students, including me, thought her weird, and a little scary, with her dark eyes and wavy black hair. She was "Edlynne," or "Ms. Sillman." She was never "Miss." She attracted a small crowd of artsy kids who were more or less on the fringe, who wore darker clothes and scruffy jeans, looked gravely sensitive in wire-rimmed glasses, or vaguely out of it, buzzed and bleary, having just rolled out of their dreams.

Rabbit was among Edlynne's most consistently good students, though not among her most inspired. He got straight Bs in her courses. He did silk screen, woodcuts, linoleum, ceramics, photography, oil painting, and watercolor. After so many years, Edlynne doesn't remember his work in detail, though she has a general impression. It was "dark" yet "floaty," "ethereal," "celestial," "psychedelic," what a lot of kids were doing then. For his final project in his senior year, he painted a dream, with her permission, on the whole back wall of the art room. It was a whorling vortex of dark shapes and colors "with a small, sharp influx of light" at the center. I imagine him up there on a ladder or scaffolding, moving his brown hand in bold, fluid strokes. What a thing that must have been for him, so big and public: to cover that dull, buff, cinder block wall with something all his own.

More than his art, Edlynne remembers *him*. She uses words like "gentle," "trustworthy," "street smarts," "intuitive good sense," and "compassion" as she describes him now. While other kids she knew went on to harder drugs, Rabbit held his distance. When, in the school year of '71–'72, she developed stress-related ulcers and colitis, he, like no one else, she says, seemed to understand her "alienation," the weight of difference in our town, for he had experienced it too. By June of '72, she was under doctor's orders to change her work environment. She resigned from her teaching position, but kept in touch with students. With a friend, she pooled her resources to rent store-space on George Street in New Brunswick, and there on September 5, 1972, after two months of hectic preparation, she opened a combination gallery/frame shop/studio called Edlynne & Friends. She gave art lessons, everything from pastels to printmaking. She hired Rabbit, part-time, to manage the store.

So, for much of that summer of '72, while I was working on my car in my parents' garage, Rabbit was catching rides to New Brunswick, where he helped make an art gallery from empty floor space. With Edlynne's boyfriend Chuck Marrero, he hung sheet rock and Peg-Board, wired wall lamps and track lighting, built box cubes and Plexiglas cases for sculpture and jewelry displays. Chuck was twelve years older than Rabbit. Born in Puerto Rico, he had worked in construction, then, later than most, he made his way through college and had just received his master's at Rutgers. He was another of those men with whom Rabbit had a short but intense friendship. Chuck has a vivid memory of Rabbit that summer, in jeans, a black short-sleeved shirt, a bandanna around his forehead. Forever, it seemed, they were hauling four-by-eight slabs of particleboard, then sawing them to make those box cubes, as sweat streamed down their arms. In my mind, I see Rabbit guiding the Skilsaw along the delicate chalk line. Particleboard is nasty to cut. The dust stinks like burning glue; the saw whines, chafes, and jumps. Now I see Chuck bending over — almost as my father bent over my engine — to brace the piece that Rabbit is cutting, what carpenters call "the work."

They worked hard together, according to Chuck, joked around, and talked about "serious stuff." Rabbit was interested in how Chuck had "made it," while at the same time he said he might never make it himself, because — how strange to think of now — "he said he would die young."

Edlynne has lent me an old photo labeled "Opening Night 9-5-72" on the back. Also on the back are three legible names: Mac, Rabbit, Lynn, and then one that begins with Hep that neither Edlynne nor I can discern. In the photo, the four of them (three men, one woman) hold glasses of champagne in front of a wall of sample picture frames. I recognize only Rabbit: the familiar afro, mustache, and goatee; a blousy white shirt, the collar open in a broad V, his hairless chest and coppery skin — I've seen it now so many times. Here, though, he looks a little heavier than I remember, a certain thickness in his neck and shoulders. On his face is a look of fun and self-satisfaction. He is enjoying the party, celebrating a job well done. He stands beside and in back of the woman, Lynn, and unbeknownst to her, he holds two fingers up behind her head, that old trick, so she looks like she's sprouting horns.

"We had really made something," Chuck says of his work with Rabbit. "It was wonderful, but we were glad it was over. I didn't want to see another piece of particleboard again."

A few weeks later, though, he would. And this time he didn't mind. Before Rabbit left for California, he gave Chuck a painting that he'd done on a scrap of particleboard, about one by four feet in size. In the jumble of his closets where he lives now in Washington State, Chuck hasn't found the painting, though he swears it's there, somewhere. He remembers it depicted "a male mythic figure, like a Trojan god." And he remembers that on the back of the board it read: "To my big brother. From Rabbit."

Talking to Edlynne these days, I sense an edge of bitterness about her, born I suppose of disappointment. Five months after opening night, and a month after Rabbit was shot, Edlynne & Friends closed down. It lost money. She broke up with Chuck. She moved to Massachusetts, lived on food stamps, looked for a job, finally found one, and eventually got back on her feet. Now she works for Cook County in Chicago, placing children into adoptive homes. It is important work, satisfying sometimes, though it isn't what she envisioned for herself. In her spare time, she still does some ceramics work, mostly miniatures of friends.

She doesn't have her own studio. She doesn't have her own kiln. But she still has a kind of tough pizzazz that makes me flinch and smile. Her hair, though graying, is still bushy. She wears wire-rimmed glasses. On the day I saw her recently, she wore a short denim skirt, an unbuttoned denim vest over a T-shirt with big cowboy boots on the front.

To this day, you don't mess with Ms. Sillman. She still speaks her mind. She still loves the students who rallied to her and hates the "male pigs" that governed our school. She hates the cops, the PTA, the Kiwanis, and country clubs. She hates what they all "did" to her and what they all "did" to Rabbit. And above all, encompassing all, she hates one particular thing. Some months after she had left our school, and some weeks after Rabbit had died, the school painted over the art room wall: that buff-colored paint, like the earth itself, burying his whirling remains.

Sunshine

Joanie Carlton was a girl who ran with the artsy kids in our school. She came from California in 1970, a junior during my senior year, and she and I never crossed paths. She lived with her family on Manor Drive, in one of those newer developments cut into the hillside north of Bonnie Brae Farm. Her father worked for a securities firm and commuted to Manhattan on the Erie Lackawanna. They had a big house with tall white pillars across the front.

In her senior photo of 1972, there is something a little different about Joanie. She has her hair long, straight, parted in the middle, a dark cape, like so many girls back then. But unlike the thin, gold link necklaces worn by others, hers is a string of narrow ceramic tubes, each with an intricate design. Her face, though, is what most catches your eye as you flip through all these photos. Except for her nose, there's a smoothed flatness — no dimples, angles, no dents at the chin, no perky, arrested motion. Her forehead is narrow, her lips full and closed, her eyes more elongated than most. She has no particular expression here, save for that wide, abundant calm, like a lake unruffled by wind.

Joanie was adopted, and like Rabbit she was part Cherokee Indian. They met in one of Edlynne's classes and soon became close friends. During their senior year, they hung out in the Bells' basement in choking clouds of incense. They got high in her father's car, and with other kids, drove out to Ravine Lake, and talked and smoked and talked. He called her "Sunshine." He was "empathetic, a good listener," she says, and he was "mushy to the bone," captivated by anything romantic and heroic. She remembers reading Arthurian legends with him: he a black/white/Cherokee Lancelot, she a white/Cherokee Guinevere. It was one of those things where you had to have been there, and you had to have been high as a kite.

She also remembers the first time Rabbit came to her home. Her father looked at him and slammed the front door in his face. But Rabbit returned again and again, and eventually her father let him in. Thinking back, Joanie says of Rabbit, "He believed that racism is learned, not innate." But I wonder, as surely Rabbit wondered, can it ever be wholly unlearned?

As I've grown older, I'm afraid, I've come to doubt it can, though Rabbit, at the time, may have clung to that hope, even in the face of slamming doors. What a thing to maintain, against so much evidence. And what was the price of its maintenance? It was, I think, the great hope of his life, the hope by which he walked among us, and the hope that was part of his dying.

When Rabbit was down in the dumps once, Joanie gave him a small, carved ivory Buddha, whose stomach he was supposed to rub for good luck. Increasingly, she says, he spoke of his death. He said he often dreamed about it, a dramatic and violent end. It was all "part of his act" of course, and yet he was also serious. It was strange, disquieting.

"You're out of your mind," she'd sometimes tell him. "Come on, don't dwell on it."

In her own mind back then, as Joanie puts it now, she and Rabbit were "friends," "soul mates," "just hanging out," what you do in your senior year of high school when you're cool, smart, and disaffected. But in Rabbit's mind, something more was happening, and Joanie knows it now. "I think that he was in love with me. He thought we were going places." And by the spring of 1972, they had come to that place where he wanted to go farther, but she was suddenly scared, confused, a seventeen-year-old kid, her parents' daughter; she "just had to tell him no." Rabbit was "delicate," "respectful," he never pursued it again. They stepped back to that place of "just hanging out," what Joanie still remembers as the warm equilibrium of "good friends."

But "good friends," when you're burning, is no consolation. You are delicate and respectful. You tell her fine, of course. You kiss her on the cheek, say see you tomorrow, then move your feet to the door.

Unbeknownst to Joanie, during the spring and early summer of 1972, Rabbit was writing maudlin poems, gushing with their lost love and his aching loneliness. Whereas his earlier poem "Comming Home" was all in brash capital letters, these lines are in the diminished lower case, as if the wind had been knocked out of him, his voice more soft and uncertain:

> she's gone
> so i cry
> when she returns
> i'll cry some more
> she doesn't love me, you see

i walk the streets . . . alone
i laugh . . . alone
i dream . . . alone
i live . . . alone. . . .

i love you too much
to lose you forever

i want to be strong
strong enough to bear
all the rain
i want to laugh out loud
so you can't hear me cry
all the tears. . . .

i am only lonely
and lonely isn't sunshine + blue skies
it's rain with little rays of friendship

you're wrong, you know
it's no fun down here
i want to climb out
but it's hard when you lose something
you love. . . .

i look at your face
and wonder who you are
you're just a dream
that never came true

you're gone from me
now you'll be free
floating in some silent sea
you're free

Joanie's "no" to Rabbit was altogether right — she has no doubt about that. But as she tells me now, some niggling part of her response to him was a "no" to his darkness, to the mixing of that with light. Some part of it was what she couldn't unlearn, even with all they shared.

They never talked directly about this, though of course it filled the air. Here was a girl more like Rabbit than any other he'd met in our town. Cool, California, adopted, part Cherokee. And still: this thing about darkness. In her yearbook he wrote but two short sentences, two facts he could not join.

> I'm the only spot in the book.
> I love you, Rabbit.

About six months later, right after he had returned from California for the holidays and she had returned from college, Joanie saw Rabbit again. He was excited and upbeat. Things were going well, panning out in San Diego, and he said he was "involved with" someone else, someone good for him, someone also named Joan. She remembers feeling happy for Rabbit. He seemed to be on his way. When they parted, they said they'd stay in touch, and he gave her a thin green folder, the kind that we always used in school to hand in reports and essays. On the lower right-hand corner of the cover, he had made a small ink doodle, a vortex. Bound inside, on lined notebook pages, were "Sunshine" and three other, untitled poems, all composed the previous spring or summer.

Joanie has sent me photocopies of these poems. They are all neatly handwritten, but the writing isn't Rabbit's. They were copied over by a mutual friend, and perhaps they were edited — I can't be certain. Still, I'm sure they are his poems. They are in his voice, about his concerns: loss, loneliness, the impermanence of human relations, the sudden changes of fortune.

> i met a man who was so kind
> but all he could say
> was hello goodbye

> i met a man who had a messed up mind
> and after i straightened it out
> he said hello goodbye
>
> i met a man who had no friends to find
> so after i became his friend
> he said hello goodbye
>
> i loved you as much as i love the sky
> you just threw me out
> you said hello, goodbye

But after immersing themselves in pain, the poems, as if to reassure the writer and reader, suddenly end with a ray of optimism and trust in some larger justice.

> someday the happiness that grew within me
> will come again and set me free.
> and the time i took to win your love
> will be repayed from above.

To me, these last lines sound more like wistfulness than conviction, a brave, hackneyed hope, born of doubt, a bright life jacket flung on the vast waves. I think of Rabbit in the Bells' basement, writing at his desk, which was a card table. I see him gravely putting his pen away and closing the cover of his notebook. He brushes earnest tears from his eyes, and washes his face in the utility sink. Then he mounts the stairs and grabs a Coke from the fridge. In the den, Charles is watching "Sesame Street," his bulbous head and stunted body sunk into the sofa. When he sees Rabbit, he brightens and makes his garbled, excited sound. "You want to fool around?" Rabbit asks, and the kid lurches as if to tackle Rabbit — he always wants to play. So they go outside and let Wretch off the rope. Then they all run around, barking, yelling, unfettered, crazed, *abandoned*, it seems, all arms and bounding legs. They wrestle in the hot, mown grass, tumbling, sweating, Charles riding on Rabbit's chest, both of them laughing, out of breath.

All of Rabbit's friends speak of his buoyancy, while many speak of his gloom. But there is no contradiction. That is who he was. Cool dude and schlocky poet. Cocky, toughassed, scared shitless. Stud and celibate. Gung ho, gun shy. A swirl of darkness, an influx of light.

The more he felt he was whirling down, the more he hurled himself upward.

A few weeks after he gave his poems to Joanie, she was back at college in Denver, and he was still in town, celebrating his twenty-first birthday at a bar in Olcott Square. He wore a vest, and around his neck, swaying against a shining silk shirt, a deer's tooth on a leather thong. He said it was a Cherokee custom. It spoke of a hunter's prowess, his aim, cunning, and speed afoot. He thought it would give him luck, this tooth, a talisman, a little pendulum over his heart.

On the Platform

If I ever saw Rabbit for a last time, it was probably at the Kiwanis Fair. The fair was always held over the Labor Day weekend, in the field between Oak Street School and the fence along the railroad embankment. More than anything else in town, it marked the beginnings and ends of things. It was here where you'd meet new kids who were coming into the school system. It was here where you'd say good-bye to friends on your way to college. And it was here where, out behind the tents at night, guys with girls in halter tops would entwine for one last exquisite evening: a summer of steamy trips to Island Beach, of "Brown Sugar" hammering the brain, all of it grinding to a close.

It was a fair like most other town fairs. Pony rides, hay rides, a dog show, an old car parade, and everywhere the smell of charred hot dogs. Of course there was a carousel and Ferris wheel, but the best thing of all was the dunking pool. There was real drama in that.

I remember that it was expensive: a dollar for three balls. But they weren't soft, fuzzy tennis balls, or something you'd throw for Kewpie dolls. These were the real thing, what Tom Seaver rocketed over the plate and Hank Aaron hit for miles. The idea was to throw each of your balls at a target the size of a dinner plate, about sixty feet away. On the adjacent platform, ten feet above a pool of water, a person would lie, usually in swimming trunks. Then, when the target was firmly struck, a latch would trip, the platform would swing down like a trap door, and the person would be plunged ingloriously into the water.

It all happened in an instant: the smack of the ball against the target, the *whooa!* of the person flailing in the air, and the splash. Often this wouldn't happen for ten or fifteen minutes, as ball after errant ball would thunk into the draped canvas behind the target and fall pitifully to the ground. But it was this long waiting with something pending that gave the thing its interest. There were the subtle alterations of the thrower's aim and motion, and there was the byplay, sometimes just a glance, between the thrower and the person on the platform. Usually they would be strangers. Younger, spindly boys, often the sons of Kiwanis Club members, tended to volunteer for the dunking. But sometimes, especially when business was slow, anyone was allowed to climb up and lie down, as long as he (or occasionally she) was accompanied by others who would pay to throw. Frequently this happened as the result of a dare. And maybe that's how Rabbit got up on the platform — or has gotten up there so vividly in my mind.

I'm not sure that he actually did this, but it *feels* like I saw him there. He was certainly capable of it. The pure, wild whimsy of it. The goofiness and drama. Was he calling somebody else's bluff? I hear his laughing, razzing voice: "So you think you're such hot shit. Put your money where your mouth is. Here, I'll go up there. Throw all you want. I won't even get my toe wet!"

This was pure Rabbit, all balls and bluster, marching up on the scaffolding, then onto the platform without removing a shred of clothing or taking his wallet out of his pocket. He'd lie on his side in his boots, jeans, and a T-shirt. "Go on, heave that thing. I'm as safe here as anywhere."

When I see this in my mind, it is Greg Easton, a friend of Rabbit's who would later be one of his pallbearers, who puts a dollar in the hand of the attendant and selects three balls. Easton was a pitcher on the high school team and good enough later to make the minors, before blowing out his arm.

"Take your time," Rabbit calls. "Find a good one! One you can throw straight."

Now Easton is serious and glowing with confidence. He's going to dunk his friend on the platform. He holds the first ball across the seams. He's going to burn it right down the middle. He stares at the target, beginning his windup.

"Wait!" Rabbit calls, sitting up.

Easton stops. And the arcing sun also seems to pause. There is no hurry here. "You scared?" Easton says. "You want to get down?"

Rabbit fishes in his pockets for his Camels and matches. He taps out a cigarette, then lights up, flicking the match, and blows a slow jet of smoke. He lies back on the platform as though he's sunbathing, and with a small smile says, "Continue."

Now Easton, pissed, winds and fires. The ball sizzles, splitting the air, but thuds into the billowing canvas, and falls to the ground like a dead sparrow.

Rabbit doesn't say anything. Just smiles that smile. The cigarette wiggles in his lips. There's the sense that he could lie there for days, months, years if he wanted, and whenever he'd get up, he wouldn't be changed from the instant he'd laid himself down.

Easton fires the two remaining balls, each to no avail.

Still Rabbit says nothing, drinking it up, milking it for all it's worth. He's lounging now on top of the world. He's made his point and rubbed it in, and vindicated, he can step down. Yet when he moves, it is only to sit up again, and he pulls a dollar from his wallet. He folds it into a paper airplane, then sails it down to the attendant. "Give that guy a couple more shots." And closing his eyes, he lies back on the platform, resting, his hands under his head. The sun is warm, his skin is moist with a coppery smell. From around and below him comes the bustle of the fair, yet it all seems oddly distant. Though he doesn't speak it, he seems to be saying, "Man, this is the life."

I don't know if Easton ever hit the target, or if he even threw those extra balls. Memory, or imagination, is an obstinate thing, and this is where this memory ends: with Rabbit up there on the platform, in the last bloom of that summer.

It is all illusory — I'm aware of that — but we live by such illusions: that there must be things that do not change, some things that last forever. You can call them God, or call them Matter, or call them the Eternal Verities. For me they are these remembered or envisioned moments that incise themselves in the mind. They are as simple as the smell of a child's breath, or the sight of a young man on a platform. He will fall, of course, in a clattering heap. I know that. I know what's coming. Yet I also know that no matter what comes, I can still see him up there — if I hold him up there — all alive in the lazy sun.

Ravine Lake

A few weeks after the Kiwanis Fair and after I had proudly returned to college in my rebuilt Volkswagen, on or about September 20, 1972, Joanne Calantoni was getting together with a
few old friends to say good-bye. She was actually going to do it:
she was heading to California, to live for a while with her older
brother in L.A., to see what the West Coast had to offer, to
settle there, she hoped. She was leaving in a week.

In the year after we had graduated, Joanne had moved away
from her sister's house on Brownlee Place where, in junior high,
she would sit on the front porch steps all those summer
evenings, talking and smoking cigarettes with Rabbit. She had
moved to an apartment over in Sterling, and had worked a lousy
job at the VA Hospital in Lyons. Little by little, she had lost
touch with Rabbit, and on that evening in September 1972, he
was not among the friends she had arranged to meet at Buona
Pizza in Olcott Square. But by one of those weird coincidences,
there he was when she went in the door, sitting at one of the
sticky, orange Formica tables, sipping a Coke, fooling with the
straw, waiting for his pizza to come.

Of course he joined in with Joanne and the group — there
were three or four others, she remembers. They pushed a couple
of tables together. They ate, laughed, had a good time. Then after they had finished, they decided to drive out into the
Bernardsville mountains, out on those narrow, winding roads,
nothing but woods, fields, and a few gravel driveways leading toward unseen mansions, way out toward Ravine Lake.

I have always loved driving those roads. They are roads that
you can somehow *possess*, even in a '63 Volkswagen. You down-
shift as you enter a turn, hugging the inside, leaning into it, two
wheels on gravel — don't touch the brakes — then accelerate
out with the whip of the turn, like a stone shot from a sling.

Joanne was driving her sister's car, and Rabbit was sitting in the passenger seat, his big legs cramped under the dash. The sun had just gone down. She had turned on her headlights. They were passing a beer back and forth, she was sliding through the turns, and they were talking in that old, easy way, like those evenings on Brownlee Place. She *was*, in fact, going to California, she told him. On the twenty-seventh. She had her ticket.

"I'm going too," she remembers him saying. But it was something he had always said, or boasted about, that he'd end up in California.

She gave him a glance.

"Really. No kidding." Then he told her he was saving up the money, that his old cottage parents from Bonnie Brae had moved to San Diego, and he could probably live with them for a while. He would get a job and go to college. He would get his own apartment. He'd be a medical photographer.

I imagine she gave him another, longer glance, then rolled her eyes. "You got your ticket yet?"

He didn't say yes or no, but drained his beer, looking straight through the windshield. "Let's take them fast," he said.

They had reached a place on Mountain Top Road that was known as Jacob's Ladder. By now the town has probably smoothed them all out, but down that long hill there used to be seven bumps right in a row — my father called them "thank you ma'ams" — bumps that if you hit them just right, you were, for an instant, for seven instants, actually flying.

I see them going over those bumps — Joanne and Rabbit — whooping with every one, each a little worse, or better, than the one before, each another threshold of excitement and fear, the glide upward and the bottom falling out, their eyes wide with wonder.

Now they come to Campbell Road and the gradual descent through the woods to the lake. This is a whole different kind of wonder, where you just sit still and silent. The lake comes first as a kind of inkling. Before you know it, before you see or smell the water, you feel, like a slow exhilaration, the wide openness above it, the light that it takes from the sky. Next come the glintings between the leaves, that cool scent, something primeval, and then a swath of it lays out before you, clear to the other side.

Ravine Lake was where most trips to the mountains ended, and where I presume that this one ended, though Joanne can't be absolutely sure. Near the inlet at the north end stands a tennis court and a shingled bath house, the only signs of human habitation. From there, for a mile, the road hugs the curving eastern shore, the water twenty feet from Rabbit's elbow, which hung out the window. The lake is about a quarter mile wide and, north to south, roughly shaped like a question mark. At its southern end stands the dam and spillway, and near it is a narrow place where you can pull your car over.

It is all private property, of course. You certainly don't belong here. Yet if you sit on the dam, with the lake spread out and that openness above, there is the sense that you could belong in *some* other place that is not the one you've always known. You are only a few miles from Olcott Square, from the tables at Buona Pizza. Still it feels like you have gone a great distance and come to a smooth, clear part of the mind, where you might start over again.

"I'll call you when I get there," Rabbit said, still speaking — and probably dreaming, she thought — of California. "We'll hit the beach. Malibu. Watch the sun go down on the waves." He made it sound like a done deal, a piece of cake, the way he made everything sound. It was what she loved and didn't love about him.

"Well, I guess we'll see," she said.

Later that night Joanne dropped Rabbit off in Olcott Square. By that time of year, there was a crispness in the air, and he might have been wearing a sweatshirt. He waved, she remembers, with a cigarette in his hand, and said, "Be cool." It was the last time she ever saw him. On September 27, she flew to L.A. to begin the next part of her life. She never heard from Rabbit again; she never got the call to meet him at Malibu — she never really expected to. Within six months she would be married. Then there would be the children, the move to Wisconsin, the terrible car accident, and the rest.

But before all that, while she was new to L.A. and California still held its glittering promise, she did get a call from her old friend Sharon Wilkerson, telling her that Rabbit was dead. He was shot within a couple of yards from where Joanne had last seen him living. She was stunned, saddened, and appalled by the news, and yet oddly tickled, all those miles away, when she learned what he would have loved to have told her himself: that he too had made it to the coast, to the place he thought he was getting to. That he had done what he had said he'd do, and that he had proven her wrong.

Joan Marie Harczku?

Many months ago I wrote in these pages, "If we are to be truthful, we must acknowledge the weight of what we do not recover; that our searches can end less in dazzling discovery than in vacancy, confusion, or exhaustion." That was a response, at the time, to the frustrating search for Rabbit's parents (his mother dead, his father unknown), for his home on Perry Street (now a vacant lot), and for his foster care records (which the state deems confidential, and thus unavailable to me). But having written that — having set it up and aside, as it were — I had thought I could move straight ahead through Rabbit's life, from discovery to discovery, without any more glaring ellipses.

I was wrong about that. And I was right in the first place. There is so much that has eluded me and such weight in all these vacancies.

In a short column titled "Citizens Inquiry Probes Shooting" in the *Bernardsville News* of February 8, 1973 (nearly a month after Rabbit died), there are these words:

> The Citizens Inquiry took information on Jan 29 from Mr. and Mrs. Robert Jeffers of Liberty Corner and Miss Joan Marie Harczku of New Brunswick, Wells' fiancée.

Joan Marie Harczku? Rabbit's fiancée?

When I first read this, toward the beginning of my research, I had never heard of Joan Harczku, or that Rabbit, at the time of his death, was engaged to be married. Who was she? Who *is* she? Was any of this true? After all these months, I still haven't found her. I still don't know for sure.

Ruth Jeffers remembers meeting "a Joan" on the morning before Rabbit's death, when he stopped by the Jeffers house to say hello and to say happy birthday to Bobby, their son. Bobby and Marian, Rabbit's old girlfriend, also remember meeting her that day, a "hippyish girl," "real nice" with long, blonde hair. She wore beads, bracelets, and she looked a little older than Rabbit. Together, she and Rabbit seemed "serious," "more than friends," but no one remembers that they were engaged.

After Rabbit's death, this same Joan visited the Jeffers a few more times to talk and share her grief, mostly, Ruth remembers, with her late husband Robert, with whom Rabbit used to talk for all those hours in the light at their kitchen table. Joan seemed "angry but reserved," "smart and sensitive." Like Rabbit, she was interested in eastern religions; she might have been in college. And Ruth remembers that she celebrated the Chinese New Year, and she had other friends who were African-American.

Very few other people who knew Rabbit, including many that knew him well, remember even hearing of Joan Harczku, to say nothing of her engagement to marry him. Not his old buddies from Bonnie Brae. Not Cy, Fred, or Doug. Not Jackie Lentzsch. Not Rusty Cook or Joanne Calantoni. Not Martha or Harrison Bell, nor any of their daughters. And yet Edlynne Sillman says that "he was crazy in love" with a young woman he had met that summer, though she doesn't recall her specifically. Chuck Marrero also recalls hearing of her. And Joanie Carlton, to whom Rabbit wrote those sad poems, has that memory of him talking about "another Joan," older than him, from somewhere else, who might have joined him on his trip to California.

From this I can only make my best guess: that Rabbit did become close to a young woman named Joan from somewhere around New Brunswick, whom he met in his comings and goings during that summer of '72 at Edlynne & Friends. I write only "a young woman named Joan" because I suspect that her last name, as reported in the newspaper, was incorrect; and I write "somewhere around New Brunswick" because I have found no evidence that she (or anyone by that reported last name) ever lived there. From 1950 to the present, the New Brunswick Directory of residents has no listing of Harczku, and nor does the Rutgers alumni office. I don't have enough information (her date and place of birth, etc.) for the Social Security Administration to bother with a search. And more disturbing still is what I have learned from a friend who has access to state records: there is no one presently in New Jersey who pays taxes or has a driver's license with that strange last name.

So I'm afraid it's come down to this. Because I can't afford a private investigator, I've swallowed my pride and called 800-U.S. SEARCH, as advertised on the afternoon talk shows. For less than forty dollars, this service claims to find old flames, prodigal sons, deadbeat dads, and the like. "All you need is the person's name" — and your credit card — and then, according to the recorded phone message, "a nationwide computer search will begin!" As I write this, "the search" is into its second month — I've envisioned switchboards lighting, a nationwide dragnet. But so far, no trace of Joan Marie Harczku. Nothing has shown up, nothing at all, except for an item on my recent VISA bill for $39.95.

More than most of us, I think, Rabbit lived his life in discrete compartments. His mother, aunt, and cousin Donald in Trenton knew nothing of his life at Bonnie Brae. His old friends from Bonnie Brae knew little about his friends on Walnut Circle. And his friends on Walnut Circle knew little about his new friends in New Brunswick, including, perhaps, his fiancée. I have made my way into some of Rabbit's compartments. Into the one he shared with Joan Harczku I've found no doors. Of course I will wait for the fruits of my forty dollars, and I will keep asking anyone who knew Rabbit if they've heard of her. But it is possible, if not likely, that I will never find her, and her part of his story — her love, anger, bewilderment — will not be told here.

This is sad and unsettling to me, for she is probably somewhere out there in the world, someone (perhaps like Rabbit's father) who could even be reading these pages. If she is living, she would be in her midforties, perhaps married; she might have a different last name. She might have kids, some as old as she was when she and Rabbit were together. Her hair is probably shorter, and she may not wear beads anymore. I imagine she isn't too different from most of us now, as we sit on our patios with our patch of lawn and a couple of dogwoods, with our small but promising mutual funds, and our wild old dreams, like bugs in amber, so strange in our children's eyes.

I suppose she doesn't think about Rabbit very much, and when she does it is not with a pang, but a slow ache, as in a tired joint, that comes and goes with the weather. It's not that she's forgotten him, however; there are just so many more things to remember. He comes to her now as if he's always been there, somewhere around, and she just hasn't noticed him for a while.

Leavings

Rabbit's leave-taking, like his arrival at the Bells', was not ceremonious. The Bells had known of his plans. By October he had saved enough money to get to California, and he told them when he was going. Through July, August, and September he had been spending more time away from the Bells, mostly down in New Brunswick, working at Edlynne & Friends and probably romancing Joan Harczku. So it seemed that, even before he left town, he was already sliding away. This was sad of course, but inevitable and right. He was getting off on his own.

The biggest problem with his imminent departure was what to do with Wretch, his dog. Rabbit couldn't take her with him, and the Bells couldn't keep her. But a Mr. Brown, a handyman who washed the Bells' windows, fell in love with her, then offered to take her home. Rabbit agreed, and one day in early October, with the Bells' windows gleaming, Wretch bounded into Mr. Brown's battered van, the van pulled away, and Rabbit took the frayed rope off the tree.

Some days later, Rabbit gathered his things, perhaps in his old canvas duffel bag — he had done this so many times before. But this time it was all his own doing. No one was kicking him out, he wasn't uncomfortable at the Bells', no one was sending him elsewhere. *So this is what leaving actually feels like.* Sad, scary, exhilarating. A choice to take some part of you elsewhere, while another part stays behind.

From the basement, he brought up his bag, once again containing all his essentials: clothes, toothbrush, poems, diploma, camera, hairpick, lava lamp. As always, a car beeped in the driveway. There were hugs all around: certainly for Charles and Martha, and for the girls, if they were home at the time. Then, I presume, a handshake for Harrison. And then, even, a bending embrace for Grandma Sally, her tired shoulders sloped as toward the grave, her cane like a spike on his boot.

"He was there," as Martha tells it now. "And then he wasn't." She washed his sheets, and took the blankets off the rope in the basement. "He had so little, he left nothing behind," no shoes, no socks beneath the bed — nothing but all she remembers.

4731 Greenbrier Avenue, San Diego

This is the part where I really lose track of Rabbit, where we all lost him for a number of months, the part where he's far away. I have heard that he had made arrangements to live with some old cottage parents from Bonnie Brae who had previously moved to San Diego. I suspect this is true, but no one remembers their names, and, as I've mentioned, all the old Bonnie Brae records are gone, destroyed in a flood. I don't know who those people were.

Possibly he went out there with Joan Harczku, if that was in fact her name. Did he (they?) fly, take a bus, or drive? What was his life like? Was he happy? Excited? Lonely? What in the world did he do?

According to the Bells, he got a job with the tuna fleet based in San Diego. But all I know about tuna is what I dig from tin cans at lunchtime and mix with mayonnaise and pepper. In my encyclopedia, I read that yellowfin tuna spawn in the central Pacific, can weigh three hundred pounds and grow six feet long, as long as Rabbit was tall. Further, I learn that a center of the tuna industry was indeed (and remains) San Diego. Seasonally, and for many weeks on end, the ships leave port to pursue and "harvest" the makings for billions of sandwiches.

So this could very well be true: for the last months of Rabbit's life, this kid from the streets and rolling hills of New Jersey may have spent more time on the rolling waves than he did on dry land. Now I try to imagine Rabbit in yellow rubber rain pants, in a squall of gulls, on a tossing, net-festooned tuna clipper, waist-deep in giant fish. But all this, while likely, feels vaguely comical to me. Rabbit riding the deep blue sea, smelling of brine, queasy of stomach? I can't quite get my mind around it. I can't quite *feel* him there.

About the only evidence I have of his life in California is a forwarding address from the New Jersey Division of Youth and Family Services, which, in July 1972, had "terminated his case." His mail, if there was any, was sent to 4731 Greenbrier Avenue, San Diego.

Many weeks ago I sent a letter of my own to that address, with an enclosed self-addressed envelope, requesting that the residents inform me if they had ever heard of William Wells or knew of the people who lived there from October through December 1972. I also requested that they tell me something about the area, or send a photo, anything. But like my search for Joan Harczku, nothing has come back my way.

I could go there of course, yet that is hard to justify, given the state of our family checkbook. A $500 coast-to-coast trip? To look at an address where Rabbit probably, though not certainly, lived for a short time? So instead of traveling, I have opened another volume of the encyclopedia and spread a street map of San Diego across my desk.

To this arid city at the bottom of California, to a place of old Spanish missions and vast military bases, of deep, fingering bays and golf courses, of watering holes for retirees, of Mexican names, English names, of freeways that wander without a hub (where is the center, the heart of town, the green, the square, the flagpole?) . . . to here — not L.A., Malibu, Haight-Ashbury — Rabbit chased his dream.

On the map I have found Greenbrier Avenue in the northwest corner of the city. I can even put my finger on a curving stretch of that street that includes his old address. It has the look of a suburban area, outside the gridded city blocks: winding "lanes," "ways," and "courts," with the usual fake pastoral names. Millbrook, Birchwood, Havenwood, Chaucer, Leicester Way, Riverdale, Kent Place, Danbury, Archwood. All places, I assume, of sun and palms. And names so redolent of olde England!

They remind me of street names in my own hometown. Arrowwood, Beechwood, Brookfield, Brookside, Cambridge, Cottage, Essex, Sherwood, Shepherd, Thackery, Wedgewood, Wexford Way. So across the continent, Rabbit had come to a place of winding roads that at least sounded like where he had come from. It must have felt strange and perhaps even comforting to know that, just a quarter mile east, his own street turned into Brunswick Avenue.

There are rumors about his time in California, most of them circulated after his death, that served to exalt or demonize him, and put his death in a certain light. Some of his friends "had heard" that he was accepted and given a scholarship to Berkeley, and some local policemen, including Bill Sorgie, "had heard" that he was involved in drug trafficking, had joined the Black Panthers, and was mixed up in some "suspicious death." But I've found no evidence of any of this in the Berkeley admissions office, or in the files of the FBI or of the San Diego Police.

I imagine Rabbit might even have found some weird humor in this, had he been around for his posthumous notoriety. I suspect that his life in San Diego was more ordinary than we all wanted to believe. He was not even there for three full months, a good part of which was surely spent in the dull rigors and happy surprises of settling into a new place. *Where is the nearest grocery store? Where can I buy stuff cheap? Where is the laundromat? Where are the bus routes? Where do I go to look for a job? What jobs are there out here anyway?*

I have only been to San Diego once in my life, and that for a day or two of sight-seeing with my aunt and cousins, in the summer of 1962, when I was nine years old. I remember the wide-openness of the zoo and a big battleship at a pier. I remember the dusty sleaze of Tijuana at dusk, and how different that felt from the crisp coolness of the Vermont–Canadian border that I had also crossed as a child.

Did Rabbit ever take a trip into Mexico, just twelve miles south of the city? And if he did, did he remember that rollicking journey to Canada when he was a boy at Bonnie Brae? I doubt that this time he ran back and forth across the border with all that youthful exuberance. Still, it might have given him some pleasure to think that in his strange, short life thus far, he had been to the top and bottom of the country, and had spanned it east to west.

San Diego de Alcala

Just two miles from Rabbit's forwarding address is California's first Franciscan mission, San Diego de Alcala, built in 1769 to spread the Christian (Catholic) faith. It is a tourist attraction, and this, too, I visited on my trip to San Diego as a kid. In my memory, it looks something like the Alamo as I'd seen it in photographs, all cracked clay or stucco, except this had a tower with a cross on top and bells in big openings like windows. I recall that the weather that day was hot in a bright, dry, lethal way that it never was in New Jersey. There was no getting out of it — too much harsh clarity for seeing, nothing indefinite, no haze to fur the edges of things, no shadows or shade, no trees as I had known them, no arching maples, oaks, elms. Just everything parched, distinct, glaring. Until we went into the mission.

It had the feel of what I imagine it is to walk into a root cellar: cool, gray, earthen; and yet this was big and airy. As I recall, the floor was dirt but everything seemed clean. The coolness had that rich, loamy smell from the ground, as though it had recently rained. Oddly, I remember nothing else inside, no other tourists, no priest, no altar, no religious artifacts. In my mind this has become a perfect place of holiness for a lapsed Protestant, like me. Dark yet airy. Fecund yet clean, ordered, empty. A holiness without the commitment and clarity of strong belief. A holiness of vague feeling and impression. Secular, quiet, peaceful, plenty of room for ambivalence — a feeling not particularly deep or long-lasting, but still convincing, true.

I have no idea if Rabbit ever visited San Diego de Alcala, or if it even crossed his mind. Yet before I take him back across the country to all that will ensue, I want, or need, to imagine him in a place such as this. Here he need not lie on the perilous platform. Here he would be protected, safe. Here all distinctions blur. Here he could be alone, at ease, where he'd feel the cool air and smell the earth, and sense the simple goodness of his living, before going out again in the sun.

Where is the smell of burning leaves? When does the season change? When is the first morning you see your breath? When do they chop wood around here?

There is no clear sense of the seasons in San Diego. So many days, even months, feel the same, one melting into another. So how do you put your finger on the calendar and say, "this is where it happened," or "this was when the die was cast," or "after this, things would be different"? Isn't that what autumn means: when things begin to *fall*, decline? Leaves, lives, the cold rain turning to sleet. How can you tell in San Diego?

And yet something did happen then and there that, unbeknownst to Rabbit, would tip him toward his end. For whatever reason, and for whatever conceived length of time, he decided to return home. Some had heard that Joan Harczku was pregnant, and that they were coming back to get engaged, married, to settle down and start a family.

Or it could have been as simple as this: like most of us after we've gone far away, he needed to come back for a while. And three months away sounds about right, the time between when I first went to college and returned for Thanksgiving. It was just enough time for him to have been on his own, to have allowed him to strut all his independence, without losing what he had depended on.

Christmas, 1972

He returned to New Jersey just before Christmas, about the same time that I returned for the holidays after the fall semester of my sophomore year at college. He didn't stay with the Jeffers, the Bells, or anyone else I know of in town, so I'm guessing that he stayed with his friends in New Brunswick, including Joan Harczku. But during these last few weeks before his death, he was around town, touching base with old friends, hanging out at his old haunts: Buxton's, Pistilli's, the Oaken Bucket, or Buona Pizza in Olcott Square.

Christmas in my hometown has always been a big deal, when we look our best, when we like to think we are still a village, and not a sprawl of housing developments. There is always a huge lighted tree in the center of Olcott Square and an even bigger one on the green in front of the Basking Ridge Presbyterian Church. Beside the tree in Basking Ridge stands a big sleigh, crammed with shining presents, and on Christmas Eve, hundreds gather round, while a small band, barely in tune, leads everyone in caroling. This is the night when my mother would drink a glass of Harveys Bristol Cream and wear her bright red winter coat with black fur around the collar. And it was the night when my father, in one of his rare forays from home, would park the car near the green and sit beside my bundled grandmother, with the heater whirring and the window half open, so she might hear, through hearing aids, the wobbling, wheezing music.

The caroling ended when, near the peak of the church roof below the steeple, a small circular window opened, and three trumpeters stuck out their horns and played "Silent Night." Then the hugs and handshakes. And then the great mahogany doors of the church would open, and Presbyterians, Methodists, and Lutherans alike, devout, lapsed, closet agnostics, and even some Catholics swept up in the tide, would pour in for the candlelight service. This was when Reverend Felmeth was at his best: solemn, loose-jowled, dark and ponderous, yet brimming with the good news. In his deep, quivering voice, he'd read the story of birth and renewal, a son of no earthly father, the savior of mankind, forgiver of sins, born in the straw, in a manger. Then we'd light our candles, and in that shivering, amber, re-deeming light, he'd give us his blessing, the benediction. We'd extinguish the flames, but still feeling their flickering, we'd go out to our cars in the night.

While I can't imagine that Rabbit ever attended such services, he seemed filled then, according to many friends, with a kind of se-rious, inward joy that might or might not have been related to the holiday season. He had been away. He had done what he al-ways said he'd do, and he was back to tell the tale. Moreover, he seemed to have a little cash in his pocket, probably tuna money. He seemed to be purposeful, optimistic, in the midst of some plan he had for himself. He talked to everyone about college.

He saw Joanie Carlton and gave her his poems. He had lunch in New Brunswick with Edlynne Sillman, and lunch some days later with Bob Saracino, an old mentor from Bonnie Brae. With Bob he talked about having a family sometime, about father-hood, and — Bob is sure he remembers this accurately — he talked about discarding the name of Rabbit ("a kid's name") to become, again, William or Bill.

Was this the time that he became engaged, if it ever happened at all? If it did happen, I have a hunch it was then, when he was riding high, feeling his oats, when colored bulbs festooned porches, and plastic Marys, Josephs, and babes garnished front lawns.

Whether engaged or not, or pregnant or not, Joan and Rabbit, like most couples, I suppose, had their secrets that gnawed or glowed, things they nestled to themselves. I imagine on one of their trips to our town, they might, on a whim, have stopped at the Minuteman, where Rabbit had been a busboy. It is still right there, a few miles from Olcott Square, heading north on 202. A big, red, barnlike building, not far from a new cluster of "boutiques" where my mother now gets her hair done. In the last six months, I have stopped in the Minuteman, as it's on the way to the Morristown Rehabilitation Clinic, where my father has been recovering from his stroke. To my eye, it's exactly as it used to be. A chalk board announces Today's Specials in the alcove as you enter:

Clam chowder
Turkey Platter w/ mashed potatoes + string beans
Jumbo Fried Shrimp w/ peas + slaw

Inside, the walls are waxy knotty pine, the color of damp french fries. There's the cash register at the end of the counter where pies lie beneath cloudy domes, upheld on chrome pedestals. Behind, the booths beckon, cozy Naugahyde grottoes with pews set face-to-face.

On either side of a Formica table, Rabbit and Joan slide in. She is blonde, in jeans, a floppy purse, a couple of silver and turquoise bracelets clinking along her arm. There are the usual looks from a few customers. (What is *he* doing with *her?*) But the waitresses in white, like elderly nurses, are happy to see him again. They want to know how he's doing and all about California. They have hair like thin, white, bobbing mists, and Rabbit relaxes in their attention. He tells Joan how just eight months before, he would set these tables and later collect the ketchup-smeared dishes, then haul them in a tub to the kitchen. Now he is sitting here, ordering dinner, with the tinny music from the little speakers overhead, and these plastic sprigs of holly and pine pinned to the ends of their benches. He sees in each of the mullioned windows the neat, repeated triangles of frost, sprayed from an aerosol can. Still, it all has its own quaint appeal, like so many things he sees now as a visitor. Like the wreaths tied to the grills of cars. And even the pallid sameness of all these faces, especially at this time of year. Like mashed potatoes without any gravy. Pasty. Bland. Blanched.

Now comes the waitress with rolls, the shrimp, extra fries. And he is with this girl, a woman really, a little older than he is. She's as white as his palm, as white as the rest, but in her hands she holds both sides of his — white palm and brown top. She drinks him all in.

Is he dreaming? No. He is in the Minuteman, with its unmistakable smell of onion rings. It is Christmas time, good will to men. Again we are bombing North Vietnam, two months after "peace is at hand." But this night here is silent and holy. All is calm, bright. Through the window, the moon skates on cars. There's a star on a distant water tower.

"I have a question to ask you," he says.

She holds both sides of his hands. "And I have something," she says, "to tell *you*."

And now they break their bread.

*   *   *

It was also a good Christmas for Bill Sorgie, and it had been a good year. He was now the father of an adopted four-year-old girl from Korea — he has her photo, today, on his desk. Between this and his work, his life seemed full, and work was busy, going well. After six months on the job, in early July, he had gotten an $800 raise. In August, Chief Kenney retired, and the position was filled by Fred Steinkoph, a straight-from-the-shoulder, no-nonsense cop, a Navy man, intensely loyal to his men, a man whom now, many years after his death, Sorgie calls his "main role model." Then in October, two more patrolmen were hired on, easing some of the work and bringing the force to sixteen. Sorgie liked both new men: Gabe Treppicone and particularly Pat Forsythe, a twenty-one-year-old baby-faced "kid," described in his yearbook as "a cute little guy," who had lived all his life in Bernardsville.

The job itself had gone pretty much as expected. A lot of traffic details. There were the usual patrols and radar traps where kids raced their GTOs. Or he'd stand for hours on the small, white-painted circle in the middle of the road, with his arms going and whistle chirping, directing cars through Olcott Square.

If anything about the job surprised and bugged him, it was the "gin mill calls" on Friday and Saturday nights. There were four bars that I recall in town. Florio's, the Claremont, and across the street from one another in Olcott Square: the Old Stone, and the Three Lights Tavern. Except for the Three Lights, I have been in all of these at one time or another. For the most part, they were typical small-town bars. Cloying smoke, dark wood, sticky bar stools, guys in jeans with drinks and cues, a wedge of light above the pool table, the smell of beer in linoleum cracks, and that sharp whiff when the men's room door opened: mentholated urinal cakes.

All during the work week, these bars were quiet, but for the occasional click of pool balls and the rustle of weary conversation. Some nights these places were almost dead, and Jimmy

Vilade at the Old Stone wouldn't even bother with last call; he'd turn off the lights early.

On weekend nights, though, guys crammed the bars, and sometimes things got crazy, especially at the Three Lights. It was the darkest and deepest of all the dives — thirty-five-cent beers on tap, leather jackets, tattoos, its clientele more "hard core." I remember seeing some of those guys around: Claude Hopson, Allan Rome, and big, bearded George Moore. There were townies and greasers, Ferrante's truckers, and sometimes even bikers and babes from out of town, from Passaic, Union, Plainfield. They'd mix it up pretty good. No one "carried metal," no knives or guns, but fists, cues, and pool balls flew. The cops called it "The Bucket of Blood," right there in Olcott Square, right next to the Brookdale Deli.

The call would usually come in around midnight from Eddie Ghilain, the Three Lights' owner, as the shifts were changing at police headquarters. Then two patrolmen, but often only one, would speed over, and carrying blackjacks and wearing leather "zap" gloves with lead-shot knuckles, they'd wade into the melee, shoving, punching, and prying people apart, then hauling a few back to the station. It sounds manly and heroic, but it quickly wore thin. The cops got bruised, bitten, spat upon; they were "pigs" rolling in sweat and beer-puke, cursing, brawling, and busting heads, to make for law and order.

When he had duty on these nights, Sorgie went to work with a knot in his stomach, though often by one or two in the morning, if no calls had come in, the knot would loosen, and he would cruise the quiet, winding streets, as cars turned soberly into driveways, then the last of the bedroom lights winked off, and the yards were smoothed in moonlight. On other nights he'd barely have his uniform buttoned when he'd be hustling to the car, heart pumping, siren wailing, hands flexing in leaden gloves — he a decorated veteran, a husband, a child's father — going to fight like a punk in an alley.

But this Christmas, he wasn't thinking too much about

that. The bars, though full, seemed to settle down, on good behavior for the holidays. At home his daughter brightened their lives; she was holding them all together. In the new year his salary would increase to $11,000, and already he was putting money away for a home out in Hunterdon County. As more men came on the force, he'd gain seniority, and he'd do less of the fighting. All in all, things were looking up. In Olcott Square, the stores were decked out. Giant candy canes and snowflakes wobbled on phone poles. Shoppers shook your hand. This year he'd hang a stocking over the fireplace, and these evenings, the lights danced along Springfield Avenue, just like when he was a kid.

Twenty-one

During high school and the years shortly thereafter, while I was entering my so-called adulthood, there were two magical birthdays, two jewels along the road, that might redeem all our sullen, acned days, and give life spark and meaning. At seventeen we could legally drive, and at twenty-one we could legally drink.

That is not to say that everyone waited until the approved moment to partake of these awesome privileges. Think of all the sixteen-year-olds who took the family car out on Whitenack Road when the folks were away for the evening. Or how many of us at eighteen or nineteen haven't piled into bottomed-out cars heading east, over the black meadows and through the tunnel, to some dive in the city to "get served," blitzed, ripped off, scared, and then to race the dawn in the rearview mirror, to stagger out a few doors from home, sneak up the stairs, holding your breath, and somehow slide back into sheets?

All of this happens long before it is sanctioned, and yet the sanctioning still has its wonder. Suddenly you are legal. You are confirmed. What was wrong one day is all right the next. You can drive through the middle of Olcott Square, waving at the cops. You can pick up your girl at her parent's split-level and hit Point Pleasant by noon. At bars, you don't sweat if you get carded. You just walk in, order, and there's your beer. You are free, or what we thought of as free.

Unlike the rest of us, Rabbit didn't have this magic on his seventeenth birthday. He never had a car at his disposal; he never had a license. But it must have happened on his twenty-first, on Friday, January 5, 1973, when according to New Jersey state law, he was no longer a "minor." From then on, he could walk into and out of any bar he wanted, hassle free.

I suppose on the night of his birthday itself, he made the rounds of some local bars in New Brunswick. It's what you do on your twenty-first birthday. Beers, bourbon, Southern Comfort. Friends stand you drinks 'til you're barely standing, bilious with all that freedom. *Here's to Jim Beam, Jack Daniels, the weed out in the glove box. Here's to life, liberty, and the pursuit of happiness, mom (mom?), and apple pie. Here's to Trenton. Here's to Bonnie Brae, Fred, Doug, Cy. To Jackie, Marian, Joanne, Joanie, Joan (all the Joans I've known). Here's to Ruth, Robert, Marty Lou, Hap. Wretch? Here girl! Where are you? And Charles, yes: hang in, hang on. Gotta get back there before I leave. Gotta get back there soon.*

According to friends, Rabbit thought he'd never make it past his twenty-first birthday; he was star-crossed, marked, a young and tragic hero. Before adulthood, he'd go down in flames, like James Dean, Jim Morrison, Jimi, Janis, Duane. He was born at 4:35 in the afternoon, or so said his birth certificate. And now, twenty-one years and eight hours later, he was crocked, reeling, but very much alive. Already it was after midnight, January 6, the day they call Epiphany. He might have felt spared or passed over. He had made it safely across some line.

*   *   *

During the next few days, Rabbit called some old friends from our town, Rusty Cook, among others. He said he'd be up here the next weekend, certainly next Friday night.

How long was he around for?

'Til he went back to Cally. Maybe a couple of weeks.

How was he doing?

Cool. Hangin' loose.

So where would they meet?

He'd drop by. They could hit the bars. "Man, you realize I just turned twenty-one?"

Shit, let's celebrate.

So the next weekend with old friends, in Olcott Square, he'd mark his birthday once more.

After Epiphany

If Bill Sorgie looked at the *Newark Star Ledger* as he drank his coffee on Monday, January 8, he couldn't have missed the headline.

1 GUNMAN SLAIN
10 Killed by Sniper at N. Orleans Hotel

Then he would have stared, appalled by the big photograph right beside the headline: a uniformed policeman sprawled on his back, eyes closed and head cockeyed against a tree trunk, his face and chest covered with blood, and another policeman, grimacing and with bedraggled hair, leaning over, trying to comfort his dying comrade.

In the long story, continuing on page six, Sorgie would

have read of a rifle-carrying "light-complexioned black with long hair," who had apparently gone on a rampage, who, perhaps with another gunman, had set fires on the upper floors of a Howard Johnson Motor Lodge, had shot and killed a couple on their second honeymoon, and then had climbed to the hotel roof, where for more than thirteen hours he had shot "at anything in uniform," wounding seventeen and killing four policemen. Finally machine-gun fire from a Marine helicopter gunship killed the gunman after he reportedly cursed and taunted police, crying "Come and get me!" and "Power to the people!"

In the next day's paper, this was again the lead story, eclipsing even the resumption of talks to achieve a cease-fire in Vietnam. A force of about two hundred police had searched the hotel and stormed the roof in a vain attempt to find a possible second gunman. Beside the headline yet another grisly photo: the "bullet-shredded corpse" of the long-haired, light-complexioned black sniper, an ooze of matter on a pebbled roof, pooled beside an air vent.

The gunman was identified in the following day's paper as Mark Essex, twenty-three, of Emporia, Kansas, a Navy man discharged for "unsuitability." His rifle, it turned out, was earlier used to kill yet another New Orleans policeman, a black man, on New Year's Eve. On January 11, Essex's history was further probed, for the first time off the front page. Here he was described as a "black militant" with "a very severe hatred for white people." According to a seaman who knew Essex, "these young blacks are educated and they know what is going on. They're not going to take it any more. That's the way he was. He was full of it and that [the rampage and killing of police] is what happens."

After running for five consecutive days — the five days before Rabbit was shot — the story left the pages of the *Star Ledger* with a wrap-up report ("New Orleans still baffled about number of snipers") on January 12. I don't know for a fact that Bill Sorgie read these exact news articles that I have dug out of the library. But I know that he closely followed this story every day — at least that's what he says he did. Today Sorgie cannot recall the name of Mark Essex, yet he clearly remembers that a black man on the roof of a Howard Johnson's shot and killed a number of policemen, and that he in turn was killed by "a helicopter strafing run." "You have to remember," he tells me now, "that cops could be targets then."

Certainly this story, like any number of others that lived in the mind of Bill Sorgie at the time, didn't cause and doesn't explain Rabbit's death. I believe, however, that it was a small part of a complicated mix, a part of a climate of heightened fear, suspicion, even paranoia, that helped make the unthinkable possible. Less than twenty-four hours after the last report from New Orleans appeared in the newspapers curled on our driveways, Rabbit was dead in Olcott Square.

I have just written of the "last report from New Orleans." But that's not absolutely true. Indeed, no more articles about the sniper appeared in the *Star Ledger,* though on page 28 of the January 14 edition, there was one more photograph. Its caption began "RITES FOR NEW ORLEANS SNIPER —" and in the photo six men carry the casket bearing Mark Essex from a church toward the open door of a hearse.

Here then, was the real last of the New Orleans story. And here, too, if you were looking closely, was the beginning of another.

In the lower right corner of the same page, about three inches below the photograph and just above an ad for maple bedroom furniture, there appeared a small headline above a short, sketchy, developing story about an "incident" in — of all places — Bernardsville:

Cop shoots man at door of tavern

A Bernardsville patrolman fatally shot a man emerging from a local tavern carrying a concrete-based "no parking" sign yesterday, authorities said. The victim was identified as William Wells, 20 [he was 21], of Basking Ridge. Neighboring police squads and the State Police tactical unit were required to disperse a crowd which formed for about two hours after the incident.

Felling the Trees

Sometime early during that week of January 7, 1973, the week of the New Orleans story, I packed my car, checked the oil and the pressure in my retread snow tires, then, hitting a blazing top speed of fifty-one miles per hour, I shot west and north back to college to begin my "January term." I didn't see Rabbit during my stay at home for the holidays; it wouldn't have occurred to me. Or if I did see him, it would have only been in passing and I don't remember it now.

It has always been during that week after Epiphany that the local road departments take down the big Christmas trees in the centers of Bernardsville and Basking Ridge. First a man in the high bucket of the cherry picker unwinds the strands of colored bulbs from around each tree, then other men loosen the guy wires on one side, while still others, holding the opposite lines, let it down, hand over hand, onto a flatbed trailer. Suddenly there is gray, empty air above the greens, and sod where the trees had stood.

These are the cold, leaden days in our towns, when Olcott Square is almost empty of shoppers, when people walk briskly to trains and cars, turning their collars up. Strapped on the trailers, the trees are hauled to the dump, shedding along the road. Beside the huge ditch where the garbage trucks unload, the men drag them off the trailers and leave them for anyone with a chain saw. For months you might see them there browning in the sun, collecting bits of paper and plastic; or even as late as the following summer, faintly, beyond all the other odors, you might smell their weeping pitch.

Friday, January 12

Here, according to the *Star Ledger,* was THE WEATHER PICTURE:

Sunny and bracing

Mostly sunny skies and cold temperatures are forecast today in North and Central Jersey, with an expected high around 30. Winds will be northwesterly at 10 to 20 miles per hour. Temperatures in the teens are forecast for tonight.

Indeed, this would be one of the colder days in New Jersey that winter, and one of the coldest nights. A mass of dry, arctic air was moving southeast through Ontario, New York, Pennsylvania, and Jersey. Temperatures would dip and winds would increase as the day wore on.

So as Rabbit dressed to go out on that last morning of his life, I imagine he wore a heavy coat, with a scarf and gloves. Like the weather, he too might have felt cold, yet sunny, braced, for today he had visiting to do, and tonight: his birthday again.

Maybe his own birthday reminded him that today, the twelfth, was Bobby Jeffers' birthday, and so, probably with Joan Harczku driving, he first stopped by, unannounced, at the

Jeffers' house. It was midmorning. Robert Sr. was at work, but Bobby was home from college. Ruth also recalls being there, and so, by chance, was Marian.

How strangely familiar it must have been for Rabbit to walk into that place where, more than two years before, he had been welcomed when he had had to leave Bonnie Brae. Marian had moved out, married now, and they had sold her horses. In the pasture where he had once seen Marian ride, now tan, brownish grasses, high as bushes, shivered in the breeze. But there's the stump where he had chopped firewood on a morning almost as cold as this. And there's the kitchen table where he'd talked with Robert, and here is the counter where he'd found his dinner on those nights he came in late. Though he doesn't go up there, he knows that at the top of the stairs is Marian's old bedroom door, where, on that very last night, he had stood shaking and clench-ing — she so sweet with that guy on the phone. And then he had done what he still can't believe, that odd little "huh" that came out with her breath. It was almost a hiccup, not even a cry. And then her hair spilling back as she fell, all crumpled and small on the floor.

Yes, he must have remembered this — in the back of his throat and in the wide bones of his hand — and she must have remembered it too, their eyes touching and flying away. But now she is married, so much has happened, and he is trying to introduce her to Joan. He is making a hash of it until, flustered, he turns to Bobby, and Marian touches Joan lightly on the el-bow, and the two of them, as though instantly familiar, go off to the living room to talk.

When they come out, Joan is smiling, and Marian looks Rabbit full in the face, then rises on tiptoe to kiss him, her lips again on his skin. It is the same and so different. *So much has happened*. There is a sense about her then that she carries to this day: that she will not forget what he did on that night, but she doesn't hate him; she might, from this distance, still even love him. She will not forget the good things either.

After this, it is all much easier. The birthday wishes. The old jive with Bobby, slaps on the back, and the talk about California. Could he surf? Hang ten? Was he still doing his photography? Sculpture? Did he have time now to chop a few cords of wood? — the maul was waiting in the garage. Or could they at least stay for lunch?

No, they had to take off soon.

Scooping mayonnaise into a mixing bowl, Ruth, I suppose, is all ears, her house filled again with their banter, with Rabbit's particular blustering banter, the way he lounges back in a chair, his legs sprawled like keys on a ring, all that space that he makes his own. Stories, memories, jokes, dreams; such earnest, wild, wonderful plans. Their lives extending and leafing out, her mind riding their veins.

Somehow they have all turned out all right. Ruth remembers feeling good that morning. She was smiling inside. *Look at them. Once they filled these hands. You make sandwiches, soothe, scold, try not to scorch. Then they are gone, everything quiet. And then they are back — "just passing by" — to show how distant, grown, how different they are. And how they haven't really changed.*

That is what I imagine her thinking when Rabbit, with one arm, hugs her shoulders, pinching her breath, and with the other dips a finger into the bowl.

"Tuna. Ichhh!"

He's doing all right. That is what she'd be thinking when, with Joan, he bangs out the door, calling, teasing, "Stay out of trouble. Don't do anything I wouldn't do."

I'm not sure where, precisely, Rabbit went from the Jeffers'. I assume he and Joan had lunch somewhere. Maybe they got subs at the Pepper Mill Deli or sat on those creaky stools at the Village Fountain. At any rate, by midafternoon he showed up at the Saracinos', where Joan dropped him off. She might have just been feeling tired or had something to do back in New

Brunswick, and Rabbit would be hanging out here in Basking
Ridge and Bernardsville, visiting and celebrating that night.
He'd be returning late, or he'd crash at some friend's and get a
ride in the morning — he'd give her a call later. So I imagine
they both said, "See you," as he shut the car door. And maybe
Joan might remember other details: his light-flecked hair in the
winter sun, or the long, billowing plumes of his breath, whipping away in the breeze. It was one of those partings that you'd
only remember — how wonderfully ordinary! — if you never
saw that person again.

The Saracinos, Bob and Bev, were thrilled to see Rabbit.
Together they went back to his Bonnie Brae days: Bev the volunteer dental assistant who made the boys gargle and floss; Bob
the recreation director; and Rabbit the freckled fourteen-year-
old from Trenton, with ears like funnels and those scared brown
eyes. The Saracinos were still working at Bonnie Brae, but that
day Bev was off and Bob didn't have to get back until an evening
event, so they had the rest of the afternoon to visit.

"It was wonderful," Bob remembers, "He seemed so at
ease and so grown-up." They laughed about the old days, the
trip to Canada, the overnight camping at Hacklebarney Park —
Bob taking sixteen city boys to the woods, all of them wide
awake, frightened of chipmunks, farting and giggling in sleeping
bags, their flashlights beaming until dawn.

Mostly, though, they spoke of the future. If Rabbit's plans
in California didn't work out, Bob, ever practical, thought he
should come back and go to Somerset County College, just
like Doug and Fred. But Rabbit was always a little different, and
determined in his difference. Bob liked that about him, though
he didn't altogether understand it — "you know, the artsy
thing."

As evening came on, Bev insisted that Rabbit stay for early
supper, and now I think of the three of them in that red Cape
Cod on South Maple Avenue, on the long straightaway where
Cross Road comes in, where Harrison Bell used to let his T-bird

unwind. Outside the front windows, traffic is picking up, people driving home from work or shopping, done for the week; people like my mother, who had spent the afternoon yawning and grading papers at her school; people now tucked into cars, their windows up, defrosters whirring, their minds, like the sun, spreading, dimming, easing through trees to the ground. On trains, weary commuters watch the gray, streaming land, dozing, their ties loosened. It is that time of day and that time of the week when we are borne back to our homes.

And this Cape Cod, though perhaps a little smaller, was much like any of our homes. Shingles, shrubs, a macadam driveway. The smell of hamburgers spill into the evening through a small, hooded exhaust fan. In the kitchen the first lights come on, and through storm windows you might see shapes reach toward cupboards, set a table, and pull up chairs all around.

This was Rabbit's last meal, an unremarkable meal, except that while eating he said he was thinking of becoming "William" or "Bill" instead of "Rabbit." Bob thought it was a terrific idea, and he still does. "He was renaming himself, becoming an individual." And so, as he speaks to me from Oregon, Bob calls him "Bill" or "Bill Wells," and never, not once, "Rabbit." He is the only person I know of who does this, something proud and obstinate in his voice.

On his way to work that evening, around six o'clock, Bob dropped Rabbit off in the Woolworth's parking lot where Rabbit said he would meet some old friends and get a ride to the Bells'. All that Bob remembers of their trip was the two of them joking about Rabbit's afro.

"How will we get *that* into the car?"

"You ought to get a sun roof!" Rabbit said.

When he got out, the air was cold, the sky dark, save for the tissue of orange light beyond the Bernardsville hills that I could see from my window as a kid. Woolworth's was closed, just the fish tanks glowing in the back. In the Shop Rite lot across 202, guys were collecting the scattered shopping carts, nesting them one into another, and pushing them like long, clattering trains, then leaving them beside the automatic doors, where shoppers would unnest them again.

Rabbit said thanks for the ride and dinner. It had been great to see them both again.

Bob said, and meant, that it was a pleasure. Then he beeped and drove off toward Olcott Square, went around the flagpole, and south on Mount Airy, heading toward Bonnie Brae.

After work that night, Bob would get home around eleven, turn off the lights, and go to bed. He was sound asleep when, about three hours later, the phone woke him.

Bev fumbled for the receiver, picked it up, and she didn't say a word. A crank call, Bob figured, or a wrong number. Then she said, "Billy Wells is dead."

"But he was just here," Bob remembers saying, as if that settled it.

She said, "They want you to go to the station."

Ridiculous.

"I'm not kidding."

So again the lights came on in the windows of the red Cape Cod, and if you were passing by, you would have seen shapes moving hurriedly about — as if hurrying could make a difference.

Bob dressed and drove back through Olcott Square, this time heading west out Route 202. He was the first to identify Rabbit's body. An officer took him into a small room and opened the end of a long bag. It seemed like a sleeping bag, the kind you'd take on a camping trip, except that it was zipped all around, even over the head. Bob says that he could barely look. A young man in a bag. "I just saw the side of his face, his hair, then I nodded and turned away."

*   *   *

But hours before this, Rabbit was standing in the Woolworth's parking lot, waving as Bob drove off. I see him turning up his collar against the wind, and shoving his hands into his coat pockets. This is an old feeling for him: waiting for someone to show up. Usually they do; sometimes they don't, and he'd walk or hitch to wherever he wanted to go. Next he is planning to visit the Bells. They should be done with dinner by now.

I don't know precisely what happened in the hour or so between when Rabbit was dropped off at Woolworth's and when he arrived at the Bells'. But I have a small scenario in mind that, though it may not have happened exactly then, did happen any number of times — or so say most of his friends.

A pair of headlights turns into the Woolworth's entrance, sweeps the lot, and fastens on him. With his hand he shades his eyes as the car approaches. Is it Rusty? Or one of the guys?

No, it's a Bernardsville police car pulling up. The car window rolls down, a breath of heated air. "You got some place to go?"

Rabbit doesn't recognize the officer. The man's voice is smooth and firm. "Yeah," Rabbit says. "I'm waiting for friends."

"Well, you better get to where you're going. It's getting cold."

Rabbit doesn't say anything.

"Soon," the officer adds, a little more firmly. Then he rolls up his window and drives slowly toward the exit, a feather of smoke behind.

Between them, they understand that in about ten minutes the officer will return, and if Rabbit is still there, hanging around, things could be less polite. It is such a small incident, one of so many such small incidents, yet it takes all the shine from the night. It reminds him of why he left this place, of what still churns in his mind: how in the same town, at the same time, he can feel so loved and so unwanted.

He waits until the police car's taillights have gone, then he walks out to the road. From behind the Shop Rite comes the rush of the train, its thin whistle like an old dream, and maybe he wonders if his hut is still back there, or if it's been taken down. He passes Gardner Volkswagen, where I used to buy car parts. Out front, the showrooms are dark behind windows, and the Dairy Queen next door is also dark, boarded up, closed until Memorial Day. He turns onto Finley Avenue, and walking backward, holds out his thumb. It occurs to him then that in this town, this life, he has walked more miles backward than forward, feeling his way with his heels.

A half mile later, he turns onto Cherry Lane where, getting close to the Bells' on a residential street, he doesn't bother to hitchhike. He quickens his pace, his toes and ears getting numb, past our house, the Guibards', the Dickinsons', Carlins', Graterexes', Normans', and Rehms' — all houses set back from the road, snug amid shrubbery, with lights behind closed curtains. He goes up the hill, breathing hard, and onto Walnut Circle. Now there is no faint orange glow in the sky, just the stars, clear and cold.

The lights are on at the Bells' house as well. As he walks up the brick path his steps seem loud. He rings the doorbell where he used to go straight in, and while he waits, he rocks from foot to foot, shivering and sweating a little.

Martha opens the door and doesn't move. "Stunned," is how she describes it now. "I thought — we all thought — he was far away, in California. But there he was, all of him."

She remembers hugging him, the bigness of him, all packed in his heavy coat. More than the words they spoke, more than the details of gesture and clothing, what she holds in her mind is what she felt in her arms: his bulk, his density, the width, height, and breadth of his live body, holding her in the doorway.

"He looked great" is all she can say of his appearance. She showed him right in. Rabbit and Harrison shook hands and embraced. Harrison remembers him wearing a snazzy vest beneath his coat, and remembers he wore no hat.

They said all the things you say on these occasions. What a surprise! Take off your coat. Judy, come on down. Guess who's here? Guess who's looking like a million bucks?

As for Rabbit, I imagine his eyes adjusting to the change of light. *How, in the same town, at the same time . . . ?* You'd think they hadn't seen him in years.

When Judy, the Bells' daughter, comes downstairs, he says, "Hi Sis. What's new?"

They hug and she stands back, checking him out. "Pretty sharp," she says.

He says, "Next time I'll have to charge you for touching these threads."

That is what she has held in her mind all these years, a little joke, a tease.

Now they all want him to sit down, relax. He looks cold. Has he had dinner?

Yes.

How long can he stay?

Just a little while. He's heading back into B'ville. "Where's Charles?" he asks.

Upstairs. He's already down for the night. But I imagine Martha saying she could wake him up. "He'd love to see you again."

Rabbit says don't bother. He'll be around for another week or so. He'll be back. He can see Charles next time.

For a while, they talk about how he's been doing in California and what's been going on around here. Then he says that what he could use is a good, hot shower, and Martha gets him a towel.

In the streaming water, as I see him there, he seems to wash away the cold, the bright headlights that passed him by, and that spinning feather of smoke, red-glowing in taillights, as the police car pulled away. The water relaxes his back and shoulders, warmth pounding softly into him, and soon, I suppose, he is David Ruffin and the Temptations, floating back to another time, those sugary harmonies, the strings coming in, and his fingers popping, even with suds in his palms.

> I got sunshi-a-ine on a cloudy day,
> When it's cold outsi-a-ide, I got the month of May.
> I guess you'd say,
> What can make me feel this way?
> My girl, my girl, my girl,
> Talkin' 'bout my gir-a-irl.
> My girl!
> Whooo-a-whooooooo. . . .

He towels off, wipes the mirror, and puts back on his boots, faded jeans, wide belt, and the new silk shirt with its big, pointed collar. From a pocket he pulls out the deer's tooth strung on the leather thong. He adjusts the thong around his neck so the tooth dangles over his chest. He slides into his vest, the front unbuttoned, cool and casual. With his pick he combs out his hair, checks its loft and sheen. He slides the pick back into his rear pocket, its shape imprinted on his ass, the handle in clear view. He *does* look like a million bucks.

Downstairs again, he throws on his coat, says his thanks and good-byes. There is often this dramatic flair about him, blowing in and whisking off, his scarf fluttering behind.

Judy remembers asking him, "When will we see you again?"

"Soon," he called over his shoulder. He was already out in the night.

He walked across the street to the Cuttings' for yet another reunion. It was the usual Friday night scene over there. Rusty Cook, Andy Cutting, Jim Gault, Tom King, among others. Hanging out, guitars in laps, smoking, drinking, Led Zeppelin booming "Whole Lotta Love," but no girls in sight. Rusty re-members Rabbit having a beer and a shot of Southern Comfort. "He loved that stuff. He was in a groove." As for himself, Rusty had a stomach bug, couldn't drink, and felt too lousy to go out. He managed to stay up until about ten when everyone else left. Then, for the first time since he could remember, he went to bed early.

With some others who were at the Cuttings', Rabbit got a ride to Olcott Square. The square, at that time, was almost pitch dark. There were none of the big, bright street lights then, and the stores were all closed, awnings rolled up tight above show-room windows. Only when a car went around the tiny green would Rabbit have seen the neat letters and logos over the shops. Mansfield's Pharmacy, Salmon's Five-and-Ten, Autumn House Furniture, or the Dutch Boy in overalls above the paint store, with his red cheeks and sandy hair: there for an instant, like some sweet reminder, and gone again in the darkness.

On that night he would have heard the slap of the long, cleated rope against the flagpole, and that peculiar, wobbling metallic sound when Stop signs are blown in the wind. Here and there on the sidewalks stood a couple of portable No Parking signs, set out by the police, each about four feet high, its post fixed in a cube of concrete. These, too, made that weird wob-bling sound when the wind kicked through the streets.

About the only real light came from the north end of the square, from the Old Stone Hotel and Tap Room, with its small, square ground-floor windows and the sallow lamp above the narrow door that went down into the bar. The Old Stone was constructed in 1840, a long, thin, shiplike building wedged into the space between Mill Street and Anderson Hill Road. It was, in fact, made from old stone, gray granite, probably from the quarry that became Ferrante's Quarry out beyond the police station. Once it was a classy carriage-stop, a place to have dinner and rest the horses before the last climb to the mansions in the hills. By the time I was growing up, though, it was down at the heels. The second-floor balcony had burned down. It was less a hotel than a rooming house upstairs, and the quaint-sounding Tap Room, a few steps below street level, was just another dive.

That is, unless it was *your* dive. In the year or so before Rabbit had left for California, he would drop in at the Old Stone, usually on weekends. He was underage but he didn't look it, and Jimmy Vilade, the bartender and a friend of Rabbit's, wasn't about to card him. He'd have a few beers, shoot pool, and shoot the breeze, his cigarette hanging on his lips. According to friends, you'd often see him chatting up girls, or leaning against the piano where Charlie "Garbage Man" Webb would play, still pungent in his overalls from work.

It was that sort of place. Low-ceilinged, warm, ripe, scruffy. And as Rabbit walked in the door that night, he would have felt the wind lift from his face and the smoky light ushering him in like a friend.

Today the Old Stone has become Freddy's, an upscale bar and restaurant for the young professionals in town. A hostess in a black jumpsuit shows you to your table with fresh flowers where guys used to shoot pool. In the back room, where the Ping-Pong table always stood, lies a small dance floor with an overhead screen for music videos and space every Friday night for live music. A huge cappuccino and espresso machine looms behind the reconfigured bar, where the bartender, in a black tie, draws imported beer on tap. The piano is gone. The place is smokeless. But the walls are still stone, the light dim, and the hand-hewn beams sag just above you, where Rabbit would have ducked his head.

So as I sit at Freddy's with a warm Watney's lager, it is still possible to imagine him here, all those years ago. The Old Stone didn't serve beer on tap, and certainly nothing imported, so he was drinking Schaefer or Pabst, and probably straight from the bottle. About seventy-five people were jammed in that night, a mix of town and college kids still around after the holidays. The mood, as Jimmy Vilade remembers, was "festive but low-key."

Word got round of Rabbit's return and recent birthday, so there were high fives and soul-brother handshakes. I suppose Rabbit tossed his coat on the pile on top of the piano, and someone handed him a beer. People remember him playing pool that night, a quarter a game, with Tom Pinson, Fred Wickemyer, Lew Morrow, John Gier, Scott Carlson, and Kip Nickerson. Between shots, he talked with "Sinful" Cindy Kline, who was showing off her legs at the bar. He was "going on about California," Tom remembers, how it was the greatest place in the world, never cold like this, how pot was cheap and good. This was Rabbit at his windiest, chalking his cue, in a groove, the deer's tooth swaying, the Southern Comfort glowing inside him — he must have been sinking some balls.

Tom Pinson is a few years older than me. I remember him as a happy-go-lucky football lineman with small, deep eyes that seemed too close together. He was a friend of Rabbit's, but a closer friend of Cy Hardy's, and at one point that night, it occurred to Tom that since they were celebrating Rabbit's birthday, he and Rabbit ought to drive over to the Killians' where Cy was staying, pick him up, and go somewhere more exciting. But then Tom remembered his horoscope for the day, which he still hasn't forgotten: "Take it easy. Don't do anything rash." So almost as fast as he had brought it up, he nixed his own idea. Today it still bugs him, that horoscope. "I wish I had ignored it. If I had followed my instincts, if we had gotten out of there, nothing really bad would have happened." Instead, he racked up again. "Your break," he said to Rabbit. They'd take it easy tonight.

At about 11:10, Pat Forsythe, who just a month before had graduated from the police academy and come on the Bernardsville force, was getting ready to go into work. He would finish watching the news, weather, and sports — all the hype for the Super Bowl on Sunday. Then he'd get his gear and go over to headquarters. On weekends, he didn't like the midnight shift. It was either too boring or too surprising. And moreover, he was recently married. At this time on a Friday night, he and his wife should be out on the town or sliding into the sheets. He was twenty-one years old, just Rabbit's age, a year older than I was. He flicked off the tube, got a cup of coffee, and he remembers saying to his wife, "I think it's going to be a long night."

Over in Basking Ridge, in his study looking across Maple Avenue at the dark swaying oak in the graveyard, Reverend Felmeth was finishing his sermon and reviewing the Order of Worship for Sunday's service, as he often did on Friday nights. He has always loved the *order* in the Order of Worship, the ritual, the giving over of himself to something larger, more or less prescribed, and the peace that often comes with it. As usual the service would begin with the Doxology, and then his Call to Worship. The choir would sing Hymn 433, "Christ is made," and he would offer a Prayer of Thanks and Our Prayer of Confession. Then he would give the Assurance of God's Pardon, the Welcome to Guests, followed by the Reading and Pondering of the Word. This Sunday he would read from Matthew 12, about Christ's healing of the man with the withered hand, in defiance of the laws of the sabbath. He would read it because, in the end, he values compassion most, even above ritual and law.

> What man shall there be among you, that shall have one sheep, and if it fall into a pit on the sabbath day, will he not lay hold on it, and lift it out? How much then is a man better than a sheep?

The reverend pushes up his glasses and rubs his puffy eyes. It is getting late, things winding down, just an occasional car on the road. He stands and turns off his lamp, his sermon still spread on his desk. He doesn't know it of course, but by this time on the following night, he will be thinking about another ritual, about what in the world he might possibly say that could make any sense, that could heal.

By 11:20, Bill Sorgie was well on the road. He had looked in on his daughter asleep in her bed, and kissed his wife good-night. In his blue '69 Cornet 500, he drove west out Springfield Avenue, then north through Millington, and over the dark Passaic. The river wasn't frozen over then, but ice had crept out from the banks, like skin on the edge of a wound. He went up South Maple, around the green in Basking Ridge, and on into Bernardsville. Olcott Square was quiet and dark, except for the seeping glow from the Old Stone and, across the street, from the Three Lights Tavern. It was windy and bitter, a night for huddling and staying put, and maybe just that, the crush of cold, would keep things quiet tonight. Pulling down the driveway and into headquarters, he could see in the starlight the frozen pond, just that long gash of water in the middle. By morning it would all be ice, a clean sheet, and there would be skaters by noon.

When he went into the squad room about 11:30, he checked the Incident Report from the previous shift — nothing happening — and talked with the sergeant on duty. Tonight he'd be on with George Salko, the old-timer, and Pat Forsythe, the kid. They were down a patrol car that was in the shop, so Forsythe and Sorgie would double up in one car, and Salko would patrol alone.

As usual he had already half-dressed at home. He was wearing his shined shoes and crisp pants with the wide, yellow stripe on either side. At his locker now he took off his coat and high-rise holster, and got into the rest of his uniform: his blue whipcord shirt and starched collar, straight off a hanger from the cleaner's; then his tie in a perfect triangular knot, and the clip with the long infantry rifle, smack above his heart. Next he pinned his name tag over his right shirt pocket, and his badge over the left.

In the eleven months since he had been suiting up like this, five days a week, on whatever shift, he had never grown tired of the process. You do one small thing and then another. Each thing has its reasoned place. The shining clip, name tag, and badge — a constellation across his chest. *This is who I am. This is what I do.* The uniform says it all. When he looks in the mirror he likes what he sees: his trim black mustache and hair, his smile, his square jaw. On one hand he wears his wedding band, and on the other his 196th Light Infantry Brigade ring with its insignia, a twisted cord, burning at both ends. Now he thrums his fingers on the top of his hat, which is pleasantly tight, a drum. He puts it on and gets it just right, pulling the visor down.

This is how, when he dreams, he imagines himself. Hard but friendly. Sharp and clean. Straight lines and right angles. It makes him feel whole, this man in the mirror. And what he sees now means it's time for work, time to do what he believes he does best. He is a husband, a father, a man in a uniform, two weeks shy of his twenty-fourth birthday. From his locker, he takes out his heavy belt, and slides his gun, his Colt .38 Police Special, into his duty holster.

January 13, 1973

At midnight, while Rabbit was shooting pool at the Old Stone and Bill Sorgie was coming on duty, "Dyno" Donnie Erwin was sitting at the bar in the Three Lights Tavern with "Rank" Rich Reijtmar. Erwin was the guy whom Sorgie had met at Berkeley Auto Body, the guy with the spray-painted Road Runner, who had played AAA ball for Cincinnati, and had the Southern Cross on his watch. In the year or so since then, Erwin had been driving a dump truck for Ferrante's Quarry. The pay wasn't bad, but he could always use more, so he was looking for a night job and had heard that the Three Lights might need another bartender and bouncer — things had been getting rough there of late.

A few days before, he had bought a new $300 camel hair sports coat, and tonight he was wearing it with a tie, as he sat there, waiting for the right moment to ask Eddie Ghilain, the owner, about giving him a job. Because he had recently been diagnosed with an ulcer, Erwin was drinking ginger ale, straight, possibly the first ginger ale ever consumed or even contemplated in the Three Lights. He was stone cold sober, and I suppose he thought that this, too, might impress Eddie Ghilain.

Rich Reijtmar, with whom Erwin was passing the time that night, was the thinnest person I've ever seen. He had that stretched, almost disappearing look of certain Giacometti figures, except that hanging on top, like some ragged pennant, was a headful of very long, scraggly hair, with an equally long and scraggly beard. Like Erwin, he drove a truck for Ferrante's and was known for his hot temper. He was called "Rank" Rich — a term of awed endearment — because whatever space there was inside his body seemed wholly occupied by gas. This tapering, insubstantial guy could clear a room in seconds.

I have mentioned that the Three Lights was the roughest of the local dives, and that, in large measure, was because people like Gus Fratesi and Rosey Tafigno often showed up. They were the inspiration behind a South Plainfield motorcycle gang called the Pagans — you could read it on the backs of their black leather jackets. They were bad news, scary, roaring into town on their Harley choppers, with tattoos and steel-studded belts, daring anyone to get in their faces.

At about 12:20, Gus Fratesi, seated near the pool table in the Three Lights Tavern, started lighting matches and tossing them one by one in the air, most of them landing, still lit, on the floor, some on the green felt of the pool table. He was well into a book of matches when Eddie Ghilain, from behind the bar, asked him to stop — and he did. But when Ghilain went out the back door to throw out some garbage, Fratesi again started tossing the burning matches. Ghilain returned and said, "Donnie, would you go tell that guy to quit it?"

Erwin, who was big but not as big as Fratesi, stood, walked up to him, and told him to cut it out. Fratesi looked up at him, and I imagine him stroking his stringy goatee and laughing a little. Then he lit another match and flipped it in the air. It landed on the sleeve of Erwin's new coat, smoldering there for a second.

That did it. As Erwin recalls, "I figured I'd better get in the first punch," though I doubt, in that moment with the match on his coat, he was doing very much figuring. He hauled off and slugged Fratesi between the eyes, spilling him over backward and onto the floor, where he didn't immediately get up. Erwin brushed off his sleeve, and thinking Fratesi had had enough for the night, he went back to his bar stool, to his conversation with Reijtmar, and his ginger ale. Maybe this would be the right time to ask Ghilain about the job.

But before he could do that, before Erwin realized what was happening, Fratesi had gotten up, pulled out a knife, spun Erwin around on his stool, and stabbed him through the mouth. Wild and wounded, he sputtered blood, and Reijtmar, all 130 pounds of him and raging hair, went after Fratesi and Rosey Trafigno until he was pulled away. Eddie Ghilain called 911 — they'd need some help here, fast. Reijtmar ran out the front door, squinting into the dark, searching for anything, anything at all — a stick, a bat, a crowbar, a tire iron — anything that he might use, as he has said to me, "to bash Fratesi's brains in." On the edge of the sidewalk outside the bar stood one of those portable No Parking signs fixed in its concrete base. This one weighed seventy-three pounds, more than half Reijtmar's body weight. But madly, absurdly it seems from this distance, he picked it up, awkwardly cradling the base, and lugged it into the Three Lights.

Back across the street in the Old Stone, Rabbit was still playing pool, taking turns buying rounds of beer, and he was thinking of making a phone call. I don't know who he wanted to talk to at that hour. As it turned out, he would never make the call. Tom Pinson thinks that, since they had been talking about Cy, he wanted to say hello to him. I have a hunch that it was Joan Harczku. He might have wanted to tell her where he was, that he was OK, having a good time, that he'd stay with friends up here tonight and be back in the morning.

In any event, the phone at the Old Stone was busy, as Tom remembers. Rabbit waited for a minute, played a shot, probably a lousy last shot, leaving a ball on the lip of a pocket. He gave his cue to Fred Wickemyer to take his next turn, and I imagine him saying with mock gravity, "Don't blow it. Don't leave anything good." He said he was going over to the Three Lights to make a phone call. Then setting his beer next to the chalk, "When I'm back, I'll clear the table!"

Without bothering to unearth his coat from the pile on the piano, he went out that narrow front door, where the cold hit him like a slap. What a night! It was now in the low teens. Beautiful, biting, the wind whipping his silk sleeves. And there was no easing into it. One instant he is in the smoky yellow light, and then out in the wheeling dark. How quickly he passes from one to the other. It catches his breath for a moment.

Again he hears those wobbling sounds, and the rope slapping the flagpole. Stars powder the sky. To his left, across a patio, the road, then beyond the curb and the far sidewalk, he sees the Three Lights Tavern. Shadowy brown light leaks out its front through its rows of square glass blocks. In the middle of the facade, a narrow alcove leads into the bar, where you enter through a door on the left. At the far end of the alcove, in a small window, a neon Pabst sign, on its last legs, flutters with pale blue light.

Now Rabbit walks briskly across the road, up the curb, across the sidewalk, and into the alcove where the light bounces over him. For an instant he looks like he's in a silent film, with that flickering, intermittent light, making his smoothness jerk and twitch as he pushes open the door.

At 12:25, George Salko has already gone off on patrol, and Bill Sorgie and Pat Forsythe are still at headquarters, doing some paperwork, when the call comes in from the night dispatcher: "A fight and stabbing at the Three Lights Tavern. Someone wounded. In progress."

Ten-four, Sorgie radios back. They're on their way. They throw on their jackets. From his locker, Sorgie grabs his black-jack and zap gloves. *Some asshole's got a knife.* Outside, he locks the door behind them. They hustle to the car. They fly up the driveway and onto Route 202, Sorgie driving, his heart racing, flooring the pedal, the siren wailing, his high beams splitting the dark. Today he still recalls a taste of sweat and leather. As he drives, he bites the cuffs of his zap gloves, yanking them on with his teeth.

Inside the Three Lights, all is swimming with trouble. Rabbit knows its look and smell. Heaving breath, beer, and sweat; blood and glass on the floor. There's a guy bleeding from his jaw, all over his tie and jacket. Other guys wrestle near the pool table, grunting, shouting, "Hold him. Get the fucking knife!" Some girls are screaming, "Stop! Please!" And there's a guy — it's Richie Reijtmar, his eyes wild — saying, "I'm going to kill him! I'm going to kill him!" He's swaying with a No Parking sign in his arms. *What the hell's **that** doing in here?*

As Rabbit entered through the door, at first no one much noticed him. He's come a long way in crossing the street — this is hardly a birthday celebration. In the back, near the men's room, the phone is open, but for the moment he's forgotten about that.

Is he showing off? Is it bravado, good will, or just common sense? It is pure Rabbit, all the above: he walks to the bar and asks Eddie Ghilain if he'd like to have the sign taken out.

As Ghilain would later testify in civil court, he says, "Yes, that would be a favor."

Then Rabbit turns to Reijtmar, who still remembers Rabbit's words: "Richie, why don't you let me take the sign for a while?"

Though they are not close friends, Reijtmar knows Rabbit. They have seen each other around. Rabbit is tall, strong, 205 pounds, and looking right at him. "Let me take the sign, Richie," he says. And Reijtmar puts it down. Then, along with Erwin, who is still bleeding profusely, Reijtmar storms outside to wait for the cops. He'll give them a piece of his mind.

Now Rabbit hoists the sign first to his waist and, with a heave, up over his right shoulder, his hands gripping the iron shaft as you'd hold a two-by-four or a baseball bat, the concrete base pointing forward. He's got it now. It's heavy as hell. Moving slowly and awkwardly, holding his balance, he turns to take it out the door.

At about this time, about 12:29, the people in the Three Lights can hear the siren wailing and see the red lights pulsing in the block glass, as the police car speeds around the green and skids up, double-parking, in front of the Brookdale Deli. Before Sorgie can even get out, Reijtmar and Erwin are at his door. In the breeze, Reijtmar looks like those old drawings of John Brown at Harper's Ferry, a whirl of indignation. Blood now, darkly shining, soaks Erwin's collar and shirt. He, too, is beside himself, the taste of his own blood. "Billy," he screams at Sorgie, "Look at me! There's a maniac inside with a knife!"

Then out in the cold, up on the sidewalk, and seeing Erwin's wound up close, Sorgie bites off his zap gloves and spits them out on the ground. He says to Forsythe, "Take out your weapon," and he draws his own, which he holds pointed downward at his side. Forsythe does the same, and slowly they all approach the alcove, their breath coming out in plumes. Sorgie is first, straight in front of the alcove, Forsythe to his right and slightly behind, Erwin and Reijtmar to his left. From somewhere comes the rush of a train, which is swallowed in a rush of wind. Near the mouth of the alcove, Sorgie stops still, like a cat in a yard, listening. At the far end of the alcove, something is happening. Someone is coming through the door and into that trembling light.

If I could stop this story — if I could stop it forever — I would do it right here at this moment. It was 12:30 on an early Saturday morning in Bernardsville, New Jersey. Something bad had happened, but nothing tragic yet, nothing that could never be undone.

With Reijtmar and Erwin outside the bar, things were quieting inside. Someone had taken Fratesi's knife, and the No Parking sign was being removed from the premises. I think of Rabbit, then, with the sign on his shoulder. Like the rest of us in crowds or especially in front of girls, he had that self-conscious, gallant way about him. He was doing a good deed. He was breaking up a fight by flexing his own muscle. He was stepping in to make peace. He must have known that he was among the few guys in the bar who could have hoisted that sign over his shoulder. He must have felt cocky, male, like winning a race, like trotting around the bases. He had a small audience. Things were under control. A little moment to savor.

At 12:30 my parents were in their beds, my father after watching the late news, having let out the dog and locked all the doors. In curlers, my mother would be falling asleep, having flicked off the chamber music on the radio. Through her closed window, she might have heard the late train pulling out of Basking Ridge, clattering across the trestle, around the embankment, then the sound fading, that soft mooing before the Bernardsville station, the silence trailing behind. Perhaps, through her dreams, she heard gusts in the trees, and the rhododendron lashing the shingles. All over town, people were sleeping or falling asleep: the Jeffers, the Bells, the Reverend Felmeth, the boys in bunk beds at Bonnie Brae. Things had even settled down at the Cuttings' — empty beer cans on dark counters, cigarettes squashed in ashtrays. Across the hills, the last lights and TVs went out, and there was only the sound of the wind.

Again, the cold hit Rabbit as he emerged through the door of the Three Lights Tavern and stepped in front of the fluttering light. What Sorgie saw, he says, was a "dark silhouette" of a large man facing him, with a sign on his shoulder, holding it like a bat. He saw the man's eyes. He says he couldn't tell if he was black or white — he says that didn't occur to him.

And yet even in that dim and quivering moment, he must have perceived in the dark silhouette the shape of Rabbit's big afro. He felt threatened, he says. He doesn't use the word, but I think he felt scared. He pointed his gun at Rabbit, about ten feet away, at the far end of the alcove. By instinct, training, and practice, he pointed at the center mass.

He said, "Put the sign down." Sorgie, Forsythe, Erwin, and Reijtmar — everyone who was there and is still alive — they all remember these words.

Then according to Sorgie, Rabbit said, "Motherfuck you." But no one else, including Forsythe, recalls Rabbit speaking then.

Sorgie gave Rabbit "a couple of seconds" to put down the sign. In Reijtmar's words, Rabbit "stood there for two or three seconds more. I guess he was just shocked at seeing us there."

Then according to both policemen, Rabbit stepped forward, raising the sign in "an aggressive action."

Reijtmar and Erwin, though, remember this differently. Rabbit was moving to get the sign off his shoulder. "He was putting it down," Erwin recalls. He was complying. Or as Reijtmar would testify, "He started to take the sign off his shoulder, and that's as far as he ever got."

Now two things happened in the same instant, one obliterating the other. Erwin cried, "No!" And Sorgie fired his gun.

A brilliant flash lit up Olcott Square — all the windows, signs, rolled-up awnings, and even the yellow-haired Dutch Boy. Erwin and Reijtmar felt the heat from the flash. Sorgie felt the gun jump in his hand. And what Rabbit felt we can only imagine, as the bullet knocked him backward.

"Oh shit!" cried Forsythe.

And spitting blood, still trying to hold himself up, Rabbit said his last words.

According to Reijtmar, he said, "You people shot me."

According to Erwin, he said, "Man, you shot me. Why?"

Then he collapsed in the alcove, this proud young man, his legs all funny beneath him. He fell with a sound like toppling luggage, and then he made another sound, alive and liquid, like water deep in a drain.

After that, there was just the wind, the pale blue fluttering light, and the rope slapping the flagpole. Rabbit's eyelids were open, as though looking out toward the road, but his eyes themselves had rolled back, leaving only their whitish bulbs. His body was still. The sign lay in the doorway beside him. The deer's tooth pendant lay on his chest, nicked by the bullet that killed him.

Dreaming of Light

When he tells me his part in this story now — and he has told me many times — what Bill Sorgie says he remembers most vividly is the feel of that fluttering light. As he describes it, his eyes squint behind his glasses, and he makes his right hand — his gun hand, I realize — tremble as with the beating of the light. He says that he wishes it never happened, but he says he "did what [he] thought [he] had to do" in much the same matter-of-fact way that he spoke of those moments of fear, courage, and killing years before in a distant land. He says he can "live with" what he's done, and I would wish no more or less for him: that he, in fact, lives with it.

He is divorced from his first wife whom he brought over from Korea, and he is remarried now, with a home in the country, where he and his wife live with their own two kids, a boy and a girl, a good, solid family. He is a girl's baseball coach and, from what I surmise, a loving, protective father. He tells me he would die for his children, and I do not doubt it for a second. Over time, some part of me has come to like him, especially when he asks about Rabbit's life, when he wants to see my photographs of Rabbit, or when sometimes, after he has seen these things, he doesn't say anything at all.

Still, I'd like him to awaken some nights, having dreamed of fluttering light. I'd like him to look at his wife sleeping beside him. Or better, I'd like him to get up and walk down to his children's room, his hands feeling for the doorway. I'd like him to stand there listening, as years ago he had stood near the mouth of the alcove, all taut, open, alive. In that dim fluttering light from his dreams, he'd see his kids sprawled in sleep, like dolls left on a floor. He'd hear snags of breath, like wind through a pipe. He'd smell washed hair, grungy feet, and sweat as familiar as his own, rich as opened mushrooms. He'd touch the smooth undersides of knees and elbows, or those birdlike bones at the back of a wrist, the vein bumping across.

How can any of this be taken away? How can it ever be re-placed? I want him to take his hands away from their skin, and look down at his trembling palms.

The Bullet

In the top drawer of Bill Sorgie's office desk, among his pencils, pens, and paper clips, is an old .38 caliber bullet, roughly similar to the one he shot into Rabbit. I ask him if I can see it, and he puts it into my hand. I have never held a bullet before, an unusual thing I suppose. This one is a dull brassy color, an inch and a half long, with a flanged end and rounded conical tip. In my palm, it seems such a small thing, gone when I make a fist. But it has a terrific weight for its size, most of it near that smug, conical front, giving it an unbalanced, expectant feel, oddly like those kids' toys, little plastic pods each with a sliding metal ball inside — we used to call them Jumping Beans.

In this brassy pod, though, the ball only moves with a great explosion behind it. And the ball is not exactly a sphere, but a lead slug, about the shape and size of my little finger if you cut it off at the first joint. Without its cartridge, it weighs 158 grains, a third of an ounce, and travels from the end of a revolver at 800 feet per second. Sorgie shot a slightly different bullet at Rabbit, a 110 grain "Super-Vel" (super velocity): a little faster, more accurate, a little lighter than the one I hold in my hand, and more likely to penetrate its target. Though it weighs just slightly more than a child's marble, it is far more dense and streamlined. It struck Rabbit's chest at about 1,000 feet per second, or 682 miles per hour.

The Heart

Again I am studying that photo, my favorite, of Rabbit in the 1972 yearbook, the "candid" one where he sits in the school library, with his huge afro, his shades in one hand and cigarette in the other, with an open book in his lap, and that serious, pensive stare, a look both proud and lonely. I have mentioned that, in this photo, the neckline of his shirt plunges down his chest in a narrow V. Crisscrossing the V and strung through eyelets is a lace that he hasn't tightened. Now I am struck by what he is showing us: a wedge of skin, a shallow valley behind the crossed leather, the place above his heart.

This, right here, is where the bullet entered. And this is what it did: "Bullet wound [in] front of chest perforating heart and lung; partial severance of pulmonary artery and aorta; hemopericardium, massive left hemothorax." That's what it says on his death certificate. His heart was torn to bits.

I have just gotten off the phone with Dr. Richard Hopkins, a heart surgeon at Georgetown Medical Center. I have described to him the circumstances of Rabbit's death and have read to him those words from the death certificate. From this, he can trace the route of the bullet, as I follow along on a diagram. He can surmise its medical effects, and even say something about what Rabbit might have felt as he died.

All in a fraction of a second, the bullet smashed through Rabbit's breastbone, deflecting slightly to the right. It ripped a hole in his right ventricle at the front of his heart, cut through the septum between the ventricles, then blew out at the base of his left atrium, transecting the left pulmonary artery and behind that the aorta, the largest vessel in the body. From there it tumbled through his esophagus, then struck his spine, slowing, wobbling, coming to rest in the soft tissue of his back.

He wouldn't have felt the bullet *going in*. It was all just suddenly *there*. Suddenly pierced. Heart broken. Inside him, blood poured through all those holes, any one of which would have killed him. A pump unable to fill itself, his heart madly clenched, compressed, "squashed," is how Dr. Hopkins puts it — "cardiac tamponade" is the medical term. Rabbit might have felt pain at the entrance wound, but he wouldn't have felt where the bullet lodged. All that, everything else in the world, was absorbed in the pain of his heart contracting. An unbearable heaviness and exploding fullness. Blood shooting up his throat. Everything squeezing, gasping, trying to hold, yet everything spewing out. "It is about the most sudden way that a person can die," according to Hopkins. Rabbit would have lost consciousness within a minute, perhaps within forty-five seconds. But during that time, Hopkins is sure, he would with effort have been able to speak, and he would have known he was surely dying.

The Sign

Holding open the big metal gate at the entrance of the Bernardsville dump on Pill Hill Road is a signpost fixed in a cube of concrete. It is forty-nine inches high, the distance from the ground to the middle of my chest, and according to my mother's bathroom scale that I brought along, it weighs seventy-three pounds, exactly the reported weight of the signpost that Rabbit carried that night.

Is it the same signpost? I can't be sure. This one has an octagonal Stop sign bolted to its rusted iron shaft, instead of a rectangular No Parking sign. Within days of the shooting, the Bernardsville road department removed all the portable signs from Olcott Square and disposed of them in the dump. This is the only one remaining; the others, like Rabbit, are buried, gone, part of the "sanitary landfill." But this one, even if it isn't *the one,* is very, very much like it.

I was taken to the dump some months ago by Allan Rome in his black pick-up, with mag wheels and a Hurst shifter. Today he works for the Bernardsville road department, which operates the dump; Rusty Cook is his foreman. Years ago Allan was a regular at the Three Lights Tavern, though he wasn't there on the night Rabbit died. He is a huge, round-shouldered, friendly guy with a thick mustache and a ponderous gut beneath his smudgy T-shirt.

With all my strength, I can barely lift the signpost, bending and cradling it under the base, heaving it up, thigh high, but not an inch further. It takes Allan's help to get it onto my shoulder, then he has to steady me as I sway.

The thing *is* heavy as hell, and ridiculously awkward and unbalanced, an anvil stuck on a stick. I can walk with it, but my legs go wobbly. With the concrete base just in front of my shoulder, and holding the shaft as I would a bat, it seems to pull me down and forward — I have to move to catch up with it. Then as I try to put it down, again I have to stagger forward, spreading my weight, before slowly sliding and tilting it off my shoulder where I can cradle it again.

At 205 pounds, Rabbit weighed 65 pounds more than I do. At twenty-one, he was half my present age, and probably twice as strong. Still, he couldn't have easily carried that sign, especially as he maneuvered it through the door of the Three Lights and turned into the narrow alcove. Nor do I think he could have used it as a lethal weapon, though it may have looked that way. It is just too heavy, too unwieldy. And even if he held it "like a bat," it was a grossly misshapen and inverted bat, with all its mass below his hands — even Allan Rome can't swing it with authority.

Then, finally, I doubt that Rabbit could have easily or

immediately put it down. You just don't drop such a thing on command. You'd break your foot, or the edge of the sign might slash your neck. He, too, would have had to step awkwardly forward to slide it off his shoulder.

The End

So, for the last time, I think of him coming through that door. There's the biting cold and the fluttering light. The rusted edges of the iron post cut into his palms, and through his vest he feels its weight grooving the meat of his shoulder. The sign pulls him forward, down, and to his right, but with a humphing, thick-muscled pleasure, mostly in his thighs and back, he steadies it, masters it, as hunters carry their prey when they leave the woods. The weight, though a pain, is a measure of his strength and the good of what he's doing. As he turns, the deer's tooth sways on his chest, a little tap on his heart.

The Three Lights Tavern is long gone. Over the years, the space has been occupied by a bike shop, a knitting store, the Aikido School of Self Defense, and who knows what else. Now, according to the sign above, it is Elegant Ensembles, a fashionable wedding arrangements shop, with photos of dewy-eyed brides in the windows. Gone are the smoky glass blocks in front, replaced by expanses of clear plate glass. What isn't plate glass has been painted pure white — you wouldn't guess it had ever been a bar. Yet the alcove *is* there just as it was, except that it is white, and the doorway has been moved to the end wall, where the Pabst sign used to flicker. The space is six feet long, three feet four inches wide, and seven and a half feet tall. When I stand right where Rabbit stood, my immediate impression is of a small, claustrophobic space, enclosed on five sides, the size of a grave.

Now I imagine Rabbit turning into the alcove and seeing its sixth side filled with the shape of a policeman. The hat. The shiny crescent of visor. The glint of badge on a chest. And then a short, shivering line of blue light: a steel tube, the black hole, so small, smaller than a marble, pointed right at him.

*What's going on here? What in the world? Put that thing away. I'm just trying to get this sign out of here. Jesus, give me a break. Look, **I'm doing a good deed! What am I doing wrong?** . . . All right, all right, I'll put it down. Give me a fucking second.*

Then all is light and sound and shuddering in his chest.

What? Whoa! What is happening? What is happening to me?

I'd like to think that Rabbit's final thoughts or memories gave him comfort. The smell of stowed hay, still sweet and warm, rain outside the mow. Or skinny-dipping that night in the Bonnie Brae pool with Fred, Doug, and Cy. Or that valley at the base of Marian's neck, thumb deep, smooth as sculpture. Or the train like a dream, a streaming ladder of light. Purple haze. Hey Joe. Hey Charles, here I come — that wild, wonderful whoop of laugh. Then Joan. The sliding click of bracelets. Holding both sides of his hands.

I'd like him to think of all these things. And maybe he did. A few of them. Or maybe his mind, like a flipped crab, for a time clawed bravely on: from here, he'd get up and head back to the Old Stone. The phone, by now, should be free. He'd call Joan. He'd say he'd see her tomorrow. Then he'd rejoin the guys around the pool table. Pinson. Wickemyer. The Garbage Man playing like Scott Joplin. "Hey, who's been sippin' my beer? . . ."

But how much can you think with a hole through your chest, and your heart clenching to stone?

I cannot know any of this. All I can do is speculate. What I do know is that, while shuddering and clenching, Rabbit fought to hold himself upright, and long enough to speak.

To stand and speak. That's what he did. And if we can know about a life by the way it dies, then we can learn something here. Often I've heard that life diffuses as it ends, blurring and fading behind autumn hills, or like the end of Mahler's Ninth Symphony, it softly dwindles, a filament of sound, sliding into silence. But perhaps, like Rabbit's heart, a life contracts at the last, concentrates, intensifies, and sometimes clenches down to this: a simple, magnificent assertion.

He stood. He made words. And he spoke not to God, not to anything greater or lesser than himself. He addressed "You people," or he addressed "Man." He left us, speaking straight at us, looking us hard in the eye.

"You people shot me," or "Man, you shot me." Either way, a simple declarative sentence, a statement of unbelievable, true, unwarranted fact. And I think also an accusation, a call to account, in the tone that he might have said, "How could you do this to me?"

And then if, in fact, he did ask "Why?" his final word was a question, a question to which I can posit answers: the endemic racism shared by so many of us; the lingering habits of war; inappropriate police training and psychological screening; the climate of fear and suspicion generated by the recent police killings; the role of chance, accident; Rabbit's obvious size and strength; the dim light; Sorgie's relative inexperience; Rabbit's bravado; and both of them still so young.

All of this is true, yet all of it together does not answer his cry. Nothing worth asking rests with answers. And this doesn't rest at all.

He leaves us living with his question, his words alive and gnawing: "Man, you shot me. Why?"

Very near the end, under all that weight, he fell in that clattering heap. I doubt, as some might have it, he felt embraced by light, disembodied, etherealized, or wafted toward another place. In his pain, I imagine he felt wholly embodied, within his skin, bound to this earth in a space like a grave — bewildered, alone, afraid.

And After

Back in 1966, Dennis Cauldron, in his early twenties, was a rookie policeman in town. For extra money, he took a weekend job as a recreation assistant and informal guard at Bonnie Brae Farm. Every Sunday, on "Family Visiting Day," he stood in his dark blue uniform at the entrance to the Farm, where he stopped each car, welcomed the visitors, and checked that they were all relatives of the boys inside. Cauldron had been doing this for some months, when a new kid at Bonnie Brae, Rabbit, asked him if he needed any help. Cauldron of course didn't need assistance, but he said fine — he liked the kid — and so, for a number of months, he and Rabbit would meet every Sunday at the end of the long, tree-lined lane where they'd "do guard duty" together.

At first Cauldron didn't think very much about this. Rabbit was probably bored, done with his chores, and like any fourteen-year-old, he enjoyed the shapes and colors of cars as they turned into the driveway. Over time, though, it became clear that more was involved, that Rabbit was avoiding the happy scenes of reunion at the other end of the lane. His friends with their brothers, sisters, or parents — it must have been tough for Rabbit to take. So each Sunday he went out to the entrance and stood with Dennis Cauldron beneath the oaks, checking out the cars streaming by.

"How's your mom?" Cauldron remembers asking once.

"Fine. I guess." That was all Rabbit said.

Now, looking back on those Sunday afternoons, Cauldron

thinks he knows what Rabbit was doing. "He was waiting for someone, probably his mother. All those times he was waiting for her."

Seven years later, on that cold January night, Cauldron was still a Bernards Township policeman, though he had left his weekend job at Bonnie Brae long before. Now he was on patrol and, having heard the report of a stabbing at the Three Lights, he was driving into Olcott Square to give the Bernardsville police assistance if needed. A brilliant flash lit up the storefronts. He thought someone was shooting at him, and he ducked, slammed his brakes, momentarily lost control of his cruiser, then skidded to a stop behind Sorgie's car. He got out and what, among other things, he saw was a figure slumped in a doorway. Almost at once he recognized Rabbit, "though he didn't look right. He seemed to be sleeping, but he wasn't sleeping. His legs were all messed up. His shoes were off. His eyes were open, but his eyes weren't there. He was staring out like he was looking for someone. He was staring out toward the road."

With his gun still in hand, Sorgie was standing on the sidewalk when Cauldron arrived. He seemed stunned, dazed, or as Cauldron says, "Bill looked out of it." "Over and over he kept saying, 'I told him to stop. I told him to put it down.'" Then Cauldron remembers seeing Pat Forsythe, the rookie cop with the baby face, take the gun from Sorgie's hand.

In the patrol car, Forsythe called on the radio for medical supplies and police backup. He remembers saying, "Get me a ten-ten! Get me all you can get!"

By now George Salko, the old-timer, had arrived. He, too, was responding to the original call, and had seen the flash in the windows of Olcott Square. It puzzled him. Tonight? This wasn't New Year's Eve. He thought it was a cherry bomb.

Next came Jim Kierstead, another Bernards Township policeman who was patrolling in Liberty Corner. From 1955 through 1961, he had been a kid at Bonnie Brae Farm, and in the seven following years, a counselor there. From 1966 through 1968, he had met periodically with Rabbit, and they talked about how Rabbit was doing in school, how he was getting along. Rabbit "was never a problem, a good kid," Jim remembers. Now he saw Rabbit crumpled in the doorway and some policemen up on the sidewalk. He got out of his car and, linking arms with his fellow officers, formed a cordon outside the alcove. Then later, after the rescue squad had arrived and tried to resuscitate Rabbit, he, Cauldron, and a few others would kneel and join hands beneath Rabbit's body, making a hammock of their arms. They'd lift and carry him out of the cold, back into the Three Lights, one of them cradling his head.

Lew Morrow was going home. He had played enough pool, had said his good-byes and was putting on his coat in the Old Stone, when from outside he heard a popping sound. He zipped his coat, put on his gloves, and went out to go to his car. He turned left, and across the road, he saw Sorgie with his gun, and Rabbit spilling down. He walked closer and saw the blood in the center of Rabbit's shirt, a whitish shirt, maybe pink — Morrow isn't sure.

Then he ran back into the Old Stone, screaming, "They shot him! They shot him! They shot him!"

The place went quiet.

Who shot who?

"The cops! They shot him! Rabbit!"

Then leaving their drinks, cues, coats, keys, and open wallets, everyone streamed out the door and into the square to see.

It was true. There he was. Some people stood and stared. Others cried. Others went wild, incensed, shouting. Pigs. Murderers. Bastards. Cubby Kurylo started swinging at cops and was eventually arrested. Tom Pinson had to be pinned to the sidewalk. Others tried to get to Rabbit while the cops were occupied, and Kip Nickerson did. He remembers crouching beside him and feeling the warm slickness of Rabbit's blood, how it stuck his shirt to his skin. He remembers an urge to close Rabbit's eyes, but someone jerked him away.

In the Three Lights, everyone heard the explosion, and saw the flash in the glass blocks. For a moment nobody moved. Then, even in the far back where Bruce Dare was standing, they heard that toppling sound.

What the hell . . . ? Still nobody moved.

For a little while it was quiet again, and then a few people, their bodies hunched, moved cautiously toward the door.

Ed Hat got there first, and saw Rabbit's "bewildered" eyes just as they rolled to whiteness. Soon the doorway, already clogged with Rabbit and the signpost, was choked with gawking, screaming people. A few spilled over Rabbit and out the alcove, but most, including Gus Fratesi, ran straight for the back door. Within moments, the Three Lights, just like the Old Stone, was empty of all its patrons.

John "Red" Lucas was the first off-duty officer to arrive on the scene. Others remember him wearing sneakers and slacks that he had thrown on, his fiery hair a tangled mess, a crotchety old veteran then, and I suppose about as crotchety today: he will not speak to me about any of this. Still, in those moments of confusion and anger in Olcott Square, he had a clear-headed idea. He ordered Sorgie and Forsythe to go back to headquarters, lock the door, and not come out.

Unlike many of the others, Jim Belcher had put on his coat as he left the Old Stone, but he sure didn't feel comfortable outside. Sirens wailed. Lurid police lights strobed the storefronts, making them leap and wobble. Everyone was pissed. Some were throwing things. A faint, acrid smell rode the wind. His friend Richie Reijtmar kept crying, "All he did was take the sign!" and cops surrounded the shadowy Three Lights alcove so you couldn't see what was in there.

In the bar, Jim had been flush with beer and bourbon. Now he shivered with more than the cold. "I'm getting the hell out of here," he told some friends who wanted to stay and confront the police. He walked to his car parked beside Autumn House Furniture, and drove carefully out of the square. He went south on 202, past the train station and the bank — he could drive this route in his sleep. He remembers pulling over as a screaming, flashing blur of police cars flew by him going in the opposite direction. Then, for some reason, he didn't turn into his parents' driveway. Instead, he drove on about a mile until he turned around at Twin Lakes Park.

For four generations, the Belchers have lived in Bernardsville. In fact, it was Jim's great-grandfather who, in the 1890s, bought the whole hillside between town and Twin Lakes, then built the house across from the quarry where Jim's grandparents and parents grew up, where he grew up, and where he now lives with his own family. But in all their days and nights in Bernardsville, probably none of the Belchers, as Jim says, had "ever seen a night like that." As if to make sure of his own perceptions, Jim drove back to Olcott Square. The police, however, had sealed it off, their cruisers parked bumper to bumper, flares burning purple-red. So Jim just kept following the road north, as though he couldn't turn back. He went out of Bernardsville, out of Basking Ridge, over the Passaic and out of Somerset County, until he stopped in Morristown at the Lackawanna Diner, and drank coffee until dawn.

Within ten minutes of the shooting, about 100 kids filled the square, and soon about thirty policemen from all adjoining towns stood shoulder to shoulder, arms linked, outside the Three Lights. Rabbit's body was still inside. That flashing blur of police cars that Jim Belcher had seen on 202 was the State Police Tactical Unit roaring in. Now, on the sidewalks and on the roofs of the Brookdale Deli and Sussman's, troopers stood in the wind, against the stars, with shotguns in their hands.

While everyone else had rushed out onto the street, Jimmy Vilade, the bartender, remained at the Old Stone. He couldn't just up and leave the place unattended. Suddenly alone, he peered out the small window at the whirling lights and shadows. In about twenty minutes, some police came in and ordered him to close up.

Right now?

Immediately. Move it. Let's go.

What about all this stuff?

Forget it. Let's go!

Vilade says it was the strangest thing he's ever done, with all those coats and scarves on the piano and chairs, those half-drunk beers and bags of nuts, those wallets, keys, and bills on the bar: to leave everything there, as though frozen, then to turn off the lights and lock up.

Slowly and fitfully, the crowd in the square began to disperse, many shivering, crying, cursing, without their coats and keys, to be driven home in strange cars, to lie awake until morning.

On the sidewalk, Dennis Cauldron held a compress to Donnie Erwin's bleeding mouth until he was taken away in an ambulance.

Soon Edwin Albano, the state medical examiner, was ushered into the Three Lights, where at 1:30 A.M. he pronounced Rabbit dead. Then Rabbit's body was zipped into a bag and laid on a stretcher.

On the front page of the January 18 *Bernardsville News*, a photo appears of four men carrying the stretcher with Rabbit's body, just as it emerged from the alcove. The translucent glass blocks on the front of the tavern catch the flash of the photographer's bulb. In the background, the alcove is but a dark rectangle. The stretcher has wheels, it could be rolled, but the men have got it in their hands, Rabbit's weight in the puff of their faces. One is George Botsko, a Bernardsville policeman, and behind him, barely visible, is an older man in a plaid lumberjack coat. The two others, probably from the medical examiner's office, wear ties and dark, heavy topcoats. They are bringing Rabbit out feet first — I can tell by the shape of the bag. At the far end of the bag, still in the mouth of the alcove, is a rounded hump that must be his head. Then a little closer, a sharper bump: either his upturned shoulder, or his hands together on his chest.

That is all I can tell. Such a cruel smoothness where the bag falls over him, like draped sculpture, eliding detail. Are his hands clenched? Enfolded? Open? What is the expression on his face? And yet even through the bag you can sense something about him, if only his size and weight. He overflows the stretcher. The men huff and grunt. Even in death, he doesn't fit our receptacles. Like a kid grown too large for a bed, his feet push over the end.

Sometime that night — he isn't sure when — the phone rang beside the bed where Doug Robb, one of Rabbit's old suitemates from Bonnie Brae, was sleeping in his apartment in Millington. It was pitch dark. Doug fumbled for the phone, got it, and the voice on the line said, "It's me, Fred. Rabbit's been shot. He's dead."

You would think that would have jolted Doug wide awake. Even now he doesn't know how he did it: he said nothing, just slid the receiver back in its cradle and pulled the blanket back over his shoulders.

Then sometime later — it was still pitch dark — Doug sat

up, sweating, turned on the light, and dialed the number he
knew by heart. He said, "Fred, did you just call? . . . What the
hell did you say?"

From the Three Lights, Rabbit's body was carried to an ambulance, then driven to the police station, as if to follow Sorgie
home. It was taken into a small room next to the locker room
where Forsythe and Sorgie were waiting.

Meanwhile, back in the square, people continued to leave
in small, muttering groups. *This can't be happening. Was he
really inside that bag?*

By 3 A.M. the Tactical Unit returned to Netcong, and the
police from neighboring towns retired to their own homes or
headquarters. An hour later the square was empty, dark. And
then a few hours after that, except for a wooden barricade outside and a pool of frozen blood in the Three Lights alcove, Olcott Square was as I've often imagined it: the brick storefronts
receiving the dawn; the first few cars, their lights on, whispering
around the flagpole; the rattling newspaper trucks, a bundled
kid in the open back, with stacks of the *Times* or the *Ledger*.
There's a whiff from somewhere, rich and sweet. The coffee
shop? Nardone's Bakery? It's a Saturday morning in the heart of
winter. And though no one gets on or off at this hour, the early
train eases into the station, glazed with frost, steam from its un-
dercarriage. It waits for what seems a long time, making a tick-
ing sound. Then with that low, weird, electrical whine, it moves
on toward Basking Ridge.

*　　*　　*

Dear William Loizeaux:

Thank you for using 800-US SEARCH. Unfortunately, after extensively searching our nationwide database for **Joan
Marie Harczku,** we have been unable to obtain any information leading to her whereabouts. . . .

Please feel free to send along any questions you may have and a customer service representative will get in touch with you. Thank you.

So. She doesn't exist in the nationwide database, and yet I believe she existed in Rabbit's life. People remember her. People remember *them.* So to hell with 800-U.S. SEARCH. To hell with the database. This I can do myself. It may not be precisely the truth, but here is the closest I can come:

Somewhere in New Jersey, perhaps in a small room in New Brunswick, a young woman gets up on a January morning, washes her face, and combs her hair. She is surprised and disappointed that she had slept through the night. She had expected a phone call to awaken her.

Well, I guess he was just having too good a time. Back in his town, with his old friends — he does lose track of himself sometimes. I suppose he'll get around to calling this morning, and I'll let him know I'm not too happy. He'll say that he couldn't get to a phone until late, and he didn't want to wake me up. I'll half believe him and half not believe him. Then he'll say he's got a ride, he'll be back before lunch. I'll say fine, good, see you soon. And when he comes in, he'll have that look that avoids my eyes, and he'll seem smaller now in that silly coat, his hands deep in the pockets. We won't hug, and we won't kiss, but I guess we'll do what people do when they're disappointed and still in love. We'll sit. We'll talk. I won't exactly say I'm pissed off, and he won't exactly say he's sorry. We'll kind of talk **around** *all that, and maybe we'll talk about us. He'll say he thinks it's time to head back to the coast, get an apartment of our own. He'll say he's done all his visiting here, seen everybody he wants to see. After all, isn't that why you come back to these places, to see the old friends, do the old things — so you can set out on your own life again?*

She finishes her hair, dresses, has breakfast with tea, the mug warm in her hand. Outside the window it looks clear and cold. People in coats and blowing scarves, venturing out for weekend shopping, like furry animals on the sidewalk. On the radio they are talking about peace in Vietnam. Kissinger, with a deal, flying back from Paris. At last, at last. Yet no rejoicing. *How many deaths did it take?*

She is startled and relieved when, around noon, the phone finally rings. She lets it ring a while — *serves him right*. But when she picks it up, it's a girlfriend of hers, her voice strange and trembling. Had Joan heard the news?

"No. Oh, yes! Peace at last. Isn't it about time?"

Then for a moment she still wishes could have lasted forever, there is silence on the line.

By January 1973, Rabbit's cousin Donald Baker, with whom he had played as a kid, was thirty-three years old, and his mother Hannah was fifty-nine, in poor health, and unable to live alone. Donald had been married, divorced, and was living again with his own mother and Hannah in a small walk-up apartment in Long Branch, New Jersey, where they had recently moved from Trenton. None of them had seen or heard from Rabbit since he had gone to Bonnie Brae. He was off in a different world.

Now on that cold Saturday morning, Donald got a phone call that he couldn't believe. Some official was telling him that Rabbit was dead, in a town called Bernardsville. Donald put on his coat, went straight to the bar where he was a regular, and knocked down a few stiff drinks. Then he drove Hannah north on I-287, through gray hills, to an old stone police station in a place he had never been. They were shown into a small room where, beneath a blue sheet, a body lay on a metal table. When the sheet was pulled partially back and Donald was asked, he said yes, of course. Who else could that be? That was my cousin. Bill.

Beside him, I imagine, Hannah stood, small and lost in a

tattered coat. Her son on a cold metal table, beneath a thin blue sheet. *How big he's grown. How long! He ought to be wearing a coat or a sweater. Don't they have blankets here?* I see that same crumpled, bewildered face as when, all those years before, she had stood in the doorway on Perry Street and watched another impossible thing: a shiny car driving away. The car, it just kept going and going, her son's eyes all wide in the rear window. She couldn't move a muscle.

As they left the station, the police gave them a detergent box filled with some of Rabbit's clothes, most of which Donald can't remember now — except the belt. It was wide, black leather, and stained with Rabbit's dried blood. When he and Hannah got home that day, Donald took off his own belt, then removed Rabbit's from the box and, without washing or wiping it, pushed it through the loops of his pants. It fit him perfectly, the metal tongue sliding into the same worn hole where Rabbit had buckled it on the day before. Donald's waist then was thirty-three inches, and as his waist grew over time, he moved the buckle from hole to hole, until many years later, after wearing it every day, the leather, still unwashed, finally cracked and broke.

"I'd be wearing it now," Donald tells me, "if it hadn't fallen apart."

All the newspapers and New York television affiliates carried the story, and reporters and camera crews, in a feeding frenzy, descended on Basking Ridge and Bernardsville. Chief Steinkopf removed Bill Sorgie from active duty, pending a grand jury investigation. An autopsy was performed at Somerville Hospital, though I'm told the report no longer exists. Then, on the evening of Thursday, January 18, there was the viewing at Galoway and Crane's Funeral Home on Finley Avenue, arranged by the Bells. A young woman, whom the Bells vaguely remember but never knew, cried inconsolably.

Cy Hardy, Rabbit's closest black friend, remembers the viewing well. To him, Rabbit looked strangely solemn, powdered and pale. He wore somebody else's suit and tie, and his hair, above all, was wrong: "It seemed uneven, mashed down or matted." So standing at the head of the open casket, Cy took his own pick from his pocket and tried to comb out Rabbit's hair. He had barely begun when a man, probably from the funeral home, came up beside him and stilled his hand — gently, discreetly, firmly.

On the next day, Reverend Felmeth presided over the funeral in our church, with six of Rabbit's friends as pallbearers. Rabbit might have rolled his eyes at all the attention, how more seemed lavished upon his death than had been on his life. Beneath the Celtic cross and directly in front of the simple steel casket adorned with a spray of white chrysanthemums and red carnations, the Reverend said to the three hundred assembled mourners, "We are here to honor him with love and remembrance. . . . We are all with him, a victim of violence, as victims of violence ourselves. Ours is a society that expects and accepts violence all too readily." After reading from the Scriptures, he recalled his discussions with Rabbit and Rabbit's aversion to the killing in Vietnam. He recited the Lord's Prayer and the Twenty-third Psalm, before the service concluded with the hymn "Be Still My Soul."

Then came the private burial in Somerset Hills Memorial Park, just a mile away, on a strange, warm, galvanic afternoon that would end with record temperatures of sixty degrees and thundershowers. Cy, Doug, and Fred were the last to leave the grave. None of them were among the pallbearers that day, and perhaps because they didn't lift and carry Rabbit then, these three especially, after all these years, have yet to lay his memory down. For five, fifteen, twenty minutes, they didn't move, or couldn't move, as the ceremony ended and the others went off to their cars. They waited until the cars were gone. They waited until they heard nothing. They waited for whatever they were getting to, and went down the hill. "That was the hardest thing I've ever done," Fred says, "turning away like that."

A memorial folk and rock concert, attended by more than five hundred, was staged on the following night in the high school gymnasium. Andy Cutting and Jim Gault, among others, played guitar, and Tom King played tambourine and maracas. The event raised $1,000 to help defray funeral expenses and buy a grave marker.

The road department removed all the No Parking signs, took them to the dump, and for a week the police enforced an 8 P.M. curfew in Olcott Square. The Three Lights Tavern was closed and padlocked, and on January 20, a week after the shooting, a circle of dried blood still lay in the alcove, about the width of a steering wheel. Eventually the sidewalk was hosed clean and the Three Lights reopened, but only for a little while. Eddie Ghilain soon went out of business. Nobody went in there anymore.

On January 27, Bill Sorgie marked his twenty-fourth birthday quietly with his family. On February 7, 8, and 9, the Somerset County prosecutor's office presented to a grand jury statements from twenty-four witnesses, and fifty-five items of evidence, including the autopsy, Sorgie's gun, the bullet, his blood-spattered shoes, the No Parking sign, Rabbit's shirt with a small, singed hole in the front, his deer's tooth pendant, and Erwin's new camel hair jacket, stained with his own and Rabbit's blood. Sorgie and Forsythe had each submitted to and passed lie detector tests, while some other "key" witnesses had refused. The grand jury visited the Three Lights Tavern, deliberated, and found "after considering all the evidence, that there [was] no basis for imposing criminal liability" on Sorgie. There would be no indictment, no criminal trial, and, according to normal procedures, all the statements and much of the evidence would be sealed for a time and then destroyed, though Sorgie eventually got back his gun and shoes, and Erwin got his camel hair jacket, with little squares of material cut out of it.

After the grand jury's decision, Chief Steinkopf determined, according to statements in the local newspaper, that Rabbit had acted in "a menacing manner," and Sorgie had acted in self-defense, "in the proper performance of his duty." So Bill Sorgie returned to the usually quiet streets of Bernardsville, patrolling, pulling over speeders, and directing traffic through Olcott Square.

In the days shortly after the shooting, the National Conference of Black Lawyers formed a special citizens committee to investigate. Testimony was reportedly taken, yet the committee published no findings and took no legal action. It remained for the Bells, particularly Martha as administrator of Rabbit's estate, to pursue any legal recourse and bring sworn testimony into the public domain. "We wanted to clear Rabbit's name," she says in her small, firm voice. "We wanted to show he did nothing to deserve his death." So in late March 1973, she filed civil suit in New Jersey Superior Court, demanding a trial by jury and seeking punitive and compensatory damages. The suit charged Sorgie with two counts of negligence, and Chief Steinkopf and the Borough of Bernardsville with inadequate and negligent training and supervision.

Then in early May, Chief Steinkopf, at age forty-one, died suddenly of a heart attack. With five other Bernardsville policemen, a grim Pat Forsythe and Bill Sorgie carried his flag-draped casket to a place on the hillside west of Mount Airy Road, just a few hundred yards from Rabbit's grave, where the faded wreaths and browned carnations still lay on the raw earth.

Finally, a year and a half after Rabbit died, Martha Bell's suit came to trial. It was settled out of court for $11,000, though not before Eddie Ghilain had testified that Rabbit was uninvolved in the bar fight and was removing the sign as a favor, and Rich Reijtmar had testified that he heard Rabbit make no remarks and saw him make no threatening gestures before Sorgie shot him. The Bells donated half of the settlement money to Rabbit's mother, and the other half to Meharry College, a predominantly black medical school, because of what they call Rabbit's "pride in his difference" and his interest in medical photography.

Twin Lakes

It feels strange now, after all this time, to let go of these people and this story with its dangling questions, and with my desk still cluttered with maps, yearbooks, yellowed newspaper clippings, and old photographs. It is impossible to make a neat end of this clutter. I suppose I'd rather it didn't end. For there are things that, if we are to hold fast to ourselves, we should never really let go.

I have but one other incident to describe, one that over time has burrowed into me.

In the late afternoon of Sunday, October 7, 1973, eight months after he killed Rabbit, Bill Sorgie was on routine patrol on Route 202, about a mile west of headquarters, along a stretch that my mother drives to and from the school where she teaches. Even today, this area is still farmland, unfurling to the south of the road, with Mine Brook meandering through rolling pastures, and with cows, like statues, under trees. The train line cuts along a ridge behind these pastures, and if you were riding then between Bernardsville and Far Hills, you would have re-marked on the slanting amber light, and the tops of the maples turning yellow-green, and the high grasses, like schools of fish, flashing in the breeze.

There was a chill in the air that afternoon, a crisp fall day very much like that day when Rabbit first came here, seven years before, along this very road. Now it was almost quitting time, and Sorgie was driving back toward the station. Near Twin Lakes Park on the north side of the road, he saw a black woman screaming and frantically waving her arms. He pulled over. She said that her six-year-old son, playing with a friend, had fallen off the dock, into the water, and he hadn't come up. He didn't know how to swim.

Sorgie radioed for emergency help, jumped out of his car, and ran across the small sandy beach to the dock that extended into the water from the spillway. The woman pointed at bubbles in the water — that's where her son had gone under. Without removing his clothing or his belt and gun — the one with which he had shot Rabbit — Sorgie plunged in and dove and dove, the brown water cold and deep, his hands in the mucky bottom.

This lower of the two adjacent "Twin Lakes" is actually a typical New Jersey pond, about a half-acre of soupy water, thick with years of rotten leaves and algae fed by leeching seepage pits. It is a good pond for bullfrogs, carp, and water moccasins, and bad for swimming and saving lives. But into this, Sorgie threw himself, and according to guys who would soon arrive with the rescue squad, he was "wild to get to that kid." I see Sorgie repeatedly coming to the surface, a flicker in the mother's eye, and then Sorgie shaking his head — no, his arms were empty. I see him spitting water, then sucking air, and with a flash of yellow stripes on pants, he turns under the water again.

For three to five minutes, Sorgie dove and surfaced where he had seen the bubbles, until the rescue squad came. Exhausted, shivering, and streaming fetid muck, he was hauled onto the dock beside the woman and wrapped in layers of blankets. He had not found her son in the pond.

It took a half hour for the rescue squad, wading arm-in-arm across the pond, to finally locate the boy. In the slow current, his body had drifted underwater, away from the bubbles where he had fallen, and settled on the deep bottom near the base of the spillway. Dave Wacker brought him up, a slender kid, all blue and brown, laid him on the dock, and tried unsuccessfully to revive him.

Even now Sorgie remembers that woman's hollowed eyes,

and I hope he'll always remember them. She was Mattie Godbolt, who worked for Dr. Brown on North Finley Avenue, near
my parents' house. Her son was Clifford Godbolt, and just that
morning their family had moved from Newark to an apartment
near Twin Lakes Park. Clifford had been out with a friend, ex-
ploring his new neighborhood, when he had walked to the end
of the dock, leaned over, and tried to touch the water.

"I might have been able to get him in time," Sorgie tells
me, "but I forgot about the current, the way it moves under the
surface." As always, he speaks in his impassive policeman's voice,
though I don't think I am wholly imagining the current beneath
his surface. He wanted, wildly, to find that kid and haul him out
of the pond. He would have laid him on his back, turned his
head to the side, draining all the water. Then he'd have tilted
back the boy's head, opened his mouth. He'd have pinched
the nostrils, and, sealing his own mouth over the boy's, he'd
have breathed and breathed, forcing air in, letting it out — as
though *this* might stand beside the other things that he can
never undo.

Today Bill Sorgie is thinking about retiring. He has been lieutenant now for five years, but the present chief isn't going anywhere, so he's pretty much at the end of his line. He likes his
work, though he's getting tired of sitting behind a desk, and he
could stand to spend more time with his kids before they're out
of the house. He thinks maybe he'll stick around for a few more
years, then hang it up, or do some work for a private detective.
It all depends on the cost of college, his pension, his health, et
cetera.

My mother has also thought about retiring, selling our
home, and moving with my father into one of those new con-
dominium complexes in town. A few years ago we even threw
her a retirement party, but each day she still seems to be driving
to work, spitting stones behind her wheels. She did, in fact, put

the house on the market. But then my father had his stroke, and they've decided that, since he seems to do best in familiar surroundings, they'll stay put for the time being.

With my own family, I get up there every three or four months. It is often a disorienting feeling. My father in his old room, with his old framed photographs, but now he lies in a hospital bed, with a push-button alarm, in case of emergencies, on a narrow chain around his neck. I'm not sure if he's aware of it, or how he'd respond, but it fills me with wonder to know that the house in Plainfield where he grew up, my grandmother's house that we'd visit each Sunday, where Frank, her black "yard-man," raked piles of leaves — that house today, with a kid's bike out front — is owned by an African-American family.

Now as I write this, the Borough of Bernardsville is refacing all the stores in Olcott Square: fancy woodwork in muted colors, fresh brick and mortar on white plinths, and new "antique lighting." With the corporate headquarters that have settled in the area, things are busier and even more upscale these days. The Old Stone, which just a few weeks ago was Freddy's, is at the moment a trendy microbrewery. The flagpole still stands, but the small, circular green has become a landscaped triangle, and there are stop lights where a policeman used to direct traffic. Even the Erie Lackawanna is now "New Jersey Transit." The old army green cars with wicker seats have been replaced, though the new trains still sound the same to me when they whistle coming into the station.

All of the Bell family have left town, and Charles Bell has been dead for many years, as has Robert Jeffers, Sr. Still, Ruth Jeffers lives in the same split-level, which now has a brown coat of paint and looks to be in pretty good shape. Rabbit's old Bonnie Brae friends, Fred and Doug, are still around, though I've just heard that Fred has had a mild heart attack that should, according to Jackie Lentzsch, "keep him off cigarettes — for a while." As for Cy Hardy, he is currently the head of security at a nearby New Jersey college. Since he graduated years ago from the academy at Seagirt, he has been a policeman. Each workday he, like Bill Sorgie, gets dressed in his uniform, straightens his hat, and puts his gun in his duty holster. He is still married to Linda Killian, blonde and blue-eyed, his old high-school sweetheart. Together they have two strikingly beautiful daughters, now about eleven and nine years old, each with bright and pestering smiles, each with long, frizzy, radiant hair, and skin that reminds me of Rabbit's.

On Valley Road, as I've said, Bonnie Brae remains, though for years it hasn't been a "Farm for Boys," but a more enclosed, state-sponsored facility, a "Community for Troubled Youths." In the early seventies, the farm operation was gradually closed down, the livestock put up for auction, acres of fields and orchards sold to housing developers. Except for Graves Cottage, which has been gutted and remodeled, the old Tudor cottages are locked and boarded, with patches of moss on their slate roofs; the mortar in much of the fancy brickwork turns to sand when I rub it with my finger. New dormitories have been built, but for only about thirty-five boys who are classified as "emotionally disturbed" or "mentally ill chemical abusers," boys with different and often greater difficulties than boys like Cy, Fred, Doug, or Rabbit. None of them enter the local school system now, and certainly none hang out in Olcott Square. They stay on the premises, and they usually stay for less than two years. So you don't hear much about "the boys of Bonnie Brae," because they just aren't around town anymore.

When I drive over there, sometimes with my wife and daughter, I am stunned by all the new houses in what used to be acres of corn and playing fields. For an instant, I nearly lose my bearings. But then, recovering, I am stunned anew by what I see in the fields that remain: those boys, in their gym suits, thick-, knobbed-, or spindle-legged, running on the grass, playing soccer or what we called speedball. Through my window, I hear them holler and cheer. They fall and get up, all in one motion, their bodies flowing against those ancient hills, their shirts all alive in the sun.

I was formed by this gentle geography, in a place of relative calm and assurance largely undisrupted, unquestioned, by difference. I still love those hills, and I find that in my middle years, more and more they fill me with yearning. I know of nothing more beautiful than the ridges stretching to the west of town, with the morning mist sifting between them, as through my mother's fingers. They kept me safe, those hills, and for a time they even kept Rabbit safe. But they could not make us whole.

I am haunted by the hills of my youth, by what was right and what was wrong in the gentle lives we lived there. I still hear the long, thin whistle of the train. I still see Rabbit's proud and lonely stare. For me, he is in the sound of that whistle, in the bells that ring each Sunday morning, in the whisk of cars around the flagpole. And it is somehow right, terribly right, that in fact he *is* inside those hills, buried in the place I call my home.

Postscript

Memorial Day, 1997

Yesterday, during a weekend visit to see my parents, my daughter, my wife, my mother, and I went to the Memorial Day parade in Bernardsville, just as I always did as a kid. We sat on the curb of the green in Olcott Square, the flag on the pole behind us at half-mast. It was a splendid spring morning, clear, brisk, and warm enough to take off your sweater.

About fifty people gathered in the square, children with balloons and parents with video recorders, and many more lined the rest of the parade route, which followed Route 202 west to the grounds of the Municipal Building and Police Headquarters, where the marchers would disband.

The parade was almost exactly like the ones I remember from years ago. First the snappy color guard; then the proud, gimpy Veterans of Foreign Wars; the high school band; fire trucks with firemen in old-time uniforms; bagpipers in kilts and knee socks; the Lyons Club and Ladies Auxiliary; Little Leaguers; Girl Scouts; Boy Scouts; then Cubs and Brownies, sitting on hay wagons, tossing candy to kids in the crowd.

Halfway through the parade, I realized that the Bernardsville policemen were not among the marchers. Of course they were on duty, closing and opening roads, directing traffic around the festivities. I got up from the curb and told my wife I'd be back shortly — I wanted to look for Bill Sorgie. He wasn't in the square, so I walked through the crowds, alongside wearying Scouts and Little Leaguers, out toward Police Headquarters.

From a hundred feet away, I saw him. He was standing alone in front of an orange barricade at the very end point of the parade. He was in his blue uniform, with short sleeves. His badge and visor gleamed. He had his arms folded in front of him, his feet apart, and he was rocking back a little on his heels, as if he were just another relaxed onlooker soaking up the warmth of the day.

Probably because I was wearing sunglasses and we hadn't seen one another in a while, he didn't recognize me as I approached. But when I took off my glasses, he smiled and said, "Hey." He stopped rocking on his heels. In the sun his mustache was mostly gray; his eyes squinted, creasing his skin, and it struck me that this was the first time I'd seen him in the open air, out from behind his desk. He is not small, but just then seemed so, not an inch taller than me. We talked for a while about the weather, our families, the Yankees' miserable pitching of late, and he joked about how it was getting harder each year to squeeze himself into his uniform.

I thought I might say something about Rabbit then, and I think he expected it too, but nothing new came to mind. Still Rabbit filled the space between us. I have become for Sorgie an unsettling but acknowledged reminder of the past. In our time together, he has come to know the person he killed, and I hope that even though our talking is done Rabbit will cling to him now as tenaciously as he has to me.

We stood awkwardly until the end of the parade came into view, a ragtag group of clowns and jugglers, a police car bringing up the rear.

"Well, I have to get back to my family," I said. "They're waiting in the square."

We shook hands, said good-bye, good luck. And indeed I wish him all the best, a long, productive, decent life that brings happiness without letting go of its deepest regrets. Then, as I walked away, I turned to look at him standing in the sunshine: a man in shirtsleeves in the midst of a life, just as Rabbit might have been.